Sutton Place, Woking
[Frontispiece]

Drawn by J. Nash, 1840
[Central Press Photos]

LIST OF
ANTIQUITIES

IN THE

ADMINISTRATIVE COUNTY OF

SURREY

Presented by the
RECORDS HISTORIC BUILDINGS AND ANTIQUITIES COMMITTEE

Chairman:
Mr. J. A. FARMER

Editor:
J. W. LINDUS FORGE, A.R.I.B.A., A.I.A.A.

FIFTH EDITION

Published by
SURREY COUNTY COUNCIL
KINGSTON-UPON-THAMES
1965

On the 1st April, 1965, the Boroughs of Barnes, Beddington & Wallington, Kingston-upon-Thames, Malden & Coombe, Mitcham, Richmond, Surbiton, Sutton & Cheam and Wimbledon and the Urban Districts of Carshalton, Coulsdon & Purley and Merton & Morden will cease to form part of the Administrative County of Surrey and will be in the area of the Greater London Council. On the same date the Urban Districts of Sunbury & Staines, formerly part of the Administrative County of Middlesex, will become part of the Administrative County of Surrey.

The necessary Addendum, showing listed buildings in this new area will be issued later.

● 7765

Printed by Adlard & Son, Ltd., Bartholomew Press, Dorking, Surrey.

SURREY COUNTY COUNCIL

RECORDS HISTORIC BUILDINGS
AND ANTIQUITIES COMMITTEE

1965

B

CONTENTS

EDITOR'S ACKNOWLEDGEMENTS

This edition is founded upon the earlier labours of the late C. D. Hawley, F.R.I.B.A. and the late Fred W. Strange, F.R.S.A.I., F.S.A.(Scot.) to whom the County is so greatly indebted for the recording of its historic buildings.

The Editor wishes to acknowledge the help of Captain A. W. G. Lowther, F.S.A., A.R.I.B.A., A.A.DIP., Mr. A. G. Martin and Mr. David Tomalin as well as the unfailing patience and co-operation of the staff of the County Council's Historic Buildings and Antiquities Office.

FOREWORD

It will be seen from the excellent Preface by the Editor that the task for which we are appointed by the County Council is difficult and often frustrating. Apart from the pressure of business concerns who generally consider an old building an obstruction to progress we have to try to balance our desires for preservation against the requirements of our own County Council Committees and the District Councils for new roads, slum clearance and land for new estates and schools.

The final factor which should decide the matter is the voice of the ratepayers themselves. This unfortunately we seldom hear. We believe that in most cases the residents of a town or village wish to preserve its traditions, the examples of ancient craftmanship in the mellow old buildings which give so much charm and pleasure to the inhabitants and to visitors especially from overseas.

It will therefore be of the greatest possible help to the County Council and my Committee if residents will quickly make their wishes known as soon as they hear of the proposed destruction of an historic building of whatever size or kind.

In the hope that residents will respond to this request this foreword has been written.

JAMES A. FARMER,

Chairman of the Records, Historic Buildings
and Antiquities Committee.

PREFACE

This List was first prepared as long ago as 1912, when it was compiled by the Ancient Monuments (Special) Committee with the help of co-opted members representing various Archaeological Societies and the National Trust.

Intended originally as a working document for the Council's officers in their difficult and often thankless task of preserving the County's historical monuments, it was felt, when the third edition came to be prepared in 1939 that it might have a wider interest. Accordingly the late Mr. C. D. Hawley, F.R.I.B.A. was invited to act as Editor and the volume was illustrated by measured drawings and photographs and provided with an introduction for the general reader. The last and greatly enlarged Fourth Edition, on the same lines and under the same devoted editor, appeared in 1951.

Now, with the approaching radical alteration in the County boundaries, the Records, Historic Buildings and Antiquities Committee (formerly called the Records and Ancient Monuments Committee) feel that a Fifth Edition is due for publication, incorporating the results of the latest investigation and research into the history and construction of the earth-works, houses and other buildings (many of which are listed by the Ministries of Public Building and Works and Housing and Local Government) over whose fortunes the Committee hold a watching brief. The opportunity has also been taken for the addition of fresh diagrams and the replacement of certain of the illustrations from photographs in the extensive collection at the Deeds, Historic Buildings and Antiquities Office, a collection which is open to the Public by appointment. The new list has been prepared with the help of the District Councils, local Societies, local architects, archaeologists and others, whose assistance is acknowledged with gratitude.

Churches used for worship and secular buildings restored out of recognition have been purposely excluded. For other, unintentional omissions and errors, perhaps inevitable in a task of such extent and involving the gleaning of information from so many and such various sources, the reader's indulgence is sought.

Finally it must be emphasized that the pace of development in the County today is so rapid that already over 350 buildings listed since 1951 have been demolished and more will disappear while the work is in the Press. On the other hand, many of the buildings included are of outstanding architectural or historic importance, so that their demolition must at all costs be avoided, while others of humbler pretensions must be preserved where they form an essential part of some piece of town-scape or land-scape. From the Past we have come into a goodly heritage, the inimitable fabric of the English countryside, woven through the centuries, and it is for us to hand it down, as unimpaired as possible, to future generations.

J. W. LINDUS FORGE.
Editor.

SOME STATUTORY ENACTMENTS

Which relate to the preservation of Antiquities

The Ancient Monuments Consolidation and Amendment Act, 1913 (Section 12), requires the Minister of Public Buildings and Works to publish from time to time a List containing—

(*a*) such monuments as are reported by the Ancient Monuments Board as being monuments, the preservation of which is of National importance, and

(*b*) such other monuments as the Minister thinks ought to be included in the List.

The Ancient Monuments Act, 1931 (Section 6), requires the Minister, before including any monument in a List published under the 1913 Act, to serve a notice of his intention so to do upon the owner and occupier of the monument, and it is an offence punishable by the fine not exceeding £100, or imprisonment not exceeding three months, for any person on whom such a notice has been served to demolish, remove, alter, add to or repair the monument without giving to the Minister three months' notice in writing of his intention to do so.

The Ancient Monuments Act, 1931 (Section 15)—

(*a*) the expression " monument " shall include

(i) any monument specified in the Schedule to the Ancient Monuments Protection Act, 1882 (none is situate in Surrey),

(ii) any monument for the time being specified in a List published under Section 12 of the Ancient Monuments Consolidation and Amendment Act, 1913, and

(iii) any other monument, or part, or remains of a monument which in the opinion of the Minister of Public Building and Works is of a like character, or of which the preservation is, in the opinion of the Minister, a matter of public interest by reason of the historic, architectural, traditional, artistic or archæological interest attached thereto, and (for the purpose of the County Council's duties under the Act) shall include any land comprising or adjacent to the ancient monument, which is reasonably required for the purpose of maintaining the monument or the amenities thereof or for providing or facilitating access thereto or for the exercise of proper control or management with respect thereto.

The Ancient Monuments Acts, 1913 and 1931, entrust to the County Councils (and Borough Councils) the following powers:—

(1) To purchase by agreement any monument in the County which appears to the County Council to be an ancient monument within the meaning of the Act (except a building occupied as a dwellinghouse by a person other than a caretaker or a building in ecclesiastical use).

(2) To become the guardians under Deed executed by the owner of any such monument.

(3) To maintain any monument of which they have become the guardians, including the fencing, repairing and covering of the monument and the doing of any act or thing required for protecting the monument from decay or injury or necessary for the proper control and management thereof.

(4) To receive voluntary contributions towards the cost of the maintenance and preservation of any monument of which they have become the guardians.

(5) To agree with the Minister of Public Building and Works for the transfer to or from the Minister of any ancient monument of which they or the Minister are the owners or guardians.

(6) To undertake, or contribute out of County Funds towards, the cost of preserving, maintaining and managing any such monument, whether they have purchased the monument or become the guardians of it or not. (Before a County Council or Borough Council can make a grant the property has to be classified as an "Ancient Monument" under Section 15, 1931 (ss(2)) and the Minister of Public Building and Works has consented to grant (Sec. 11).

The Historic Buildings and Ancient Monuments Act, 1953 provides for the preservation and acquisition of buildings of outstanding historic or architectural interest and their contents, and amended the law (Ancient Monuments Acts 1913-31) relating to ancient monuments and other objects of architectural interest. Under the provisions of this Act the Minister of Public Building and Works can make grants towards the cost of the upkeep of such buildings and in certain circumstances of objects in them and of amenity land (upkeep of grounds and gardens); it further provides for the acquisition, management and disposal by the Minister of such buildings, including those vested or in which the National Trust have an interest. The Minister is advised by the Historic Buildings Councils for England, Scotland and Wales, an authoritative body which is required to make and submit to Parliament annual reports. The Council has now set up an Historic Buildings Bureau to compile lists of such outstanding buildings which are threatened with demolition and might be available to likely purchasers who with the help of Government Grants would be willing to repair, use and preserve such buildings. (Applications for grants should be addressed to The Secretary, Historic Buildings Council for England, Abell House, John Islip Street, London, S.W.1.)

The Minister may also make grants for the purpose of defraying in whole or in part any expenditure of a local authority in the acquisition of property under Section 69 of the Town and Country Planning Act, 1962.

The Local Authorities (Historic Buildings) Act, 1962 empowers all local authorities to contribute, either by a grant or a loan, towards the cost (including Architects' fees) of preserving buildings of special architectural or historic interest and, with the consent of the Minister of Housing and Local Government, of non-listed buildings of a similar type. At the same time as a contribution is made, a local authority may also make a grant towards the upkeep of any garden occupied with such buildings. Conditions may be imposed requiring public access to the property and also if the property is sold within three years of the date of making the grant, a local authority may recover the amount of the grant or any part of it. (Applications for grants should be addressed to the Clerks of County and/or District Councils).

TOWN & COUNTRY PLANNING ACT, 1962 (re-enacts similar provisions in the Town & Country Planning Acts, 1944 & 1947).

In this Act (Sections 32 and 33) the Minister of Housing and Local Government is empowered to consult persons or bodies having special knowledge of or interest in buildings of architectural and historic interest, and to compile Lists of these buildings, or approve Lists compiled by other persons or bodies of persons and from time to time amend such Lists with a view to the guidance of Local Authorities in the performance of functions relating to such buildings under the Town and Country Planning Acts. The Act further provides that so long as a building of special architectural or historic interest is included in a List compiled or approved by the Minister it shall be an offence punishable by fine not exceeding £100 for any person to execute or permit any works for the demolition of the building or for its alteration or extension in a manner which would seriously affect its character, without giving the County Council two months' written notice of his intention so to do.

Section 62 further empowers the County Council to serve on the owner or occupier of such a building a notice requiring the reinstatement of any part of the building which he has demolished, altered or extended as aforesaid, and to enforce such notice.

Sections 30 and 31 empower the County Council and other Local Authorities for the preservation of any building of special architectural or historic interest in their area (except an ecclesiastical building in actual use or a building which is the subject of a scheme or order or included in a List published under an enactment with respect to ancient monuments), to make a Building Preservation Order restricting the demolition, alteration or extension of the building. The Order may—

(1) require the consent of the County Council for the execution of works of any description specified in the Order,

(2) enable the County Council to require the restoration of any building dealt with in contravention of the Order, and

(3) provide for payment to the owner of the building of compensation for damage or expenses caused to or incurred by any person in consequence of the Order.

DEVELOPMENT NEAR BUILDINGS OF SPECIAL ARCHITECTURAL OR HISTORIC INTEREST

The need for care in considering, and publicity for, applications for planning permission for development affecting buildings of special architectural or historic interest has been stressed by the Ministry of Housing and Local Government in a circular to Local Planning Authorities (Circular No. 51/63). In addition to the physical protection of the buildings themselves equal importance is attached to assessment of development proposed near such buildings in the light of the effect it may have on the building or on the scene of which it forms part. It is expected that there should be no hesitation in publicising applications in suitable cases so that public opinion may be tested before decisions of importance are taken nor in obtaining appropriate professional advice if that is not already available to the authority concerned.

The Housing Act 1957 (Section 17), provides that where Statutory Lists have been prepared under Section 32 of the Town and Country Planning Act, 1962, or Building Preservation Orders are in force under Section 30 of that Act, all listed houses or houses subject to an Order must be freed from any Demolition Orders and Closing Orders must be substituted. Such houses will then enjoy the protection afforded under Sections 30 and 31 of the 1962 Act. The Minister of Housing and Local Government will issue Notices covering all houses proposed for statutory listing so that the Housing Authorities can change existing Demolition Orders to Closing Orders and in future make only Closing Orders on those houses. The Local Planning Authorities and the Minister will be kept informed of all contemplated improvements to those houses.

HOUSING (FINANCIAL PROVISIONS) ACT 1958.
HOUSE PURCHASE AND HOUSING ACT 1959 & HOUSING ACT 1961

Under the provisions of the Housing (Financial Provisions) Act, 1958, as amended, a local authority may, subject to conditions, make a loan for the purpose of acquiring or "altering, enlarging, repairing or improving houses" provided that the house is in all respects fit for human habitation when the work has been carried out (Section 43(1) and (2)).

A local authority may also make improvement grants under the Housing Acts for older houses, very briefly on the following basis:

Standard Grant—

House owners and certain leaseholders can obtain as of right, half the cost, up to a maximum of £155, of installing five basic improvements: a bath or shower, wash-hand basin, hot water system, water closet and food store, subject to conditions. The house must be reasonably fit to live in for 15 years after the work has been done.

Discretionary Grant—

At the discretion of the local Council, up to half the estimated cost of more extensive improvements may be paid, subject to a maximum grant of £400 per unit subject to conditions. The period of useful life must be at least 30 years after the work has been done, or exceptionally 15 to 30.

If an old house is converted into flats a grant per flat may be obtained.

Improvements eligible for grant are specifically listed and repairs are not eligible. The property must be put into a good state of repair in order to qualify for a grant.

The Minister has power to waive conditions which are impracticable in any particular case and also to authorise grants in excess of the normal maximum. In one case he did authorise an additional grant of £82 per dwelling towards the additional cost involved in safeguarding architectural features of special interest. (Applications for grants should be addressed to the Clerk to the Local Authority who will also supply a pamphlet issued by the Minister of Housing and Local Government, giving details and conditions relating to these grants.)

The three Lists now existing may be briefly described as follows:—

I. The List published by the Minister of Public Building and Works comprises Ancient Monuments the preservation of which is a statutory obligation; its contravention involves liability for heavy penalties. Additions are constantly being made to this List.

II. The List of Buildings of Special Architectural or Historic Interest compiled or approved by the Minister of Housing and Local Government is intended for the guidance of Local Authorities in the performance of their Planning functions relating to such buildings. Its contravention also involves heavy penalties. Certified Statutory (Grade I & II buildings) and Supplementary Lists (Grade III buildings) approved by the Minister have been deposited with the County Council covering 31 County Districts and the Crawley New Town area. Provisional Lists (Grade I, II & III buildings) for the Rural Districts of Dorking and Horley and Guildford have also been deposited.

III. The Surrey County Council List is more comprehensive than the Ministers' Lists and provides an exhaustive record of antiquities in the County in addition to Ancient Monuments and Buildings of Special Architectural or Historic Interest. It lacks the statutory authority possessed by Lists I and II.

BRIEF NOTES FOR THE GUIDANCE OF OWNERS AND OTHERS
in connection with alterations and/or additions to historic buildings.

1. It is advisable, from the start, to consult an architect or surveyor experienced in such work and have it carried out under his supervision. This is obviously of particular importance where matters of aesthetics and knowledge or architectural history are so closely concerned.

2. Where structural additions are contemplated every effort should be made to ensure harmony with existing work. This should be achieved by the use of suitable form and materials, but on no account should the old be slavishly copied. Pseudo period work, which may mislead, should certainly be avoided.

3. The external application of rought-cast or plaster rendering of any kind to old brick walls, in order to arrest the penetration of damp, should never be permitted as these are detrimental to the architectural or antiquarian character of the building. There are several reliable colourless water-proofing solutions obtainable which serve the same purpose without obviously affecting the buildings appearance. Tile-hanging, however, may be used with advantage in certain cases.

4. The roof covering is important. Clay tiles (preferably hand made) should be used rather than slates (unless the existing building is already slated) and a dark sand-faced texture is much to be preferred. Semi-vitreous faced tiles, corrugated sheeting or asbestos-cement slates should on no account be used.

5. The use of imitation half-timbering in the form of cement bands, or wood battens (such as often seen in speculative building) or imported old woodwork on the face or in the body of the wall should be avoided.

6. Repairs to chimney stacks require careful consideration and any rebuilding should accord with the architectural character of the original work. Particular care should be taken with the mortar mix and the type of pointing.

7. Owners are advised not to permit ivy, creepers or other vegetable to cover walls. These may conceal valuable architectural features and certainly tend to encourage dampness. Ivy in particular may, in course of time, cause considerable damage to masonry or brickwork.

8. To preserve exposed timbers it is suggested that two coats of a reputable colourless wood preservative should be applied with subsequent application of a solution of turpentine and beeswax; the timbers should certainly not be painted or distempered. Any internal timber-work where exposed should also occasionally be treated with a similar wood preservative.

9. It is of course essential to keep all underfloor air vents clear of obstruction and where possible ensure that the ground is kept at least 6 in. below floor level or damp-proof course.

PHOTOGRAPH OF THE IDENTIFICATION PLAQUE TO BE AFFIXED
TO CERTAIN BUILDINGS OF HISTORIC INTEREST.

The cast bronze plaque measures 10 inches in diameter and contains the Coat of
Arms of Surrey in coloured vitreous enamel with enamelled lettering. The number
is for reference purposes and should be quoted if further information regarding
the property is required.

[*Facing p.* 1

INTRODUCTION

PREHISTORIC

c. 500,000 B.C.–43 A.D.

Man, we are told, first walked this Earth about half a million years ago. During the Old Stone Age he hunted great beasts like the mammoth over steppe-like plains and, having to follow his quarry, was necessarily a nomad, sheltering at night in caves or, judging from wall paintings, in skin tents like tepees or yourts. He left behind only weapons, ranging from the 'eoliths' of dawn man, which only archaeologists can discern from pebbles, to the beautifully finished flint weapons from the Thames and Farnham gravels, which can be found in most Surrey museums.

About 12,000 B.C. the climate seems to have become much warmer. Forests filled the lowlands and Middle Stone Age man made smaller weapons (microliths) with which to hunt woodland birds and beasts and catch fish. It was he who left us the earliest of our 'antiquities': the 'pit-dwellings' of Farnham and Abinger, the oldest man-made homes in England.

Then, something like five thousand years ago, there came the Agricultural Revolution; the arrival from the Continent of the peoples of the New Stone Age who knew how to grow a few primitive crops and who had domesticated cattle. Grain meant baskets, milk meant pottery and wool meant weaving; farming, moreover, meant permanent homes and barns and byres. Both solid-walled and timber-framed houses have been found elsewhere in England, but none has yet been discovered in Surrey and we have to be content with a single (destroyed) 'long barrow' (a communal grave), and flint workings.

A thousand years later and there are new arrivals, men with the first bronze weapons, who buried their dead in the round barrows that still stud our heaths, though elsewhere many more must have been ploughed out. Finally, about five hundred years before Christ come warriors with weapons of iron who built the great hill forts: Anstiebury, Hascombe and Holmbury, 'Caesar's Camps' at Farnham and Wimbledon, with others at Weybridge and elsewhere. As evidence of their artistry they have left us the superb enamelled bronzes, like the Battersea shield in the British Museum.

1

FARNHAM PIT DWELLINGS. (Mesolithic).

These are grouped near the head of the Bourne Spring and consist of irregular hollows surrounded by banks of excavated material. They contain hearths and, it is now suggested, may possibly have had wooden floors. At one end is a post hole which probably held a forked upright, supporting one end of a sloping ridge pole against which branches may have been laid as a foundation for a rough thatch. There is evidence of a microlith industry.

BADSHOT LONG BARROW, FARNHAM. (Neolithic).

This was about 1¾ miles East of Farnham and had already been largely destroyed by quarrying and ploughing when Mr. Rankine discovered it in 1936. It appears to have been about 140 feet long and 40 feet wide, with a post-hole (which can be paralleled elsewhere and probably contained some ritual 'totem') on the approach road.

> (For the Farnham Pit Dwellings and Long Barrow see:—
> Oakley, Rankine & Lowther; 'A Survey of the Pre-history
> of the Farnham District.' Surrey Archaeological Society.
> 1939).

ROUND BARROWS. (Bronze Age).

Unlike long barrows, these were circular mounds thrown up over individual burials: inhumations in a crouched position and, later, urns containing the ashes of cremations. They vary in size from about five to fifty yards across and are called 'bowl', 'bell' and 'disc' barrows respectively depending whether the 'berm' separating the mound from the surrounding ditch is missing, moderately wide or so wide that the central feature has shrunk to a tump.

In Surrey round barrows are found on the commons of Crooksbury, Chobham, Banstead, Frensham and Horsell and on Reigate Heath. There is the uncommon arrangement of four in one entrenchment on Crooksbury Common.

ST. GEORGE'S HILL CAMP, WEYBRIDGE. (Iron Age).

Although only about 250 feet high, this hill was obviously chosen as the site of a camp because it commanded the junctions both of the Mole and the Wey with the Thames at a time when rivers were of greater importance than track-ways, while at the same time it was within striking distance of three important fords: over the Thames at Cowey Stakes, the Wey near the future Wey Bridge and the Mole at Cobham.

The fortified area is about 13 acres in extent, a rough rectangle running NW-SE, with a projection like a Vauban artillery bastion on the SW and a subsidiary enclosure round a dell where a stream may have been dammed to provide a water supply on the NE. The ditch is even now over twenty feet deep and very impressive; once it must have been much higher while on the West side, where the summit breaks out into spurs impracticable to include in the defended area, the ditch is doubled.

Eighteenth-century afforestation makes the camp invisible except at close quarters and it is partly inaccessible in gardens.

(See: Surrey Archaeological Collections. Vol. XXIV. 1911.)

THE ROMAN OCCUPATION

43 A.D.–c. 410 A.D.

During Roman times, Surrey seems to have been of little importance. It belonged to no particular tribe but appears to have been shared between the Atrebates and the Cantii; consequently there is no tribal capital or any town of real size. Much of it was probably woodland or waste, across which drove the great military road to Chichester: Stane Street, with a branch to Portslade through Caterham and Godstone. A third road crossed and re-crossed the border with Kent on its way to Lewes, while the great road to the West nicked the N.W. corner of the county as it passed from Staines into Hampshire. Numerous branch roads, some doubtless awaiting discovery, connected these arteries with centres like Farley Heath, Ashtead and Titsey.

About two dozen villa sites are known, but none so far excavated has proved of any great size; Surrey has nothing to show remotely comparable with the splendours of Bignor or Fishbourne. Some are associated with local industry: brick and tile making at Ashtead and Farnham, fulling at Titsey. Romano-Celtic temples have been unearthed at Farley Heath and Titsey.

STANE STREET

Stane Street ran from London to Chichester via Juniper Hill, Leith Hill and Ockley. Two of the four 'mansiones' (staging points for troops) were at Merton and (probably) Dorking. There are good stretches to be seen at Holmwood, Mickleham Down and elsewhere.

Between the two boundary ditches, 84 feet apart, construction varied considerably. The 'agger' or raised, cambered platform might be about 30 feet wide, half of which was metalled, and was flanked by drainage channels. The depth of the metalling and the foundation to it depended on the nature of the soil.

(See: 'The Stane Street' by Hilaire Belloc, 1903, corrected by 'The Topography of Stane Street' by Capt. W. A. Grant, 1922, also 'With A Spade on Stane Street' by S. E. Winbolt, 1936.)

ROMAN VILLA, ASHTEAD.

'SIX BELLS' ROMAN SITE, FARNHAM.

In both these cases a separate Bath building and a villa are associated with a tile works. The bath building is the earlier and was presumably for the workmen; the Roman bath being, of course, as much a social centre as a place of ablution.

At Farnham the bath house is a small rectangular building to which an apsidal plunge was added in the early IV c. when the house was built. At Ashtead there was a circular calidarium, as in many similar military buildings, while a singular chimney-pot was unearthed, with convex sides pierced by triangular openings.

The villa at Ashtead was of the usual type with a verandah in front and central porch. Interesting box-flue tiles were found, including one pattern with stags and hunting dogs. At Farnham the ground floor had a small bath suite and a single heated living-room, but two walls a few feet apart almost certainly supported a stair to an upper storey.

(see S.A.C. Vols. XXXVII–XXXVIII. 1927–8 (Ashtead). Vol. LIV. 1955 (Farnham).)

FARLEY HEATH, ALBURY. ROMANO-CELTIC TEMPLE.

Perhaps built on a prehistoric sacred site, this was a typical Romano-Celtic temple on a plan widely distributed over North-West Imperial territory and of which the best example yet found in Britain is at Sheepen Farm, Colchester. The cella, 46′ 6″ square, rose above a surrounding verandah eight feet wide, and was probably lit by a clearstory. Auxiliary buildings stood in the sacred enclosure in which the temple was always off-centre, suggesting a central cult object. Here this 'temenos' was twelve-sided and is almost exactly duplicated at Coblenz, in Germany. Unsolved problems are a stretch of inner wall close to the temple and outer embankments forming three sides of a rhomboid.

The site was excavated by Martin Tupper (rather unscientifically), in 1848, by S. E. Winbolt in 1926 and by A. W. G. Lowther and R. G. Goodchild in 1939.

(see S.A.C. Vols. XLVI & XLVIII 1938/43).

THE MIDDLE AGES

1066 A.D.–c. 1510 A.D.

1. RELIGIOUS HOUSES.

Communities of monks and nuns built their living quarters opening from covered walks around a court, called the cloister which, unless site peculiarities dictated otherwise, lay in the angle formed by the Nave and South Transept of the Church.

In the buildings of the oldest order, the Benedictines, the East range contained a Chapter house and undercroft on the ground floor, with the Dorter over, the South range a Refectory and the West range offices and a Parlour. An Infirmary for old and sick monks lay away to the South-East and an outer court contained the Guest-house, stables, brew-house, bake-house, etc.

The Cluniacs and Augustinian Canons followed the same plan but the Cistercians and Premonstratensian Canons, who wanted the greater part of the West range for lay brothers, turned the Refectory at right angles to the cloister walk so as to allow a common kitchen also in the South range.

The Carthusians, who led a strictly secluded life, had an entirely different plan, with individual cells, each with its garden, round the cloister, while the various orders of Friars, who built in towns, had less regular, more compact lay-outs for their living quarters and usually 'hall' churches adapted for preaching.

CHERTSEY ABBEY. (Benedictine Order).

One of the greatest abbeys in England, Chertsey was originally founded by Erkenwald in 666, but entirely destroyed by the Danes in the Ninth Century when the Abbot and ninety monks were slain. It was re-colonised from Abingdon in 936 and new buildings were begun by Hugh of Winchester in 1110.

The church, which has entirely disappeared, had the unusual arrangement of chapels opening off an ambulatory running round a square Eastern arm, a combination of the two customary Norman arrangements.

Especially outstanding are the encaustic tiles which were fired and used at Chertsey and which illustrated, inter alia, the legends of King Arthur and his Knights. Specimens can be seen in the Victoria & Albert and Guildford Museums.

The Abbey was surrendered in 1538 and the stone looted for Hampton Court and other buildings. Only a blocked doorway and fragments of walling remain, incorporated in barns and other structures.

WAVERLEY ABBEY, near Farnham. (Cistercian Order).

Founded in 1128 by William Giffard, Bishop of Winchester, Waverley was the first house of this order in England. The original church, excavated 1899–1903, was small and aisle-less, with side chapels forming embryo transepts. It was rebuilt to the North (1203–78) on a much grander scale, with triple chapels in each transept and the usual square Cistercian East end with, in this case, five chapels abreast.

The conventual buildings, originally also very humble, were similarly re-built; the chief remains are part of the lay brothers frater, which is vaulted, and the south wall of the dorter, with three lancets. The latter was unusually built on the ground floor South of the Chapter house; a singularly inconvenient arrangement since there was no direct access to the church at night and the Wey was liable to invade it at flood-time.

Although the first, Waverley was never one of the richer Cistercian houses and, falling on hard times, was suppressed with the lesser monasteries in 1536. However, it is perhaps assured of immortality as having inspired Scott, while it also figures in Sir Arthur Conan Doyle's historical romance: 'Sir Nigel'.

(See 'Waverley Abbey' by Harold Brakspear. S.A.S. 1905).

NEWARK PRIORY. (Augustinian Canons).

Founded by Ruald de Calna, 1199. The Church had the presbytery and choir rather unusually cut off from the transepts by a solid wall and this was carried through and returned to enclose the East bay of the Nave. The transepts each had two Eastern chapels which, for no apparent reason, were built out separately without a common dividing wall. There was a detached belfry to the south-west.

The Priory was dissolved in 1539 and the conventual buildings have disappeared. The walls of the Eastern arm and the South Transept remain to a fair height but stripped of almost all their ashlar so that they are best viewed from a distance as a picturesque feature in the Wey water meadows.

(See Captain Pearce's report of his excavations. S.A.C. Volume XL. 1929).

OTHER HOUSES.

Little survives of other Surrey monasteries. There were Augustinian Canons at Merton, where a Norman arch has been re-erected in the churchyard, at Reigate and at Tandridge. A splendid Carthusian monastery founded by Henry V, and a house of Friars Observant, founded by Henry VII, both at Richmond, have disappeared, as has also the Dominican Friary at Guildford. In addition there was a hospital at Sandon (Esher), wiped out in the Black Death, and collegiate churches at Kingston, Malden and Lingfield.

2. Castles.

Like the Romans a thousand years before, the Normans speedily
ran up wooden forts to hold down a restless, subject race. These
consisted of living quarters and stables built in a large enclosure,
the 'Bailey', linked to a watch-tower on a conical mound, the 'Motte',
each defended by its own stockade and ditch. No motte-&-bailey
castle survives today, since security demanded something more
durable and less inflammable than wood, but interesting light was
thrown on their construction at Abinger in 1950.

At first the motte was replaced by a stone keep, which might be
either a lofty, isolated tower or a 'shell keep', i.e. a high stone wall
built around the top of a flattened motte with independent buildings
against its inner face. Then it was the turn of the bailey stockade to
be replaced by a stone 'Curtain', eventually supplied with projecting
towers, to allow flanking fire on assailants, and protected by a moat
as a defence against mining. Finally the keep disappeared entirely
in favour of concentric curtains, only to return in the form of a heavily
defended gate-house in the later middle ages. By Tudor times,
artillery was sounding the knell of castles, though in England they
had one final hour of glory during the Civil War, before the Parlia-
mentarians acquired an adequate siege train.

Abinger.

What was thought to be a barrow turned out, on excavation, to
be a motte, erected about 1100 and heightened about fifty years later,
perhaps by a 'robber baron' during the chaos of Stephen's reign. It
was surrounded by a moat, not the customary dry ditch, crossed by a
light, wooden bridge which could doubtless be hauled away in time
of peril. From this a ladder led to the top of the motte, which was
about thirty-five feet across and defended by a palisade of split tree-
trunks with perhaps a sentry-walk around the inner face. More post
holes in the centre showed the size and position of the watch-tower,
which probably had an open lower storey and a platform reached by
a ladder. The bailey has disappeared beneath a later manor house
and the whole was probably dismantled as 'adulterine' during
Henry II's reign.

(see 'New Light on Mottes' by Brian Hope-Taylor. 'Country
Life'. 18.5.1951.).

Farnham Castle.

As originally built by Henry of Blois, c. 1138, the keep appears
to have consisted of a high tower of which the lower thirty feet was
embanked with earth, an original arrangement calculated to give
excellent protection against either battering or mining.

The upper part of the tower was rased by Henry II and the keep was subsequently converted into a 'shell', but with the encircling wall built at the bottom, not the top of mound, so that the area so enclosed is considerable and the lowest 'storey' is practically solid earth. Although a few buildings were later constructed in this shell, perhaps to allow the bishop more privacy, the main buildings of the castle seem from the first to have been constructed round the triangular bailey below, an unusual arrangement at so early a date.

Neglect, 'slighting' after the Civil war and subsequent rebuilding means that little of the Norman core of the buildings surrounding the bailey can be seen today. A carved, wooden capital in a cupboard shows that the Great Hall once had timber arcades, one of which is still buried in later masonry, while there is a Transitional arch from the screens passage to the kitchen quarters and a blocked arcade of the same period on the North side of the Chapel.

Later work, to be considered in their proper places, includes Waynflete's magnificent brick gate-tower and Bishop Morley's rich Restoration woodwork.

(see 'Farnham Castle'. M.P.B. & W. Official Guide book, by M. W. Thompson. H.M.S.O. 1961).

GUILDFORD CASTLE.

A shell keep was superseded *c.* 1170 by a small tower keep, built of Bargate stone, chalk and Roman tile on the side of the motte, perhaps through fear of settlement, and relieved externally only by the usual flat buttresses and twin windows at high level. Internally it was typical of the smaller type of Norman keep with timber floors, a single room on each storey, linked by a newel stair, and an entrance on First Floor level. The only feature of much interest to-day is an oratory in the thickness of the wall, with a wall-arcade decorated by graffiti, including a Crucifixion and a St. Christopher, dating from the time when the keep served as the county gaol.

The domestic buildings, on which Henry III spent a great deal of money, were grouped around two baileys stretching downhill towards the river. Only fragmentary walls remain, standing in a public garden or built into surrounding property. Next to 'Castle Arch', the gateway on Quarry St. is the headquarters and museum of Surrey Archaeological Society.

(see 'Guildford Castle' by Dr. G. C. Williamson. Guildford. 1926).

OTHER CASTLES.

Of Surrey's other castles, mottes & baileys alone survive at Reigate and Bletchingley, later ruins at Betchworth and a moat at Sterborough (Lingfield).

3. HOUSES.

The heart of the Mediaeval Manor was the Great Hall, open-roofed and with a central hearth. A raised platform, the dais, ran across one end, to elevate the high table, while at the other a screen with two openings gave on to a passage between external doors. Off the dais end was the Solar, a private room for the lord and his lady, with perhaps a Bower for the women-folk. From the screens passage a way led between Buttery and Pantry to the Kitchens.

Poor people lived in huts with perhaps a ladder to a loft; accommodation little if any better than their Iron Age ancestors.

Surrey was not a rich county at this period. Much land was waste, much en-chased and the arable and pasture areas were split up between farmers rather than great estates. (There are Kentish-type yeomans' houses in the Eastern part notably at Brewer Street, near Bletchingley).

Higher living standards and a greater love of privacy has inevitably meant that most mediaeval houses have been altered and enlarged, often out of all recognition. Had there been better building stone available, more might have endured. Half-timber, on the contrary, can be easily dismantled or re-faced and mediaeval work must therefore be sought in roof-spaces or buried behind later facades.

PACHENESHAM MAGNA. ('The Mounts', Leatherhead).

The site of a Manor-House, rebuilt by Sir Eustace de Hacche in 1290–91 and altered by Robert Darcy c. 1310–20. The Hall and portions of the Chapel and Gateway were excavated by Captain Lowther 1947–9. Only the moat is visible.

(see S.A.C. Vol. 55. 1957).

WALTON-ON-THE-HILL MANOR HOUSE.

A Fourteenth-Century stone manor-house, of which the Hall and Chapel survive, though the latter has details which suggest that it may have been built somewhat earlier. The Hall was divided into two floors in the Sixteenth Century and the whole incorporated into a house of 1891.

(see S.A.C. Vol. 22. 1910).

WALTON-ON-THAMES MANOR HOUSE.

A timber-framed house of c. 1500, which looks older. The Great Hall has been given a plaster ceiling but retains its screen and gallery, the latter with a Jacobean balustrade. At either end are two-storeyed wings.

OLD SURREY HALL, LINGFIELD.

Incorporated in a mock-mediaeval house of 1922 and 1937 is a Fifteenth-Century hall with a superb roof of braced scissors beams and, at intervals, massive tie beams supported by four-centred arches. (The same architect, George Crawley, restored another mediaeval roof, this time a double hammer-beam, at Crowhurst Place).

(see 'Country Life'. 15.10.1959).

FARNHAM CASTLE. ('FOX'S TOWER').

Really built by Bishop Waynflete, 1470–75. The late mediaeval Keep/Gate-house has now been replaced by a prestige symbol, with ornamental battlements and false machicolations. An early specimen of the revival of brickwork but completely assured in its craftsmanship, e.g. the way the off-centre archway bites into the angle turret. (The same bishop built a more orthodox gateway—John Cowper, master 'brekke-mason'—at Esher: 'Waynflete's Tower', which was later Gothicised by Kent).

OTHER MEDIAEVAL REMAINS.

Space only allows mention of the late XIII c. or early XIV c. undercrofts at Nos. 52 and 115, High Street, Guildford, and at 16a, West St., Reigate, a XIV c. king-post roof at The Crown, Chiddingfold and a XIII c. oratory at The Old Rectory, Albury.

4. BRIDGES.

Upstream from Guildford are a group of six mediaeval bridges: Tilford (2), Elstead, Eashing (2) and Unstead. Narrow and rather crudely made, with thin voussoirs to the arches and cutwaters pointed on the upstream side only, they may have been built after the great floods of 1233.

(see Jervoise—'The Ancient Bridges of The South of England'. S.P.A.B. Arc. Press. 1930).

The Clattern Bridge, over the Hogsmill River at Kingston-upon-Thames, has three round-headed arches of c. 1180, with no breakwaters, embedded in a later structure.

THE RENAISSANCE

c. 1510 A.D.–c. 1800 A.D.

1. THE TUDOR PERIOD.
c. 1510 A.D.–c. 1610 A.D.

The classical revival, called the Renaissance, reached England tardily and then infiltrated only gradually since, like France, we had a still vigorous Gothic tradition. It began when Henry VIII competed with François Premier for artist-craftsmen from Italy, but these drifted away after the Reformation and for the remainder of the period our designers found their inspiration in the debased classicism of the pattern books imported from the Low Countries.

The plan of the Tudor house reflected a higher standard of living and a greater desire for privacy. At one end of the Great Hall a dining parlour and other reception rooms, bedrooms and guest chambers, at the other a 'squillery', 'spicery', 'chawndry', 'accatry' and other culinary departments resulted in wings which give the typical 'E' and 'H' plans. The great hall itself, now perhaps only a grand entrance, is often ceiled over, while a long gallery appears on an upper floor.

Externally the only evidence of the Renaissance is often an increased regard for symmetry and perhaps some more or less accurate classical trimmings around the main entrance. Otherwise the house might be mediaeval, except for an enormous increase in window area, evidence of an enhanced respect for law and the greater availability of glass, and the re-appearance of brick—especially important in a county with little good building stone. Internally walls are panelled in the 'linen-fold' pattern or hung with tapestry, fireplaces and doorways have comparatively plain four-centred arches while ceilings, at first with exposed and moulded rafters, are later decorated with a net-work of narrow plaster ribs.

NONSUCH PALACE, Ewell.

This palace, involving the destruction of the mediaeval village of Cuddington, was begun by Henry VIII in 1538. There were two main courtyards and the decoration of the inner was unique to England: half-timber covered with carved slate and framing mythological scenes in plaster. (There are parallels at Fontainebleau, etc.) At the South-east and South-west angles, octagonal towers, heavily 'jettied' at the top and adorned with 'King's Beasts' completed this gay, rather unsophisticated extravaganza, while away to the South-West, in the gardens, was a detached banqueting-house.

The Palace, perhaps by then in poor condition, was given by Charles II to Lady Castlemaine and promptly sold by her for the value of its materials. The site was excavated by John Dent and Martin Biddle, 1960–61.

(See John Dent—'The Quest for Nonsuch'. 1963).

RICHMOND PALACE.

The palace of Sheen was built by Edward III, demolished by Richard II in his extravagant grief at the death of Anne of Bohemia and again destroyed by fire in 1497. In Henry VIII's time there were two courts with a great tower and a forest of cupola-ed turrets fronting the river.

The gateway of the outer court survives and there is much Tudor brickwork in the Gothicised 'Old Palace' adjoining and in Wardrobe Court beyond.

OTHER PALACES.

At Woking only a moat, a ruined gate-house and a barn with a king-post roof survive of a favourite palace of the Tudor kings, the birthplace of Queen Mary.

At Oatlands a blocked gateway and red brick walls remain above ground, and some passages and chambers (drains?) below the surface. Otherwise this palace, built in the same year as Nonsuch, had an even shorter life, for it was pulled down by Cromwell (to avoid maintenance) and some of the bricks went to build the locks on the Wey Canal.

On Kingston and Coombe hills there are three conduit houses and a 'tamkin', part of the elaborate system which fed the twin pipe-line that ran three miles across country and below the river to Hampton Court.

SUTTON PLACE, Woking.

Built by Sir Richard Weston in c. 1523 and practically contemporary with that other landmark in the history of Early Renaissance in England, Layer Marney Towers in Essex, which has the same lavish use of terra-cotta in window dressings and parapets. Here the hollow window mouldings have arabesque ornament and there are some curiously naive panels of cherubs above the doorways, while the search for symmetry has resulted in the main entrance being located in the centre of one long wall of the Hall (if this is really the original arrangement). The North side of the courtyard, which included a great gate-house, was demolished in 1786.

(see Frederick Harrison—'Annals of An Old Manor House).

LOSELEY HOUSE, Artington.

A dignified, many-gabled, much more conservative house, built by Sir William More in 1561–69 with stonework from Waverley Abbey. Alterations were carried out c. 1680, when decoration from Nonsuch Palace was introduced: canvas panels painted with heraldic badges and wooden panels inlaid with trompe-d'oeil designs. A very large Jacobean West wing, nearly as big as the original house, which contained a chapel and long gallery, was pulled down in 1830. Of the same period is the great chalk chimney-piece in the drawing-room, a very rich example of the contemporary taste for heraldic display and barbarous caryatids.

(see 'Country Life'. May 25th, 1935).

GREAT TANGLEY MANOR, Wonersh.

Built c. 1540 on an old moated site and given a new front in 1582 when the Hall, with its king-post roof, was divided into three floors. Very elaborate half-timber—small square panels with quadrant braces—which can be paralleled elsewhere in Surrey, e.g. at Lythe Hill Farm, Chiddingfold, but is much more typical of the Welsh Marches than the South-East. Additional wings and a covered way across the moat, were added by Philip Webb.

Other notable Tudor houses in the county are Crullings, (Small-field Place), Burstow, in stone: Great Fosters, Egham and Baynards, Ewhurst, in brick: Crowhurst Place and Brewer Street, Bletchingley, in half-timber.

2. THE EARLY SEVENTEENTH CENTURY.
c. 1610 A.D.–c. 1660 A.D.

Peace with the Catholic powers meant a resumption of cultural links with France and Italy and the appearance of the first great English classical architect: Inigo Jones. As far as Surrey is concerned, however, his principal work was for Anne of Denmark at Oatlands, where a great gate-way, based on Serlio, is said to have survived the destruction of the remainder of the Palace until as late as 1860.

Such sophistication was chiefly for Court circles and most of the architecture of the period affected by the new movement was what has been termed 'artisan mannerist'; the work of master craftsmen, untravelled and imperfectly read who had to grapple with the demand for up-to-date houses and in the process produced buildings which, if technically incorrect, often have considerable vigour and a naive charm.

In plan there is a tendency for the old wide-spread 'E' and 'H' plans to contract into more compact blocks of greater height. In external appearance detail is often coarse with too many mouldings, eccentricities like 'eared' architraves and a fondness for curvilinear

'Dutch' gables. Internally panelling gets more 'architectural', ceilings have broader, flatter ribs and fireplaces are incredibly ostentatious with a display of debased heraldry flanked by half-barbarous caryatids.

ABBOT'S HOSPITAL, Guildford.

One of the grandest almshouses in England, built by Archbishop Abbot, 1619–22, to house twelve poor men and twelve poor women. In the centre of the High Street front there is a great turreted gatehouse, said to be the last of its type to be built in England (until the romantic revival) linked to wings crowned by 'dutch' gables and giving on to a quiet courtyard. Within there is very good Jacobean woodwork and a chapel with Gothic windows (from the Dominican Friary?) filled with late XV c. glass.

SLYFIELD MANOR, Great Bookham.

An assymetrical main façade, perhaps part of an uncompleted, larger scheme. Seven bays are separated by giant Ionic pilasters and at one end there is a wing with a shaped gable above a segmental window flanked by smaller, superimposed pilasters. Behind this window is a Great Chamber with an elaborately decorated plaster barrel vault of West Country type. The staircase has carved 'strapwork' panels instead of balusters, rusticated newels and elaborate dog-gates.

KEW PALACE.

A typical London merchant's house, built by Samuel Fortrey in 1631, which only later got its grandiloquent title because it suited the simple tastes of 'Farmer' George III. It is one of a group (e.g. Broome Park, Kent, and Swakeley's, across the river) in which the details are more elaborate than those of the average 'artisan' house and more sensitively handled. The windows, for example, have the classical proportions which facilitated their conversion from casements, with mullion and transome, to double-hung sash. This is reputed to be the first instance in England of the use of Flemish bond for brick-work.

PENDELL HOUSE, Bletchingley.

Built in 1636, the roof, although top-heavy, foreshadows the hipped pattern, with central flat, of the Restoration, while the massive keystone and voussoirs of the entrance doorway are pure Baroque. Another curious feature is that between the windows are 'pilasters' which are recessed instead of advanced.

(see Pevsner & Nairn. 'Surrey' (BB) p. 342).

GUILDFORD (formerly CHILD) HOUSE. No. 155 (formerly 25), High Street, Guildford.

An excellent example of that rarity, a comparatively unspoilt prosperous merchant's house of *c*. 1660. The Entrance has the eared architrave and flanking volutes beloved of the contemporary master builder, between XVIII *c*. bay windows with the original oak panels, carved with a floral motif, below. Above, there are high casement windows between pilasters, and at the rear, a delightful oriel with ends typically rounded on plan and with a pargetted panel under.

Inside there is a rich plastered ceiling in the First Floor rear room and a splendid staircase, the balustrade upheld by panels of floral carving and the newels crowned by vases, as at Ham House. The most enjoyable features, however, are perhaps the window fastenings, elegant, functional and a triumph of wrought iron.

(Part occupied by Borough Public Library.)

THE GUILDHALL, Guildford.

Artisan Mannerism having its last, most glorious fling as late as 1683. A boldly cantilevered First Floor has three high pedimented windows below an overall flat-topped pediment on which is set an outsized lantern. An elaborate clock of the period, by John Aylward, is thrust on a moulded beam supported by elaborate ironwork right out above the High Street. To quote Pevsner & Nairn 'completely wrong by Academic standards, completely right in the particular circumstances', i.e. 'at the critical part of the High Street'.

Among other notable houses of the period are West Horsley Place (an older house re-faced), Crossways Farm, Abinger (immortalised by Meredith), Fulvens, Shere and Brook Place, Chobham.

3. THE AGE OF WREN.
c. 1660–*c*. 1720 A.D.

This period saw the Renaissance house, which had been slowly evolving since the time of Inigo Jones, brought to perfection in the so-called 'Queen Anne' style. During the following century it was to be varied in detail and in materials and it was to be refined to the point of losing much of its virility, but never again was it to possess the same quiet beauty.

Externally the walls of a warm, red brick have regularly-spaced windows with thick sash-bars and broad, white sash-boxes (at least after *c*. 1680, when the double-hung sash-window mysteriously appears from nowhere). The roof is tiled and, where isolated, usually hipped with a central flat carrying a balustrade and lantern. The eaves over-sail to end in a wooden cornice supported on brackets and the entrance doorway is flanked by pilasters and crowned by a pediment or sometimes a canopy supported on richly-carved brackets.

Internally the walls are boldly panelled in two stages, with a single marble bolection mould around the fireplace and the ceiling divided into a simple pattern of panels by broad, elaborately-moulded ribs. Staircases, which to begin with have carved panels supporting the balustrade, later have a wealth of turned balusters, often three to the tread.

Shortly after the turn of the century came the short-lived Baroque. Its two chief protagonists were Vanbrugh and Hawksmoor, but the sprawling house at Claremont, Esher, originally built by the former for his own occupation, is now represented by the Belvedere and some stable buildings, and of the latter's works, Ockham Park was much altered, then burnt.

HAM HOUSE, Petersham.

A Tudor house, modernised by the Earl of Lauderdale, 1673–5. Some earlier additions of 1637–8 have left behind a fine staircase, an early example of the type where carved panels support the balustrade (*cf.* 155, High St., Guildford), although here, instead of foliage, they are unusually in the form of military trophies.

The chief interest of the house is the way in which the Restoration furniture and decor have survived almost complete, even to the silver fire sets. Nowhere else can one get a better idea of an ostentatiously wealthy interior of the period. (Quite near is a superb exterior, at Ormeley Lodge, Ham Common).

TRUMPETERS' HOUSE, Richmond.

Built on the site of the Inner Gate-house of Richmond Palace, this noble house has a better claim than most whose design has been attributed to Wren. (It may have been begun by James II and only completed by Richard Hill, brother of Queen Anne's Mrs. Masham). The central portico on the garden front, tetrastyle with widely-spaced central columns, smacks of Chelsea, the wings of Kensington. (The end pavilions, with Palladian windows, look later). Inside there is a splendid room with a rococo plaster ceiling, *c.* 1740, decorated with busts of Shakespeare & Milton.

(see 'Country Life'. 21st April, 1944).

MAIDS OF HONOUR ROW, Richmond.

A terrace of four, five-bay, three-storied houses on the Green, built for the maids-of-honour of the Princess of Wales, in 1724. With fine door-cases and magnificent ironwork, the Row is the best example of this earliest urbanisation of Surrey, as yet confined to towns made fashionable by the Court, as here, or by a spa, as at Epsom.

2

WILLMER HOUSE, Farnham.

Prosperity, first from corn and later from hops, gave Farnham in the Eighteenth Century a quantity of fine houses constructed by bricklayers with a tradition going back to 1473. One of the finest is The Grange, Castle Hill, with a painted staircase attributed to Thornhill. Willmer House, however, in West Street, which was built in 1718, is outstanding, 'perhaps the most remarkable elevation in cut and moulded brickwork extant' (Nathaniel Lloyd). An elaborate cornice, rusticated quoins, string courses and bold bolection architraves to the upper windows leave scarcely any plain wall surface. The building now houses Farnham Museum.

SUDBROOK PARK, Petersham.

Gibbs's work spans the gap between English Baroque and Palladianism, but here, in 1726, he followed his earlier allegiance. Its glory, the Cube Room, runs from front to back, the walls decorated with Corinthian pilasters and trophies of arms, the ceiling vaulted and the Vanbrughesque fireplace topped by a magnificent achievement of arms.

Other notable houses of the period are Tadworth Court, c. 1700, and Carshalton House, 1714.

4. THE PALLADIANS.
c. 1720–c. 1760 A.D.

The reaction against the Baroque was centred on Lord Burlington and his circle, of whom Mr. Ralph Dutton has said: 'Palladio was their god, Inigo Jones was their prophet and "The Book of Architecture" their Bible.' Convinced that even the limited freedom that Wren took with classical precedent was inadmissable, they sought to return to first principles and, setting up as arbiters of Taste, roundly condemned anything that they deemed to offend against the canon.

About 1745 there was some revolt against such inflexibility which, except when exercised by genius, too often resulted in dullness. The rectangular blocks with central porticoes and balancing wings gave way to more interesting arrangements of masses, often innocent of column or pilaster and sometimes adorned by bays. Internally there was more variety in the shape and height of rooms with a lighter touch in their decoration.

There were, however, two other ways in which some escape from formality was secured. Within, walls and ceilings bore a froth of rococo swirls and goddesses. Outside the stately formal lay-outs of canal and parterre, inherited from the previous century, were ruthlessly swept away in favour of a great tide of grass which lapped the very walls of the mansion, studded with clumps of trees carefully composed to form a 'landskip' which should appear the work of Nature and not of Man. Man, however, could intrude with carefully sited 'features', usually temples, but on occasion sham ruins, grottoes, and even, at Kew, a pagoda.

Finally mention must be made of the few bold spirits, like Walpole over the river at Strawberry Hill, who dared ridicule by reverting to 'Gothick'. Technically inaccurate, since it was conceived as applied decoration and not a structural language, it often has considerable charm, especially when mixed with rococo, but often also it has a paste-board insincerity. Henry Pelham, who commissioned Kent to add two wings to Waynflete's Tower at Esher, was a pioneer, some twenty years before Walpole; the wings have disappeared but there is some curious plasterwork remaining in the tower itself.

WHITE LODGE, Richmond Park.

Designed by the Earl of Pembroke and his architectural 'ghost', Roger Morris, in 1727 as a hunting-box for George II. A neat, 'correct' Palladian villa with a rusticated base and five bays over, the central three with attached Tuscan columns bearing a pediment. The interior is not so fine as the same collaborators' other villa at Marble Hill, Twickenham. Wings of c. 1750, some Victorian additions and landscaped grounds altered by Repton.

CLANDON PARK, West Clandon.

This, the home of the Onslows, was officially the work of Giacomo Leoni, between 1713 and 1729. Certainly the cold, splendid Entrance Hall, with two superlative fireplaces by Rysbrack and a rococo ceiling by Artari, is first cousin to Moor Park (Herts), and the remainder of the interior, except for three rooms redecorated in an Adamesque manner and a heavily Regency dining-room, is worthy of him. Note an especially fine flock wallpaper of the late Eighteenth Century in the Palladian Room.

Externally the building suggests a provincial designer of Baroque leanings, but the West Front is Palladian behind Victorian additions and the East Front has a central feature with meagre, skied pilasters, not bonded to the wall behind.

(see 'The Onslow Family' by C. E. Vulliamy. 'Clandon Park' by The Countess of Onslow. 'Country Life', 24th November, 1960).

ASGILL HOUSE, Richmond.

Built by the immensely successful City architect, Sir Robert Taylor, for Lord Mayor Sir Charles Asgill, c. 1767. Comparison with White Lodge of forty years before underlines the difference between an early and late Palladian villa; indeed, this might stand as an unusually distinguished type of the latter were it not for the exceptionally prominent eaves, a foretaste of Regency. Internally the planning is ingenious, the staircase especially rising with a serpentine balustrade to a First Floor landing flanked by Venetian arches. The principal bedroom also has delicate detail to the bed recess and the octagon room wall paintings by Casali.

(see 'Country Life'. 9th June, 1944).

PAINSHILL PARK, Cobham.

Kent 'first leapt the fence and found all Nature was a garden', but his most notable lay-out in Surrey, of which Walpole has left a lyrical description: Esher Place, has disappeared, and the seed is surely found in the 'wildernesses' which intruded into earlier, formal gardens, like that which surrounded Vanbrugh's tower at Claremont.

What was once the most glorious of the county's landscape gardens was constructed by the Hon. Charles Hamilton at Painshill, in the middle of the century. It was centred on a wooded lake, fed by a giant iron water-wheel (by Bramah) which must have been turning for over a hundred years. In this respect it resembles Stourhead, but the 'temples' can never have been so fine though considerably more varied, ranging from a 'Turkish Tent' to a hermit's cell. (The best surviving is a Gothic pavilion, said to be by Batty Langley).

(see 'Country Life'. 2nd/9th January, 1958).

5. LATE GEORGIAN.
c. 1760–c. 1800 A.D.

After forty years of Palladianism, there was an excellent opportunity for an architect who could offer something not too radically different, yet more in accordance with the spirit of a gayer, less formal Age. The opening was seized by a young Scotsman, Robert Adam, who speedily evolved a style based on Roman domestic ornament— the first shafts were being sunk at Pompeii—but also combining elements taken from French and Italian Renaissance. All this was welded together into something both rich and delicate, enhanced by another novelty: the subtle use of colour. Soon he and his four brothers built up an enormous practice and had numerous imitators, but the Adam style is very poorly represented in Surrey, for Hatchlands is not typical and The Oaks, Carshalton, has been pulled down.

Meanwhile the Palladian flag was kept flying by more conservative designers, led by the great Sir William Chambers, while there are lesser figures who deserve to be better known like Robert Mylne, a most accomplished architect and a brilliant engineer. Their work, however, was the exception to an output which underlined the fact that here was a vein that had been practically worked out.

Some of the work of the Adam's 'Middle' period had tended to be over-elaborate, inspiring Walpole's celebrated gibe about 'snippets of embroidery'. Nevertheless it was more the desire of a fickle society for change than any falling off in their powers that led to the waning of their popularity and the last of the brothers, who had given such beauty to English architecture, dying in poverty.

Henry Holland was the most distinguished of their successors. Externally he favoured what may be termed a 'pruned' Palladian, internally his decoration is often related to Adam's, but used with enormous restraint and with a greater admixture of French motifs, so that his work is much more closely related to the neo-classicism that had been evolved across the Channel.

HATCHLANDS, East Clandon.

In 1759 the young Robert Adam, fresh from Spalato and Rome, was given by Admiral Boscawen his first commission: the decoration of his new house at East Clandon. (It was through the same client's influence that the architect was to get his first London assignment: the Admiralty screen in Whitehall). Hatchlands is a four-square, red brick block, the work of a designer of vast ingenuity, (the admiral, himself?), who contrived two, three and four storeys at different places in the same overall height, involving cunningly-contrived staircases and numerous false windows.

Here the chief interest is to watch the slick designer of the future essaying for the first time some of those 'gimmicks' which were later to make him famous. The Drawing Room has probably the finest ceiling with a central oval in an octagon, rather incongruous trailing foliage that is purely Palladian and, in the angles, charming little amorini holding dolphins by the tail. The library also has nautical motifs incorporated in a Maltese cross design. Some of the fire-places are fine, but the grandest, in the drawing-room, is unexpectedly flanked by caryatids.

The house was altered in the Nineteenth Century, by Bonomi and later by Ricardo, while Sir Reginald Blomfield added a rich, baroque music-room in 1903.

(See 'Country Life'. 17th September and 1st October, 1953).

PEPER HAROW HOUSE.

Built by Sir William Chambers for two Viscounts Middleton, 1765–75. The exterior probably looked better before the third storey and porch were added, but can never have been very rewarding. Inside the Entrance Hall is 'stripped' Palladian, but the elegantly garlanded Drawing-Room ceiling and the effective stair balustrade, (wrought-iron 'Ss' between twin verticals) show the architect's command of detail.

CLAREMONT, Esher.

The great Empire-builder, Sir Robert Clive, who had Palladian tastes, commissioned designs both from Sir William Chambers and Lancelot ('Capability') Brown, and, to the Royal architects's chagrin, employed the latter. Presumably the landscape architect's reputation for convenient planning won the day, for the elevations are run-of-the-mill Palladian with no great distinction.

The interior design is probably due more to Henry Holland, Brown's assistant and son-in-law, than to the older man. Certainly the bold and delightful ceiling of Lord Clive's dressing-room and the arrangement of the Stair Hall are later duplicated at Holland's masterpiece, the magnificent Berrington Hall in Herefordshire.

Another famous architectural name is connected with the house, for the basic design of the Entrance Hall, an oval of scagliola columns in a rectangle, was apparently due to the young John Soane, then a pupil in the partners' office.

THE WICK, Richmond Hill.

Built by Robert Mylne, in 1775, for Lady St. Aubyn, The Wick can be termed by Mr. Christopher Hussey 'one of the most perfect of small Georgian houses', without fear of contradiction. The Entrance front is an essay on how simple features: five windows and an elegant doorway, recessed into a brown brick wall with white dressings, can be composed into a small masterpiece. On the river front, a wide bow gives a foretaste of Regency, though the decoration of the oval room behind is Palladian in its high relief. The plan is as ingenious as the elevations are beautiful.

THE NINETEENTH CENTURY

1. REGENCY.
c. 1800–c. 1830 A.D.

The Regency Style is the swan-song of the English Renaissance, but seldom can a great age have passed more gracefully. It is true that walls are of stucco, but when this is kept well painted what can look pleasanter through the greenery of Regents Park or Cheltenham! The delicate cast-iron work which supports the tent roofs of balconies and verandahs is mass-produced, but to what elegant patterns! The new canals are distributing Welsh slate throughout England, but it is not particularly noticeable on the low-pitched roofs with their heavily projecting eaves. In the green-shuttered windows, sash bars have shrunk to mere lines across the glass and, after centuries, casements are returning, often as French doors. Often too the windows are placed in shallow bows, than which there are few happier shapes, inside or out.

Not that these gently classical buildings are inevitable. By now the Romantic Revival is under way, Gothic has become respectable and some of the villas have pointed gables, hood moulds over the windows and other tributes to the popularity of Sir Walter Scott. John Nash has a thriving side-line to his practice designing sham castles and Wyatville is employed to make Windsor yet more mediaeval.

Within, too, pomp and circumstance are usually absent and all is gay with flowered chintzes and striped wallpaper. Ornaments on the mantel-shelf above the soberly-classical fireplace are reflected in the tall mirror behind and the staircase spirals upwards with a severely delicate iron balustrade. It is, indeed, the age of the smaller house; the great mansions of the eighteenth-century aristocrats are left behind and those of the Victorian iron-masters are yet to come.

Let us admire all this while we can. Unfortunately much Regency architecture is in our towns on increasingly valuable sites and, unappreciated, is being ruthlessly torn down for yet more blocks of flats or terraces of shops. The Thames villages are suffering especially. This is the more ironical because so many of these modest dwellings are so easily adaptable to modern living. But already, in 1803, the writing is on the wall, for the first public railway in the world has been opened, the Surrey Iron Railway, from Wandsworth to Croydon, later to be extended to Merstham. We are in the world of Jane Austen, but that of Charles Dickens is only just round the corner.

23

SOUTHBOROUGH HOUSE (formerly SOUTHBOROUGH PLACE), Surbiton.

Built by John Nash for Thomas Langley in 1808. The plan is L-shaped, with a domed porch in the internal angle, an echo of the cupolas of Sussex Place, Regent's Park. The south elevation has deep, bracketted eaves, round-headed first floor windows and a bay crowned by a balustrade in the centre of the ground floor. Within there is an oval cantilevered staircase with 'S' balusters and much agreeable detail.

(A charming villa at Kingston-upon-Thames: Port Pleasant, c. 1797, by the same architect, has disappeared).

DEEPDENE, Dorking.

A late Palladian house altered in 1819–26 by Thomas Hope, the wealthy collector and neo-classicist, to his own designs but with some advice on construction from an architect, William Atkinson. The surviving front has a rusticated base storey and above five single-storey bays between two-storey, three-bay pavilions, with pilasters between the windows. Elsewhere both within and without the house has been much mauled about and the splendid collections have been dispersed, including Greek and Egyptian furniture designed by the owner to harmonise with his antiquities and described in his 'Household Furniture & Interior Decoration', (1807).

FORT BELVEDERE, Windsor Great Park, Egham.

The core of Fort Belvedere is a triangular tower with angle turrets, part of the landscaping of the park done by the Duke of Cumberland with the help of Paul Sandby, c. 1757. The architect was probably Henry Flitcroft and some of his elegant plasterwork survives.

In 1827 Wyattville was instructed by George IV to lay out a great half-moon bastion to accommodate the Duke of Cumberland's collection of guns, and to enlarge the tower to provide living quarter's for the gunners. Later additions included an octagonal banqueting-room for the king himself.

Further alterations were made in 1910, when the fort became a grace-and-favour residence and between 1930 and 1936 for the Duke of Windsor.

(see 'Country Life'. 19th–26th November, 1959).

2. VICTORIAN ECLECTICISM.
c. 1830–c. 1900 A.D.

No one has satisfactorily explained the steady decline in taste which affected English Architecture in the thirty years before about 1860. It is not a question of a style now unfashionable; if we apply to most of the buildings produced during this period the criteria by which all architecture should be judged, we find that mouldings grow progressively coarser, ornament over-done, proportions unhappier and materials less harmonious.

Of the contending styles, Classical perhaps comes off best, since there were rules to which lip-service was paid and the remnants of a tradition handed down through Regency. The Goths, on the other hand, were too often apt to thumb through their Continental sketch-books and produce buildings alien to the English scene and marred by that mechanical precision which so many Victorians mistook for ultimate beauty. Their best work, however, was ecclesiastical and is outside the scope of this book.

There were, of course, exceptions to the rule. The Victorians can at least claim that they were never timid; they had a prodigious self-confidence which led the less sensitive into the artistic disasters already mentioned, but enabled architects like Hopper at Penrhyn, Salvin at Harlaxton, Burges at Cardiff or Crossland at Egham to pull off remarkable tours-de-force in the way of period recreation. The great disappointment is Pugin. No architect could have been more scholarly, none had a greater devotion to his art, which was indeed part of his religion, yet the best of his uneven output never quite fulfils our hopes.

We must always remember, too, that for every building put up by an architect, hundreds were erected by speculating builders. In 1838 and 1841 respectively, the London & Southampton and the London & Brighton Railways drove their main lines through the Surrey countryside. Between them grew up the dense network later to be known as 'Southern Electric', transforming peaceful rural villages into dormitory suburbs, 'commuter country'. Mean terraces and later 'semi-detacheds' for clerks spread over the inner suburbs while the tycoons, whose office hours were shorter and purses longer, could afford to build further out on the hitherto-neglected Surrey hills. A century was to pass, however, before the last pockets of unspoilt countryside were to be threatened by the ubiquitous motor-car.

MOUNT FELIX (formerly WALTON HOUSE), Walton-on-Thames.

This was a Palladian house, of which the main staircase survives, transformed into an Italian villa in 1837–40 for the Earl of Tanker-ville. Here Sir Charles Barry is at his best, working in an idiom he liked and understood and the result is a building worthy to stand beside his great clubs in Pall Mall.

The long, low wings have brown stuccoed walls and pantiled roofs (an innovation), while the main entrance is beneath a high, narrow, triple-windowed tower which is magnificently sited as a focal point in the landscape on its bluff above Walton Bridge.

The gardens, needed to complete the effect of this particular style, have disappeared beneath bungalows and the building itself, divided into flats, is in some danger of demolition.

ALBURY PARK.

There are remains of a late mediaeval house and its early seventeenth-century successor incorporated in the present house which was built in 1697, altered by Soane in 1800 (the stair remains) and refronted by Pugin in 1846–52.

The elevations are in red-brick and rather dull, the best feature being the variety of the brick chimneys. Pugin did much better with his gateway and barn at Oxenford Grange, in Peper Harow Park.

Apart from its art treasures, the house repays a visit for the great terraced gardens, laid out by John Evelyn, the diarist, of Wotton, with a yew walk, semi-circular pool, bath-house and tunnel, as an 'English Pauslippe' (Posilipo).

ROYAL HOLLOWAY COLLEGE, Egham.

This enormous pile was built in 1887 for Thomas Holloway, the manufacturer of patent medicines, as the second college for women (after Girton). He wished it to be modelled on the great chateau of Chambord in the Loire valley and his architect, W. H. Crossland, a pupil of Sir Gilbert Scott, spent two years studying the prototype and paraphrasing its detail.

The plan is a double quadrangle, 550 feet long and 376 feet broad. At each corner is a lofty tower, complete with tourelles and between them, on the short sides are further towers crowned by open-work lanterns. There is yet another elaborate tower in the centre of the lower block separating the quadrangles.

The forest of chimney stacks, lucarnes, and pinnacles thrusting up from this five-storey palace on Mount Lee look across to Holloway's other benefaction, on St. Anne's Hill: Holloway Sanatorium, built by the same architect in continental Gothic.

3. THE RETURN TO TRADITION.
c. 1870–c. 1914 A.D.

In 1851 a seventeen-year-old boy, William Morris, sat resolutely down in the Entrance of the Great Exhibition and declined to go any further, declaring, with pardonable exaggeration that it was all 'wonderfully ugly'. Eighteen years later Philip Webb was to build for him the famous 'Red House' at Bexley, in Kent, and the return to tradition was fairly launched. The following year Webb was to build the first of a group of houses in Surrey: Benfleet Hall, Fairmile, Cobham.

The greatest figure, however, in this movement to return to the use of traditional materials using traditional techniques was Webb's old chief, Norman Shaw. His career was in some ways extraordinary for he developed in turn a passion for Half-timber, Elizabethan, Jacobean, Carolean, Queen Anne and Palladian design, doing good work in all but having some difficulty in carrying his clients along with him in his aesthetic odyssey.

Shaw had a much less gifted rival, Sir Ernest George, and to his office came the young Edwin Lutyens, destined to become one of the greatest of all English architects. Reared at Thursley, he numbered among his friends Tickner, the Milford builder and Gertrude Jekyll, the formidable gardener. His first building was Crooksbury, Seale, fundamentally 'George-ean' (as he termed it) but twice radically changed for successive clients. Others of his early works show him fumbling towards his mature style, but he first found himself in 'Munstead Wood', Busbridge, for Gertrude Jekyll herself. Profoundly versed in both the geometry and sophisticated vocabulary of the Renaissance and in the traditional usages of vernacular building, he used either with almost invariable success and was even capable of mixing them without incongruity. Many of his houses, too, owe much of their beauty to their settings, in gardens where Lutyens expertise in lay-out combined with Gertrude Jekyll's flair for planting and colour.

An architect without Lutyens' dazzling range but with possibly more influence on the modern movement was Charles Annesley Voysey. Externally his buildings were revolutionary only in their restraint in an over-decorative age but internally, although much of his detail 'dates' as 'arts-and-crafts', much also is surprisingly clear-cut and modern in feeling. Of all English architects his is the nearest approach to that of his great contemporary in America, Frank Lloyd Wright.

Of course the story of late Nineteenth-Century architecture in Surrey is much more complicated than this brief mention of its three most significant architects. The reader wishing to learn more is referred to Pevsner & Nairn's 'Surrey', (Buildings of Britain). The authors' erudition, the fruit of so much research and travel, places anyone who writes on Surrey architecture heavily in their debt, even though he may not always be prepared to endorse their rather trenchant judgements.

PIERREPONT, Frensham.

Built in 1876 and one of the earliest of Norman Shaw's at-the-time revolutionary buildings. It has the usual straggling plan, with most rooms opening off a spinal corridor, and is in the architect's earliest half-timber vein, though the service quarters are tile-hung, a traditional Surrey wall-covering he did much to revive. Internally there is a

Great Hall with a collar-braced roof and some good contemporary decoration.

MUNSTEAD WOOD, Busbridge, 1896.
TIGBOURNE COURT, Witley, 1899.

Munstead Wood was built for Lutyens' old friend, Gertrude Jekyll, who specified 'no random choosings, no meretricious ornament, no moral slothfulness, nothing poky or screwy or ill-lighted'. The result has sandstone walls, tiled roofs and brick chimneys with much old oak internally, especially in the gallery with its cantilevered window and glazed cupboards.

(see 'Home & Garden' by Gertrude Jekyll, 1900).

Tigbourne Court, built only three years later of Bargate Stone with garretted joints already shows Lutyens' mastery in the handling of masses and his remarkable sense of texture, as well as exhibiting such favourite motifs as great, sweeping roofs, curved walls and massive chimney stacks.

LITTLE COURT (formerly VODIN), Pyrford. (C. A. Voysey)

Built in 1902 and, except that the roof is tiled and not slated, typical of the architect's work, i.e. long and low with a deep roof, rough-cast walls with sloping buttresses and long rows of small casement windows. It is grouped with a stable block of 1904 to form a small courtyard.

POSTSCRIPT

FUNCTIONAL ROOTS.

The revival of traditional materials and techniques which had resulted in so much rewarding architecture in the fifty years before the First World War, petered out in what Mr. Osbert Lancaster terms "Stockbrokers' Tudor" and "Bankers' Georgian" before the second. In one respect, also, its early successes must be regretted for no opening was left for the introduction of a style which should take full advantage of new materials and techniques unknown to our ancestors, and as a result the modern movement was almost entirely evolved abroad.

It is, of course, a common accusation that modern architecture is an alien and upstart art, without roots in the past. Those roots, however, must not be sought in academic products or among the famous names but in the work of hundreds of nameless designers, mason-contractors and mill-wrights and engineers, who would never have dreamed of themselves as 'architects' or of their works as 'architecture'. But it is because they endeavoured to satisfy contemporary requirements in an entirely straight-forward, honest and logical way, without self-conscious 'artistry', that they appeal to us, in our flight from shams and pretences towards a saner, simpler expression that should accord with a changed world.

The most impressive examples of functional architecture, however, have come down to us from the industrial areas and not from a county like Surrey whence industry early fled, leaving behind only a few dozen reedy hammer-ponds and the trenches of old iron workings scarring our commons. Even the railways can contribute no monumental viaducts or impressive stations and we are left with rather a heterogeneous collection of examples to illustrate this last section of the introduction.

The reader may possibly have noticed that certain Twentieth-Century items appear in the List, a contribution of the Ministry's advisers. We feel ourselves, however, that it is as yet too early to select what is of most significance in modern architecture; we cannot yet see the wood from the trees or view everything in its proper perspective. The task we accordingly leave to future editors making as our plea that, whatever their merits, such buildings cannot yet properly qualify as 'Antiquities' of Surrey.

WOLSEY'S WATER-WORKS.

Believing the water good for the 'Stone', Cardinal Wolsey in 1516 tapped springs on Coombe and Kingston Hills and carried them in twin lead pipes over three miles across country and beneath the Thames to his new palace at Hampton Court.

The three conduit houses still exist though one, Ivy Conduit, has been wrecked by bombing and looters. Gallows Conduit has only one of the original twin buildings, but both survive at Coombe Conduit, linked by an underground passage. Of the intermediate inspection points, called 'Tamkins', only one, over-restored, stands on a golf-course; the remainder have disappeared without trace.

(see S.A.C. Vol. LVI. 1959).

OUTWOOD MILL, Burstow.

This is the oldest working windmill in England, proved by the surviving lease from Richard Paine of Westhoathly to Thomas Budgen of Nutfield, Miller, dated 1665. It originally probably had an open trestle, now raised on piers within a round-house, while the sails would have been spread with canvas and not have patent shutters. The smock mill that once stood beside it has gone.

(see M. I. Batten: 'English Windmills'. Vol. 1. S.P.A.B. 1930).

NEWARK MILL, near Ripley.

This almost certainly stands on the site of the mill belonging to Newark Priory, and though the earlier part of the existing building, that with the gable, only dates from the seventeenth century, it is possibly the oldest water-mill in the county. Originally there were two internal wheels, fourteen feet in diameter, but a third wheel was added externally, also under-shot, so that four pairs of stones could be driven.

(see J. Hillier: 'Old Surrey Water Mills'. 1951).

THE WEY NAVIGATION.

Between 1651 and 1653, Sir Richard Weston of Sutton Place, famous for his innovations in crop rotation, joined with other 'undertakers' in making the Wey navigable from the Thames to Guildford, involving numerous stretches of canal and among the earliest locks in England, some of which still have earthen sides while others are lined with bricks from Oatlands Palace. In 1760 the canal was extended to Godalming, while from 1813–1868 the ill-fated Wey & Arun canal gave a link with the sea. On the quay at Guildford is a crane worked by a giant tread-wheel. (Part transferred to National Trust in 1963.)

(see L. T. C. Rolt: 'The Inland Waterways of England'. 1950).

THE SURREY IRON RAILWAY.

This, the first public railway in the world, was horse-drawn and ran from Wandsworth to Croydon. After its opening in 1803, it was extended as the Croydon, Godstone & Merstham Railway, but this later section was abandoned, the overgrown cutting being visible alongside the Brighton Road, particularly near Merstham. The seemliness of the buildings of Mitcham Station, now serving Southern Electric, makes one regret that our railways were not built fifty years earlier.

THE ADMIRALTY SEMAPHORE LINES.

These were designed to allow rapid communication between the Admiralty and the chief naval stations, the messages being relayed by pensioners armed with telescopes. Lord George Murray's system, of 1796–1814, which had frames carrying shutters and huts for the operators, was abandoned after the defeat of Napoleon, but revived with more permanent buildings carrying semaphore arms in 1823.

There were six stations on the Portsmouth route in Surrey and two more on the never-completed Plymouth branch. Three survive: at Cooper's Hill, Esher; Chatley Heath, Cobham; and Pewley Hill, Guildford. The system was abandoned, in favour of the electric telegraph, in 1847.

THE PALM HOUSE, Kew Gardens.

Built by Decimus Burton, Architect, and Richard Turner, Engineer, between 1844 and 1848, this great building was very closely modelled on its prototype, Paxton's earlier conservatory at Chatsworth. Now, however, that the latter has been blown up and its famous successor, the Crystal Palace, has been burned down, the Palm House must be preserved as the surviving representative of those earlier experiments in the logical use of glass and iron which were to reach their culmination in Barlow's superb vault at St. Pancras.

THE CITY CORPORATION BOUNDARY POSTS.

From early times the City Corporation intermittently took tolls from coal and wine entering London and these duties were levied continuously from 1666 until they were repealed in 1892 under the Coal Duties Abolition Act of 1889. The money was devoted to the extinction of the City's debt, (paid off in 1834), the rebuilding of the City after the Great Fire and subsequently on Metropolitan Improvements. Under the Coal Duties Acts of 1841 and 1851, the fiscal area was respectively defined as 25 and 20 miles from the G.P.O. and marked by stone obelisks bearing the City arms, erected on the banks of the Thames and canals and beside turn-pike roads and railways. (A typical example will be found between Epsom and Ashtead Stations.) In 1861 the area was re-defined as the London Police District and numerous smaller posts of cast-iron employed as markers.

(The Council acknowledges with gratitude the help of Mr. W. Bindoff, who made his researches available in compiling this list and who contributed an article to 'The Times' on the subject—17.5. 1961). (See also 'Country Life', 8.2.1962).

J. W. L. F.

PLATES

PLATE 1

Two Barrows, Horsell Common, Woking   *Major G. W. G. Allen*

Roman Bath Buildings, Roman Way Housing Site, Farnham   *N. B. Cookson*

PLATE 2

(a)   *Newark Priory, Ripley*   *D. Yel*

(b)   *Waverley Abbey Ruins, Farnham*   *D. Yell*

PLATE 3

Norman Oak Pillar in wall at Farnham Castle, Farnham *D. Yellan*

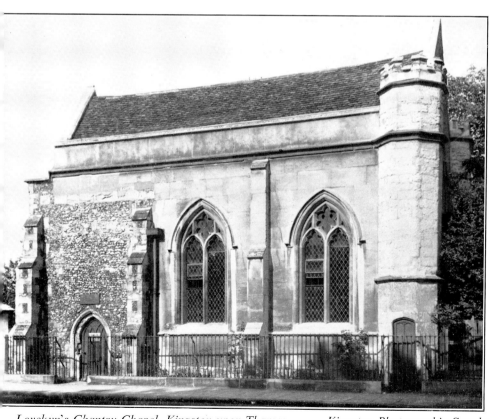

Lovekyn's Chantry Chapel, Kingston-upon-Thames *Kingston Photographic Supply*

PLATE 4

Guildford Castle, Guildford

Vivian Hu

PLATE 5

Clattern Bridge, Kingston-upon-Thames   *F. W. Strange*

Eashing Bridge, Shackleford   *D. Yellan*

PLATE 6

(a) *Crown Inn, Chiddingfold*

Topical Pr

(b) *Old Manor House, Walton-on-Thames*

D. Yel

PLATE 7

Osbrook's Farm, Capel   D. Yellan

Brewer Street Farmhouse, Bletchingley   D. Yellan

PLATE 8

(a) *Homewood Farmhouse, Newark Lane, Ripley*   *D. Yella*

(b) *Nos. 2, 4 and 6 (Sweech House), Gravel Hill, Leatherhead*   *Austin Youe*

PLATE 9

Pennypot Cottage, Chobham   *D. Yellan*

Privett (or Guildables), Cottages, Limpsfield   *W. Scott Henderson*

PLATE 10

(a) *Lythe Hill Farmhouse, Chiddingfold* D. Ye

(b) *Great Tangley Manor, Wonersh* D. Yel

PLATE 11

rance Porch, Crullings and Smallfield Place, Burstow   *Cosser Photographic Service*

PLATE 1.

(a) *Great Hall, Old Surrey Hall, Lingfield* D. Ye

(b) *Fox's Tower, Farnham Castle, Farnham* D. Ye

PLATE 13

aynflete's Tower, Esher D. *Yellan*

PLATE 14

(a) *Crullings and Smallfield Place, Burstow* *Cosser Photographic Serv*

(b) *Loseley House, Artington* *D. Yel*

PLATE 15

Nonsuch Panels, Loseley House, Artington   *J. T. May*

Great Fosters, Egham   *D. Yellan*

Abbott's Hospital, High Street, Guildford   *D. Ye*

PLATE 17

. 155 (*Child House*), *High Street, Guildford*   *D. Yellan*

(a) *Brook Place, Chobham*   *D. Yell*

(b) *Kew Place, Royal Botanical Gardens, Kew*   *D. Yella*

PLATE 19

Guildhall, High Street, Guildford   *D. Yellan*

(a) *Crossway's Farm (front gable), Abinger*   *D. Ye.*

(b) *Pendell Court, Bletchingley*   *D. Ye.*

PLATE 21

) *Ashtead Park Farmhouse, Ashtead*　　　　　　　　　　　*Michael Hall*

Ham House, Petersham　　　　　　　　　　　*Jane Bown*

No. 38 (Wilmer House), West Street, Farnham

D. Yell

PLATE 23

ircase, Reigate Priory, Reigate

D. Yellan

(a) *The Trumpeter's House, Old Palace Yard, Richmond*   D. Yel.

(b) *Nos. 1–4 Maid of Honour Row, The Green, Richmond*   D. Yel.

PLATE 25

) *Tadworth Court, Banstead*   *D. Yellan*

) *Clandon Park House, West Clandon*   *J. W. Lindus Forge*

(a) *Asgill House, Old Palace Lane, Richmond*

D. Yell

(b) *The Wick, Richmond Hill, Richmond*

D. Yella

PLATE 27

Claremont, Esher   *D. Yellan*

Southborough House, Surbiton   *D. Yellan*

Royal Holloway College, Egham

D. Yel

Palm House, Royal Botanical Gardens, Kew

D. Yel

PLATE 30

Pierrpont School, Frensham   *D. Yellan*

Gallery, Munstead Wood, Busbridge   *D. Yellan*

(a) *Tigbourne Court, Witley*   *D. Yel*

(b) *Little Court, Pyrford*   *D. Yel*

PLATE 32

The Granary, Peper Harow Farm, Peper Harow   *D. Yellan*

Newark Mill, Ripley   *D. Yellan*

(a) *Elstead Mill, Elstead*   *D. Yel*

(b)*Wheel at Elstead Mill*   *D. Yel*

TITLES OF THE FOLLOWING PLATES

PLATE 34

(a) *Doorway, No.* 44 *Quarry Street, Guildford*   *Arthur J. Mason*

(b) *Gallows Conduit House, George Road, Coombe*   *D. Yellan*

PLATE 35

(a) *Reigate Heath Windmill, Reigate*   *D. Yellan*

(b) *Coal and Wine Tax Post, New Road, Esher*   *D. Yellan*

QUARRY HILL HOUSE.

PLATE 36

(a) *St. Peters Cross and Village Cage, Lingfield* *H. Courland*

(b) *Old Wheel and Crane, Guildford Wharf, Guildford* *D. Yel.*

SURREY COUNTY COUNCIL

LIST OF ANTIQUITIES IN THE ADMINISTRATIVE COUNTY OF SURREY

NOTE.—The undermentioned symbols set against certain of the listed Antiquities have the following meanings:-

   * Included in a List of "Scheduled" Ancient Monuments by the Minister of Public Building and Works under the provisions of the Ancient Monuments Acts, 1913 and 1931.

  ** Recommended for addition to the List of "Scheduled" Ancient Monuments.

   φ Included in Certified Statutory List as a Grade I Building of Special Architectural or Historic Interest by the Minister of Housing and Local Government under the provisions of the Town and Country Planning Act, 1962.

   ‡ Included in a Certified Statutory List as a Star Grade II Building of Special Architectural or Historic Interest by the M/H. & L.G.

   † Included in a Certified Statutory List as a Grade II Building of Special Architectural or Historic Interest by the M/H. & L.G.

  †† Included in a Supplementary List as a Grade III Building of Architectural or Historic Interest, issued with the Certified Statutory List by the M/H. & L.G.

C.P. Crown-owned property—listed by M/H. & L.G. but not subject to the above named 1962 Act provisions.

N.T. National Trust property.

P... S.C.C. Identification Plaque affixed to property.

NORTH-WESTERN PLANNING AREA

BAGSHOT RURAL DISTRICT

BISLEY   *GENERAL*

1   †† The Old Cottage (16c.), Church Lane
2   †† Newbridge Cottage (16c.) Newbridge,

BISLEY GREEN

3   †† Combers Cottage (15c.)
4   †† Ford Farm Cottage (18c.)

CLEW'S LANE

5   ‡ Clew's Farm (15c. & 16c.)
6   † Holy Well of St. John the Baptist (near Clew's Farm)

CHOBHAM   *GENERAL*

7–9 †† Scotts Grove Farm (17c. altered) and barns (2) (early 18c.), Scotts Grove Road
10   * Earthwork on Albury Bottom
11   †† Fowlers Wells (mid 18c.)
12   †† Gracious Pond Farm (16c.)
13   ** Barrow at Heatherside, Ridgemount Road, Sunningdale
14   †† Home Farm (16c.), Steep Hill
15   † Fosters Farm (16c.), Woodcock Lane
16   Lovelands Farm (17c. & 18c.)

BAGSHOT ROAD

17   ‡ Brook Place (1654) P.47
18   †† Timbers (16c. & 17c.)
19   Whitedown Cottage (17c.)

BURROW HILL

20   †† Brimshot (15c. and later)
21   †† Burrow Hill Farm (16c. and later)
22   Heneage Farm (17c. and later)
23   †† Jasmine Cottage (15c. and later)
24   †† The Four Horse Shoes (P.H.) (18c.)
25   †† Virginia's Cottage, adjoining Burrow Hill Farm (16c. and later)
26   †† Wayside (16c.)

CASTLE GROVE ROAD

27   † Castle Grove House (1643)
28   † Pond House (16c. and later)

Borough or District Civil Parish	No.	Name or Description of Antiquity

CHOBHAM—*cont.*

CHERTSEY ROAD

29 †† Cooper's Lodge (early 18c.)
30 † Fish Pool Cottage (16c.)
31 †† Old Pound Cottage (16c.)
32 † Pear Tree House (early 18c.)
33 †† Three Ways Cottage (16c.)
34 Copyhold (17c. and later)

CHOBHAM PARK LANE

35 †† Chobham Park House (18c. and earlier)

HIGH STREET

36–8 †† Nos. 1, 2 and 3 (early 19c.)
39–40 † Baker's shop (Mitchell) and house (16c. with alterations)
41–2 † Cannon Cottage and Laurel Cottage (16c.)
43 † Chemist's shop (Herbert) (18c. with 19c. shop front)
44 † Florida House (mid 18c.)
45 †† Grant's Cottage (mid 18c.)
46–7 †† House and shop (Chobham Stores) (16c. with 18c. alterations)
48–9 † House and shop (Grimditch) (17c. or 18c., part modernised)
50–53 † Westminster Bank, Hairdresser, Spong Cottage, Telephone Exchange (17c. & 18c.)
54 †† King's Head P.H. (early 18c.)
55–6 † Lynton House and Belcher's Shop (late 17c. & 18c.)
57 †† Myrtle Cottage (18c.)
58 †† Saddler's Halt (early 19c.)
59 †† The Sun (P.H.) (early 18c.)
60–2 †† Two Cottages with baker's shop (Burrows) on corner (mid 18c.)
63 † White Hart Hotel (16c. & 17c.)

LUCAS GREEN ROAD

64 †¹ Lucas Green Manor (16c. and later) P.74
65 †† Manor Cottage (16c.)

¹ See Surrey County Journal, January, 1953

Borough or District Civil Parish	No.	Name or Description of Antiquity

CHOBHAM—*cont.*

PENNY POT LANE
66 †† Hatchgate Farm (late 18c.)
67 † Penny Pot Cottage (16c.) P. 85
68 † Yew Tree Cottage (16c.)

PHILPOT LANE
69 † Brooklands House (early 18c.) and small House (17c.)
70 †† Emmett's Mill (18c.)

STANNERS HILL
71 Stanners Hill Manor (17c. and later)
72 † Stanner's Cottage (17c.)

WEST END
73 † Malthouse Farm, Benners Lane (16c. & 17c.)
74 Brentmoor Dene (c.1610)
75 †† Brooklands Farm, Blackstroude Lane (16c. & 17c.)
76 ** Three Barrows on West End Common
77 Fellow Green (16c. and later)
78 † Hookstone Farmhouse, Hookstone Green (16c.–18c.)

WINDLESHAM ROAD
79 †† Biddle Farm (15c.)
80 † Buckstone Farm (15c. & 16c.)   .
81 † Steep Acre Farm (16c.)

WINDSOR ROAD
82 † The Cloche Hat Restaurant (formerly Sundial Cottage) (14c.)
83 The Dial House (c.1720)
84 †† The Homestead (16c. and later)

WINDLESHAM

BAGSHOT
GENERAL
85 † Queen Anne House (early 18c. and later) Bridge Road
86 Brookside Bridge (17c. and later)

Borough or District Civil Parish	No.	Name or Description of Antiquity

WINDLESHAM—cont.

HIGH STREET

87–90 †† Nos. 17, 15, 13 & 11 (formerly Nos. 1, 2, 3 & 4) (early 19c.)

91 †† No. 63 (Rural District Council Offices) (18c.)

92–5 † The Three Mariners Inn and three houses to the west, comprising former Lyon Inn (16c. and later)

96–7 Bridge House Tea Rooms and adjoining offices to the west (site of The Bell Inn) (16c.)

WINDLESHAM
GENERAL

98 †† The Cedars (Early 18c. and later), Church Road

99 Hatton Hill Lodge (18c.)

POUND LANE

100 †† Pound Meadow (formerly Ivy Dene Cottage) (16c.)

101 † Pound Cottage (16c.)

CHERTSEY URBAN DISTRICT

CHERTSEY

GENERAL

102–4 † Abbey Barn (Youth Club), Abbey Barn Cottage (17c.) and remains of early ovens in garden

105–7 † Nos. 1, 2 & 3, Manor Farm Cottages (formerly Nos. 1, 2 and 3, Abbey Farm Cottages) (16c. altered)

108 * Barrow 120 yards N.N.W. from Flutters Hill House

109 * Barrow S. of Flutters Hill

110 * Barrow S.E. of Longcross House

111 † "Wheelers Green" (formerly Wheatsheaf Cottages), Nos. 1 & 2 Bittams Lane (16c.) P. 98

112 †* Chertsey Bridge (1780–1785)

113 * Earthwork near Childown Hall, known as the Bee Garden, Chobham Common

114 † Crockford Bridge Farm (16c. & 17c.), Crockford Bridge

115 * Earthwork on Laleham Burway

Borough or District Civil Parish	No.	Name or Description of Antiquity

CHERTSEY—*contd.*

GENERAL—*contd.*

116–20††[1]Nos. 1, 3, 5, 7 and 9 (Late 18c.) Guildford Road

121–2 †Hardwick Court Farm and Barn (early 16c.), Hardwick Lane

123   †Redlands Farm (16c.), Lyne Lane P. 111

124   ††Manor Farm Barn (17c.)

125–6 *Site of the Abbey of Chertsey and Old Fish Ponds

127   *St. Ann's Hill Camp

128–9†**St. Ann's Chapel (remains of) and St. Ann's Cottage adjoining

130–1††The Old Parsonage and Kilree Cottage (18c. and earlier)

132   The Old Farm House (16c.), Woodham Grange Road

133   Brick Bridge over the Bourne (Late 18c.), Woodham Park Road

134   Anningsley Park, Ottershaw

135   ††The White Cottage (formerly Thatched Cottage) (17c.), Murray Road

136   C.P. Mediaeval doorway in garden wall of Abbey House, Colonel's Lane

137   †Botleys (*c.*1750)

138   Green Lane Farmhouse (17c.)

139   ††Hunters Wynd, Holloway Hill (early 18c.)

140   Anchor House, Longcross Hill (18c.)

141–3 ‡The Grotto, Tea House and †temple of Freedom, St. Ann's Hill House

BRIDGE ROAD

144   ††No. 7 (18c.)

145   ††No. 9 (early 18c.)

146–7††Nos. 34 and 36 (early 19c.)

148–50††Nos. 46, 48 and 50 (early 19c.)

151–2††Nos. 66 and 68 (mid 18c.)

153–4 ††[2]Nos. 78 and 80 (mid 18c.)

155   †Belsize Grange (early 18c.)

156   ††The Vine (P.H.) (early 18c.)

157   No. 88 (18c.)

[1] Demolished 1959–60
[2] Demolished 1957

Borough or District Civil Parish	No.	Name or Description of Antiquity

CHERTSEY—*contd.*

GUILDFORD STREET

158 †† No. 86 (early 18c.)
159–66 †† Nos. 94 to 108 (17c. & 18c.)
167–8 † Nos. 118 and 120 (19c.)
169 †† No. 126 (The Prince Regent (P.H.)) (18c.)
170 †† Guildford House (Late 18c.)
171 † No. 45 (The George Inn) (17c.) P. 110
172–3 †† Nos. 71 and 73 (18c.)
174–5 †† Nos. 83 and 85 (late 17c.)
176 † No. 101 (early 18c. and later)
177 † No. 103 (King's Head Hotel) (17c. & 18c.)
178 †† No. 121 (18c.)

LONDON STREET

179–82 †† Nos. 6 to 12 (late 17c. & 18c.)
183–4 † Nos. 11 and 13 (early 19c.)
185–6 †† Nos. 17 and 19 (*c.* 1700)
187–92 †† Nos. 22 to 32 (17c., 18c. and early 19c.)
193–8 †† Nos. 29 to 39 (early 19c.)
199–202 †† Nos. 36 to 42 (17c. & 18c.)
203–5 † Nos. 44 to 48 (16c.–18c.)
206 † No. 60 (Dover House) (18c.)
207–9 † Nos. 62, 64 and 66 (Calais Cottage) (18c.)
210 No. 84 (18c.)

PYRCROFT ROAD

211 † Golden Grove (P.H.) (17c.)
212 † Pyrcroft House (18c.)

ROW TOWN

213 †† No. 4 (formerly No. 2) (18c.)
214 †† Hall Farm Cottage (16c.)
215 †† Thatch Cottage (17c.)
216 Myrtle Cottage (18c.)

STONE HILL ROAD

217 †† Ivy Cottage (16c.)

WINDSOR STREET

218 † York Corner (early 18c.)
219 † York House (18c.)
220 † York Cottage (18c.) P.113

Borough or District Civil Parish	No.	Name or Description of Antiquity

CHERTSEY—*contd.*   *WINDSOR STREET*—*contd.*

221–3   † Nos. 2, 4, 6 (17c.)

224–8   † Nos. 8, 10, 12 (Curfew House), 14 and 16
             (18c.)

229–43 †† Nos. 18 to 46 (17c. & 18c.) including The
             Sun (P.H.)

244–7   Nos. 13, 15, 15A and 17 (18c.)

248   ‡ No. 25 (early 18c.)

249   † No. 29 (Denmark House) (18c.) P. 123

250–1   † No. 33 (The Cedars and Little Cedars)
             (18c.) P. 112

252   †† No. 27 (The Swan) (P.H.) (18c.)

ADDLESTONE
GENERAL

253–5   Hamm Court Farm (early 18c.) †Dovecot
             and Moat

256   Ongar Place (18c.) Ongar Hill

257   †† Woburn Hill House (early 19c.), Woburn
             Hill

258   †† Entrance Pillars to Addlestone Park (prob-
             ably 18c.)

CHERTSEY ROAD

259–60 †† Nos. 114 and 116 (early 19c.)

261   † Hatch Farm (17c. with 18c. alterations)

262   †† Ivy Cottage (early 19c.)

263   † The George Inn (16c. with 18c. alterations)

EGHAM URBAN DISTRICT
EGHAM   *GENERAL*

264–8   † Almshouses Nos. 1 to 5 (1624, restored
             19c.), Egham Hill

269   †† Bulkely House (late 18c.)

270   Cumberland Obelisk (18c.)

271   † Dalkeith House (18c.), London Road

272   †† Englefield Green House, Englefield Green
             (mid-late 18c.)

273   †† Fort Belvedere (18c.)

274   ‡ Lych Gate at St. John Baptist Church (15c.)

275   Magna Carta Monument Stone near Runny-
             mede Lodges, Windsor Road

Borough or District Civil Parish	No.	Name or Description of Antiquity

EGHAM—*contd.*

GENERAL—contd.

276 Magna Carta (No. 4, The Glanty) (mid 18c.)

277 †The Old House (formerly Englefield Green House) (18c.), Englefield Green

278 Warren Farm (16c.), Portnall Park

278–(1) Royal Holloway College (1879)

HIGH STREET

279–81††No. 53 (White House Tea Rooms) (18c.) 53A and 54

282 ††No. 159 (Constitutional Club) (18c.)

283 ††King's Arms (P.H.) (17c. & 19c.)

284 †Literary Institute (18c.)

285 ††Old House Cafe (17c. & 18c.)

MIDDLE HILL

286 No. 1 (18c.)

287 No. 9 (18c.)

288–91††Nos. 20, 21, 22 and 23 (Prospect Place) (18c.)

292 ††Englefield Lodge (c.1730 with later additions)

STROUDE

293 ††Stroude Farm (17c.)

294–5 †Great Fosters (1550) and Stables, P. 29

296 Memorial Stone on site of Roman Road

296(1) Royal Holloway Sanatorium (1884)

THE AVENUE

297 ††Milestone (18c.)

298 ††The Red House (18c.)

THE HYTHE

299–309††Nos. 1 to 11 (18c.)

310–316 †Nos. 20 to 26 (17c. & 18c.)

317–8 Nos. 27 and 28 (17c. & 18c.)

319 †No. 29 (The Free House) (17c.)

320 †No. 30 (Ye Anne Boleyn Hotel, formerly Ye Old Bridge House) adjoining No. 29 (18c.)

321 †The Jolly Farmer (P.H.) (17c. & 18c.)

322 ††The Swan Hotel (18c. and earlier)

Borough or District Civil Parish	No.	Name or Description of Antiquity

THORPE

GENERAL

323–4 †† Nos. 1 & 2, Church Approach (formerly Carl Hawes Cottages) (16c. with 18c. alterations)

325 † Eastley End Cottage (16c. & 17c.), Norlands Lane

326 † Little Manor House (18c.), Crockhurst Lane

327 † The Rose and Crown (P.H.) (16c. & 17c.), Thorpe Green

328 †† Thorpe Mill (17c. & 18c.), St. Ann's Hill Lane

COLDHARBOUR LANE

329 † No. 25 (Renald's Herne) Coldharbour Lane (formerly Gardener's Cottage, formerly Thorpe House Cottage) (17c. & 18c.)

330 †† Black House Farm Cottages (Early 18c.)

331 †† Manor Farm (18c.)

332–4 †† Spelthorne St. Mary Anglo-Catholic Home (early 19c.), †wrought-iron gates (early 18c.) and ††stable block (now laundry) (16c.)

335 † Thatched Cottage, adjoining above stable block (16c.)

336 The Vicarage (18c. restored)

337 ‡ Thorpe House (17c., with 18c. front)

338–9 †† Thorpe Place Cottage (18c.) and †Old Wall (1613) adjoining Spelthorne St. Mary

340 † Village Hall (formerly Tithe Barn) (17c.)

ROSEMARY LANE

341 †† Ivy Cottages (17c.)

342 †† The Chimneys (formerly Eglantine) (16c. & 17c.)

VILLAGE ROAD

343 † The Cottage (16c.–18c.)

345 †† Little Timbers (16c.)

344 † Curl Hawes (16c. or 17c.)

346 † Thorpe Farm (late 16c.–early 17c.)

Borough or District Civil Parish	No.	Name or Description of Antiquity

FRIMLEY AND CAMBERLEY URBAN DISTRICT

FRIMLEY

GENERAL

347 †† Bristow Farm, Frimley Road (17c.)
348 †† Bowling Green Cottage (early 17c. much restored), Frimley Green Road
349 Frimley Lodge (19c.)
350 †† King's Head (P.H.)
351 Mytchett Place (*c.*1780 and later)
352 †† The Manor House (late 18c.)
353 † The Old Rectory (late 18c.)
354 The Pilgrims' Well
355 †† The White Hart (P.H.) (17c. and later)

FRIMLEY GREEN

356–7 †† Bedford Farm (15c.) and Barn (17c. restored)
358 † Cross Farm (15c. & 16c.)
359–60 † Cross Cottages, Nos. 1 and 2 (1713) Cross Lane
361–2 †† Moor Farm and Barns (17c.)
363 †† Whitewell Farm (16c. & 17c.)

FRIMLEY STREET

364–5 †† Nos. 30 and 32 (17c. restored)

CAMBERLEY

GENERAL

366 Milestone (1819) opposite site of Golden Farmer (P.H.)
367 †† Ruins of the Obelisk

LONDON ROAD

368–9 †† Nos. 141 and 142 (early 19c.)

WALTON AND WEYBRIDGE URBAN DISTRICT

WALTON-ON-THAMES

CITY OF LONDON CORPORATION BOUNDARY POSTS

370 North side of A.244 approach to Walton Bridge
371 West side of Molesey Road at junction with Pool Road

Borough or District Civil Parish	No.	Name or Description of Antiquity

WALTON-ON-
   THAMES—*contd.*

GENERAL

372–4 †† Nos. 1, 3 and 5 (Early 19c.) Ashley Road
375   †† Belfry House
376   †† Burhill
377   †† Burwood House (Convent of Notre Dame) (18c.)
378   † Burwood Park School (18c.)
379   †† Squirrells Drey (formerly Catts Hill Cottage) Burwood Park (17c. & 18c.)
380   † Old Manor House (*c.* 1500) Manor Road P. 26
381   †† Park Cottage (17c.) Burhill Park
382–3 † South Waylands Farm, moated and Barns (17c.), Esher Road
384   †† Southwood Manor Farm (formerly Beres Farm) (16c. and later)
385   * St. George's Hill Camp
386   †† Thames Cottage (17c. & 18c.), Thames Street

BRIDGE STREET

387   †† No. 34 (Park House) (early 19c.)
388–9 † Mount Felix and stables (18c. and 19c.)
390   †† The Duke's Head (P.H.) (18c.)

CHURCH STREET

392–4 † Nos. 13, 15 and 17 (17c. & 18c.)
395–6 †† Nos. 26 and 28 (18c.)

HERSHAM ROAD

397   †† No. 106 (16c. and later)
398   †† Elm Grove (early 19c.)

HIGH STREET

401   †† No. 47 (Henry Ireton's House) (*c.* 1650)
402   †† No. 68 (early 19c.)

MOLESEY ROAD (LOWER GREEN)

403–6 † Nos. 1, 3, 5 and 7 (16c. and later)
407   † No. 9 (16c. and later)
408   †† No. 94 (early 18c.)
409   †† Barley Mow (P.H.) (early 18c.)

Borough or District *Civil Parish*	*No.*	*Name or Description of Antiquity*

WALTON-ON-
THAMES—*contd.*

PAINS HILL PARK (*Nr. Cobham*)

410 †† Bath House (late 18c.)
411 †† Garden Urn on Pedestal
412 †† Gothic Temple (late 18c.)
413 † Pains Hill House (1780)
414 †† Rockworth Bridge
415 †† The Chapel (late 18c.)
416 [1] The Grotto
417 † The Lodges (18c.)
418 †† The Tower (19c.)

WEYBRIDGE

GENERAL

419 † Brooklands Farm (16c. & 17c.)
420 Eastlands (18c.), Brooklands Lane
421 †† Queen's Head (P.H.) (early 18c.), Bridge Road
422–6 †† Oatlands Palace. Sections of Garden Wall, including Tudor gateway (blocked). Underground chambers and drains (16c.) Oatlands Park Hotel (19c.), possibly incorporating parts of 18c. building)
427 † Robin's Nest (1767), High Street
428 † School Cottage (late 17c. and early 18c.), Springfield Meadows
429 † The Old House (18c.), The Quadrant
430 † York Column (1822) (originally at Seven Dials; former dial-stone in front of Council offices), Monument Square

CHURCH STREET

431 †† No. 42, Ye Old Curiosity Shop (16c. & 17c.)
432–3 † Nos. 54 (Portmore House) and 56 (Portmore Cottage) (18c. and later)

HEATH ROAD

434–5 †† Nos. 2 and 3 (mid 18c.)
436 † Nutfield (mid 18c.)

MONUMENT GREEN

437 † No. 23 (The Old White House) (early 18c.)
438–40 Lavender Cottage and †† two cottages adjacent (18c.)
441 † Ship Inn (17c. and later)

[1] Now Derelict

Borough or District Civil Parish	No.	Name or Description of Antiquity

WEYBRIDGE—*cont.*

THAMES STREET

442 †† No. 51 (late 18c. and early 19c.)
443 † Gate piers to Portmore Estate (17c.)
444 †† St. Maur's Convent (late 18c.)
445 † The Old Crown (P.H.) (17c. with later alterations)

WOKING URBAN DISTRICT

BYFLEET

GENERAL

446–7 † Byfleet Mill House (mid-late 18c.) and † Water Mill (18c.)
448 †† Grasmere (early 18c.), Green Lane
449–51‡ The Manor House (late 17c. with later additions), (gate piers and walls) early 17c.

HIGH ROAD

452 †† Foxlake Farmhouse (18c.)
453 †† Manor Cottage (late 18c.)
454 †† Oak Tree Cottage (early 18c.)

RECTORY LANE

455 † No. 18 (Hedges) (16c. and later)
456 †† Stream Cottages (18c.)

HORSELL

GENERAL

457 ** Barrow at Lynwood, Woodham Lane
458 Bluegates (17c.)
459 † Boylett's (formerly Coombe Place) (16c. and later), Carthouse Lane
460 Castle House (17c. and later)
461–2 Pear Tree Cottage and Lawrence Cottage, Cheapside (late 17c.)
463 Elm Cottage (17c. & 18c.)
464 † Esgairs, High Street (16c.–18c.)
465 Ivy Cottage (17c. & 18c.)
466 †† Horsell Grange (early 18c.), Chobham Road
467 Scotcher's Farm (17c. & 18c.)

BULLBEGGAR'S LANE

468 † Well Farm (16c.–18c.)
469 †† Whopshott Farm (16c.)

Borough or District Civil Parish	No.	Name or Description of Antiquity

HORSELL—*contd.*

KNAPHILL

470 †Inwood (16c.), Barrs Lane

LITTLEWICK ROAD

471 ††Longcroft Cottage (early 18c.)

472–4 ††Whitfield Court, outbuildings and barn (mid 18c.)

PYRFORD

GENERAL

475 †Bluegate Cottage (16c.), Bolton's Lane

476 †Garden House (17c.), Pyrford Place

477–8 †Henry VII and Henry VII East Cotts. (formerly Pyrford Green Cottages) (16c.)

479 †Pyrford Place Cottages (16c.), Wisley Road

480 Pyrford Stone

481 The Old Almshouses (17c.), Byfleet Road

481(1) Little Court (formerly Bodin) (1902) Old Woking Road

LADY PLACE

482 Church Farm (16c.)

483 ††Church Farm Cottage (16c.)

484 ††Lady Place Cottages (16c.)

485 †Stone Farm (17c.)

PYRFORD ROAD

486 †Grove Cottage (16c.)

487 †Lees Farm Barn (17c.)

488 †The Old House (16c. & 17c. front elevation 1710)

489 ††Thorley Cottage (*c.* 1740)

490 ††Woodland View (formerly Nos. 1 and 2 Toss Cottages) (early 18c.)

491 ††Wheelers Farmhouse (16c.)

WOODHAM LANE

492 The Glebe Cottage (16c.)

WOKING

GENERAL

493 †No. 17 (The Old Oak Cottage) (16c., 17c. & 18c.), Vicarage Road

494 ††Brookwood Farm (16c.), Robin Hood Road

495 ††Cripplegate Cott., St. John's Road (17c. or earlier)

Borough or District Civil Parish	No.	Name or Description of Antiquity

WOKING—*contd.*

GENERAL—*contd.*

496 †† Dunmore Nursery Cottage (16c.), Smart's Heath

497 †† Ellis Place (16c. & 17c.), Berry Lane

498-9 † General stores and cottage (formerly The Old Cricketers' Inn) (16c., 17c. & 18c.), Westfield Common

500 †† Ramwick Cottage, Park Road

501 †† Roundhill Farm (16c.), Old Woking Road

502-4 *† Remains of Woking Palace with Barn and Moat (15c. and later)

505-6 * Two Barrows S.E. of Horsell Common

507 †† The Old Thatched Cottage (18c.), Loop Road

508 †† The Row Barge (P.H.) (Early 18c.), St. John's Road

BASINGSTOKE CANAL

509 Goldsworth (or Langman's) Bridge (*c.* 1790)

510 Woodend Bridge (*c.*1790)

CARTERS LANE

511 †† Roundbridge Farmhouse (early 18c.)

512 † The Old House (early 17c.)

513-4 † Woking Park Farmhouse (16c. & 17c.) and Barn (16c.)

CHURCH STREET

515 † The Old Vicarage (17c. & 18c.)

516 †† Weylea (early 18c.)

GUILDFORD ROAD

517-8 †† Hunt's Farm (16c. with later alteration) and †† The Old Cottage (16c.) Mayford

HIGH STREET

519 †† No. 12B (mid 18c.)

520 † No. 29 (16c.)

521 No. 34 (17c. & 18c.)

522 †† No. 61 (Kate Lodge) (early 18c.)

523 †† No. 63 (mid 18c.)

524-5 † Nos. 80 and 82 (late 17c.)

526-8 † Nos. 84, 86 and 88 (early 18c.)

Borough or District Civil Parish	No.	Name or Description of Antiquity

WOKING—*contd.*

HIGH STREET—*contd.*

529 ††Nos. 144 (Ashdean and Hanway) (16c. & 17c.)

530 No. 165 (15c.)

531–5 ††Nos. 193 to 201 (odd) (formerly Market House, see V.C.H. Vol. 3, p. 383) (much altered early 20c.)

536–7 †Nos. 130 and 132 (Magnolias and Ye Olde Brew House) (1715)

538 †No. 159 (The Old Manor House) (16c. & 17c.) P. 33

HOE BRIDGE ROAD

539 ††Hoe Bridge House (18c.)

540 †Hoe Place (1708) and stable block

KINGFIELD ROAD

541–2 ††Nos. 1 and 2 (Crowley Cottages) (18c. and earlier)

543 †Elmbridge Cottage (16c.)

544 ††Wingfield Arms (P.H.) (16c.)

SMARTS HEATH ROAD

545 ††No. 30 (Ivy Cottage) (16c.)

546 ††Little Housen (17c. & 18c.)

547 ††Thatched Cottage (17c., altered)

SUTTON GREEN

548–9 ††Nos. 5 and 6 (Sutton Green Cottages) (late 18c.)

550–1 ††Nos. 7 and 8 (Sutton Green Farm) (16c. & 18c.)

552 †Post Office (private residence) (16c.)

553–4 Whitmoor House and Falconry (16c.–18c. and later additions)

555 *Woking Old Manor House (site of) W. of R.C. Church

SUTTON PARK

556 †Bull Lane Cottages (16c. or earlier)

557 †Lady Grove Farmhouse (16c. & 17c., restored)

558 †Manor House (mid 18c.)

Borough or District Civil Parish	No.	Name or Description of Antiquity

WOKING—*cont.*

SUTTON PARK—contd.

559 †[1] Sutton Place (1525) P. 36
560 ††Sutton Park House (17c. & 20c.)

WHITMORE

561 †Cox's Farm (15c. or 16c.)
562 †The Old Cottage (15c. or 16c.)

RIVERSIDE PLANNING AREA

BARNES BOROUGH

BARNES

GENERAL

563–600 ††Nos. 84–124 and 93–125 Castlenau
601 Milestone at West end of Red Rover (P.H.) (1751)

BARNES COMMON

602 ††Mill Hill (early 19c.)
603 ††Mill Hill House (*c.* 1840, with 17c. & 18c. oak panelling)
604 ††Mill Hill Lodge (early 19c.)

BARNES TERRACE

605 †No. 3 (18c.)
606 ††No. 6 (18c.)
607 ††No. 6A (18c.)
608–9 †No. 7 & 7A (late 18c.)
610 †No. 8 (18c.)
611 †No. 9 (early 19c.)
612 †No. 10 (early 19c.)
613–4 †Nos. 13 and 14 (early-mid 18c.)
615 †No. 28 (18c.)
616 †No. 30 (late 18c.)
617 †No. 31 (Ivy House) (early-mid 18c.) P. 102

CHURCH ROAD

618–9 †Nos. 43 and 45 (Convent of the Sacred Heart) (18c. & 19c.)
620–1 †No. 113 (formerly The Homestead) including forecourt wall (*c.* 1700–1720)
622 †Strawberry House (formerly The Rectory) (18c.)

[1] See Surrey County Journal, March, 1950

Borough or District Civil Parish	No.	Name or Description of Antiquity

BARNES—*contd.*

CHURCH ROAD—contd.
623 ††Sun Inn (18c. and earlier)
624 †The Grange (*c.* 1700–1720)

MILL HILL ROAD
625 ††Toll House adjoining Putney Cemetery (early 19c.)
626 ††The Cedars (late 18c.)

STATION ROAD
627–8 ††Nos. 66 and 68 (18c.)
629 ††No. 70 (Gothic Cottage) (early 19c.)
630 ‡Milbourne House (17c. & 18c.) P. 87

MORTLAKE

GENERAL
631–2 †Gate piers (mid-late 17c.) and gates (early 18c.) to entrance of Cromwell House, Williams Lane
633 Milestone on island at junction of Upper Richmond Road and Sheen Lane (1751)
634 †West Hall (early 18c.) West Hall Road

CHRIST CHURCH ROAD
635–6 ††Nos. 60 and 58 (formerly Nos. 1 and 2) (early 18c.)
637–8 ††Nos. 52 and 50 (formerly Nos. 5 and 6) (18c.), Merton Cottages
639–41 ††Nos. 48, 46 and 44 (formerly Nos. 7, 8 and 9) (early 19c.)
642 ††Gates to Highgate House (early 19c.)
643–4 †Percy Lodge and West Lodge (late 18c.)

HIGH STREET
645 No. 105 (The Cottage) (18c.)
646 †No. 115 (Acacias) (18c.)
647 †No. 117 (Afron House) (18c.)
648 †No. 119 (Suthrey House) (17c.) (with later additions)
649 ‡No. 123 (*c.* 1720) including forecourt piers

RICHMOND PARK
650 C.P. Bog Lodge (18c.)
651 C.P. White Lodge (Mid 18c.)

Borough or District *Civil Parish*	*No.*	*Name or Description of Antiquity*

MORTLAKE—*contd.*

SHEEN LANE

653 †† Sheen House Garage (early 19c.)
652 †† East Sheen Lodge (18c. and later)

THAMES BANK

654 † Leyden House (16c., remodelled *c.* 175(
     and 1962) P. 88
655 Riverside House (17c. & 18c.)
656 † Thames Bank House (*c.* 1730)
657 † Thames Cottage (18c.)
658 †† Tudor Lodge (*c.* 1750)
659–60† Nos. 1 and 2, Thames Bank Cottages (18c.

UPPER RICHMOND ROAD

661 †† Hare and Hounds Hotel (Early 19c.)

ESHER URBAN DISTRICT
COBHAM

CITY OF LONDON CORPORATION
BOUNDARY POSTS

662 West side of Stokesheath Road, 50 yard
     east of Railway Bridge
663 South side of Birchwood Lane, 500 yard
     west of its junction with New Road
664 East side of New Road at Holroyd's Plan
     tation

GENERAL

665 †† No. 51 (Joanne), High Street
666 † Appleton's Cottage (17c. and later), Leigh
     Hill Road
667 † Benfleet Hall (formerly Sandroyd), Green
     Lane, Fairmile (1860 and later)
668 †* Chatley Semaphore Tower, Telegraph Hill
     Chatley Heath (early 19c.)
669 †† Chilbrook Farm (early 18c.)
670 †† Cottage to Pointer's Farm (17c.), Pointer's
     Green
671 † Downside Bridge (1782)
672 ** Earthwork on Chatley Heath
673 †† Norwood Farm (18c.), Fairmile
674 Pains Hill Cottage (early 19c.)
675–82 †† Postboys Row (8 Cottages) (early 19c.)

Borough or District Civil Parish	No.	Name or Description of Antiquity

COBHAM—*contd.*

GENERAL—contd.

683 ††The Old Cottage (adj. Teegen's Shop), River Hill
684–5 ††Upper Court and Stables, Fairmile (19c.)
686–8 ††Three Cottages, facing car park (16c.), Mill Hill

CHURCH STREET

689 ‡Church Stile House (1432) P. 56
690 †Lime House (18c.)
691 †Over-Bye (early 18c.)
692 ††Pyports (18c.)

DOWNSIDE ROAD

693 ††Bridge Cottages (early 18c.)
694 ††Park Cottage (17c.)
695–7 ††Plough Cottages (3) (17c.)
698 †Pump on S.E. side of Downside Common
699 ††The Plough Inn (18c.)

GOOSE GREEN

700–1 ††Goose Green Cottages (two) (16c. restored)
702–3 ††Old Wells Cottages (two) (17c.)

MILL ROAD

704 †Cobham Water Mill (early 19c.)
705 ‡Ham Manor (early 18c.)
706 ‡The Cedars (15c. 17c. & 18c.) (N.T.)
707–8 †The Old Mill House (17c. & 18c.) and Barn (18c.)

PORTSMOUTH ROAD

709 †Cobham Bridge (1782)
710 Milestone near East Lodge, Fairmile Hotel (18c.)
711–2 †The Old House and Vine House (18c.)
713 †White Lion Hotel (17c., with 18c. front)

TARTAR HILL

714 ††Bennett's Buildings (Early 19c.)
715 ††Ivy Cottage (Early 19c.)
716 ††Rambler Cottage (Early 19c.)

Borough or District Civil Parish	No.	Name or Description of Antiquity
ESHER		*CITY OF LONDON CORPORATION BOUNDARY POSTS*
	717	S. side Lower Green Road opposite footway under railway
	718	300 yards W. of Marquis of Granby (P.H.) Portsmouth Road
	719	Junction of Milbourne Lane, Arbrook Lane and Littleworth Road
	720	400 yards N.W. of Arbrook Farm
		GENERAL
	721–3	Nos. 1, 2 and 3, Castle Cottages (*c.* 1800) Catos Hill, The Green
	724	No. 146 (Southdown) Lower Green Road (19c.)
	725–6 ††	Esher Place (1749) and Esher Place Garden (early 18c.)
	727 ††	Few's Cottages (mid 18c.), Church Street
	728 †	Friend's Meeting House (early 19c.), Claremont Lane
	729 ††	Garson Farm (18c.), West End Common
	730 *	Milestone at Hill House Farm, Portsmouth Road (1768)
	731–6 ††	Six Cottages (Endcott, Westeria, Fleetwood, The Cottage, Myrtle Cottage and Forge Cottage) (early 18c. and later), Catos Hill
	737 ‡**	St. George's Church (disused) (1540 and later)
	738	The Old House, Portsmouth Road (19c.)
	739 †	Waynflete's Tower (*c.* 1480 and 18c.) Waynflete's Tower Avenue P. 81
		CLAREMONT PARK
	740 †	Claremont (1770) P. 24
	741 *	Milestone in Park (1747) inscribed "15 miles from Standard in Cornhill, London"
	742 ‡*	The Belvedere (early 18c.), Claremont
	743–5 †	The Gardener's House, Stables and Coach house (18c. and later)
	746 †	The Obelisk, Claremont Home Farmhouse
	747–8 ‡	The White House and walling to kitchen garden (18c. and later)

Plan of Esher Place, dated 1606.

[Facing p. 54

Barne feilde

Rayled Close

Longe meadowe

fyshing pond

The olde ponde

Orchard

P.t of y.e lawne

The garden

orchard + garden

Stable yarde

he hope yarde

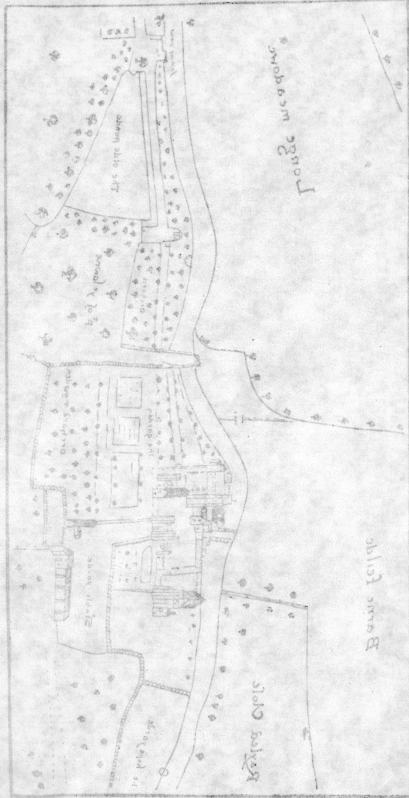

Plan of Tyster place, dated 1606. [Hering p.]

Borough or District Civil Parish	No.	Name or Description of Antiquity

ESHER—*contd.*

HIGH STREET

749 †† No. 51 (18c.)
750–1†† Nos. 75 and 77 (late 18c.)
752–3†† Nos. 83 and 85 (early 18c.)
754 †† No. 91 (early 19c.)
755–7†† Nos. 99 to 103 (odd) (early 18c.)
758 †† 115A (early 18c.)
759–60† †Nos. 136 and 138 (late 17c.)
761 †† Belvedere House (early 18c.)
762 †† Clive House (early 18c.)
763 †† Clive Place (early 18c.)
764–9†† Nos. 1–5 Dawes Court (early 18c.), and †† Dawes Cottage (18c.)
770 †† District Council offices (early 18c.)
771 † Moore Place Hotel (late 17c. & 18c.)
772 †† The Bear Hotel (early 18c., much altered)
773 † The Grapes (1616)
774 † The Traveller's Rest (Wolsey's Well)

MILBOURNE LANE

775–84† Nos. 32 to 50 (late 18c. and early 19c.)
785–7†† Nos. 76 to 80 (late 18c. and early 19c.)
788 Milestone between Nos. 24 and 26 (19c.)

WEST END LANE

789–90†† Nos. 55 and 56 (18c. or early 19c.)
791–2†† Nos. 59 and 60 (early 18c.)
793–4 † Nos. 68 and 69 (1742)
795 †† Chequers (early 18c.)
796 †† Clover Cottage (early 19c.)
797 †† Wayside Cottage (early 19c.)

LONG DITTON

GENERAL

798 †† Cumbrae Cottage (17c. and later), Ditton Hill Road
799 Remains of early Church of St. Mary's (now Garden of Rest)
800 The Old Manor (19c.), Thorkhill Road
801 The Manor House (18c.) adjoining Church, Woodstock Lane

Borough or District Civil Parish	No.	Name or Description of Antiquity
EAST MOLESEY		*CITY OF LONDON CORPORATION* *BOUNDARY POSTS*
	802	N. bank of River Ember S. of Island Barn Reservoir
		GENERAL
	803	Ice House in grounds of No. 10, Beauchamp Road (18c. restored)
	804	† Matham Manor (14c., with 17c., 18c. & 19c. alterations and additions), Matham Road
		BELL ROAD
	805–10	†† Nos. 14, 16, 18, 20, 22 and 24 (early 19c.)
	811–3	† Bell Inn (*c.* 1550) with coach houses, and No. 2 (16c., with 18c. alterations and additions)
	814	†† Green Arden (early 18c.)
	815–6	† Old Manor House and Quillets Royal, (16c. and later) P. 89
		BRIDGE ROAD
	817–8	†† Nos. 95 and 97 (early 18c.)
	819	† No. 117 (17c. & 18c.)
	820	†† No. 154 (late 18c. and early 19c.)
	821	†† Post Office (late 18c.)
		CREEK ROAD
	822	No. 3 (*c.* 1690)
	823–4	Nos. 5 and 7 (18c.)
		WALTON ROAD
	825	† No. 2 Olde House (Early 18c.)
	826–31	†† Nos. 8 to 18 Providence Cottages (18c. and later)
	832	†† No. 20 (early 19c.)
	833	‡ Radnor House (1720)
WEST MOLESEY		*CITY OF LONDON CORPORATION* *BOUNDARY POSTS*
	834	E. end of Sunbury Lock Ait at Middle Thames Yacht Club
	835	N. side of Hurst Road, opposite Bessborough Reservoir

Borough or District Civil Parish	No.	Name or Description of Antiquity

WEST MOLESEY—*contd.*

CITY OF LONDON CORPORATION BOUNDARY POSTS—*contd.*

836   S. side of Walton Road at junction with Molesey Road

HIGH STREET

837–9 †† Nos. 9, 11 and 13 (18c. or early 19c.)
840   †† No. 23 (18c.)
841   †† No. 47 (18c.)
842–3 †† Nos. 54 and 56 (18c.)
844–7 †† Nos. 59, 61, 63 and 65 (late 18c.)

NEW ROAD

848–51 †† Nos. 416, 418, 420 and 422 (late 18c., much altered)
852   †† Mole Abbey (formerly called The Lodge) (18c., much altered)

WALTON ROAD

853   † Church Farm (18c., with later alterations)
854   The Vicarage (early 19c., with later additions)

STOKE D'ABERNON

GENERAL

855   † Ashford Farmhouse (*c.* 1610)
856   Ivy Cottage, Tilt Lane (17c., restored)
857   C.P. Jessop's Well (18c.), Princes Coverts
858–9   ‡ Manor House and Tithe Barn (15c., 17c. & 18c.) P. 62

OXSHOTT—HIGH STREET

860   C.P. Danes Hill Farmhouse (16c.)
861   † Highwayman's Cottage (16c.)

THAMES DITTON

CITY OF LONDON CORPORATION BOUNDARY POSTS

862   W. side of Littleworth Road at junction with New Road
863   W. side of Littleworth Road at junction with Sandown Road
864   W. side of Copsem Farm, Copsem Lane
865   W. side of Copsem Lane at junction with Sandy Lane
866   N.E. of Stokesheath Farm Cottages

Borough or District *Civil Parish*	*No.*	*Name or Description of Antiquity*

THAMES
    DITTON—*contd.*

GENERAL

867   Laurel Cottage, Angel Lane (19c.)

868   †† Pine Tree Cottage (formerly Vine Cottage) (early 19c. and later), Manor Road North

869   †† Semaphore House, Telegraph Hill, Hinchley Wood (early 19c.)

870   St. Leonard's Farm Barn (18c.) Sugden Road

871–2 † Yew Tree Cottages (two) (late 18c.), Ditton Common

ALMA ROAD

873–4 † Nos. 1 and 2 Holly Cottages (17c. with alterations)

875–6†† Nos. 3 and 4 (early 19c.)

CHESTNUT AVENUE

877   †† The Old Red Cottage (early 18c.)

878   †† The Old Red House (18c.)

CLAYGATE

879   †† No. 12 (Rose Cottage) (late 17c.) with later alterations), St. Leonards Road

880   † Fee Farm (early 18c.), Fee Farm Road

881   † The Orchard (late 17c., with later alterations) Hare Lane

GIGGS HILL GREEN

882   † Angel Hotel (16c.)

883   †† Giggs Hill Cottage (18c. and earlier)

884   †† Honeysuckle Cottage (18c. and earlier)

885   †† Shop (Regent House) (18c. and earlier)

GIGGS HILL ROAD

886   †† Roseneath (early 19c.)

887–92† St. Leonard's Cottages (6) (18c. and later)

893–4†† Woodbine Cottages (two) (18c.)

HIGH STREET

895–7†† Nos. 3, 5, and 7 (17c. with later additions)

898–9†† Nos. 9 and 11 (early 19c.)

900–3†† Nos. 43 to 49 (late 18c.)

Borough or District Civil Parish	No.	Name or Description of Antiquity

KINGSTON-UPON-THAMES—*contd.*

HIGH STREET—contd.

965–7 † Nos. 37, 39 and 41 (*c.* 1600, with later alterations)

968 †† No. 52 (18c. & 19c.)

969 *† Clattern Bridge (three stone arches) (*c.* 1180 and later)

970 † Coronation Stone, beside Guildhall

LONDON ROAD

971 † No. 143 (Vine House) (early 18c.)

972–3 †† Nos. 155 and 157 (Artington Coombe Manor House) (late 17c.)

974 ‡ Cleaves Almshouses (1668) P. 4

975 †† Elmfield, in grounds of Tiffin Boys' School (early 19c.)

976 *† Lovekyn's Chantry Chapel or St. Mary Magdalen's Chapel (1305)

MARKET PLACE

977 Staircase in Hide & Co. (formerly site of Castle Inn) (1651)

978 † No. 23 (John Quality's Shop) (15c. & 17c.)

979–80 Nos. 32 and 33 (15c. & 16c.)

981 †† No. 41 (early 18c.)

982 † Boots (Chemist) (part) (15c.–18c.)

983–4 †† Market Hall (formerly Old Town Hall) (1838–40) and Statue of Queen Anne (1706)

RICHMOND ROAD

985 No. 3 (early 18c., with late 18c. front)

986 †† Old School building (1818)

SURBITON ROAD

987 † No. 3 ("The Elms") (18c.)

988 † Milestone at junction with Portsmouth Road (18c.)

VILLIERS ROAD

989 † No. 79 (The Old Mill House) (Late 18c.)

Borough or District *Civil Parish*	*No.*	*Name or Description of Antiquity*

RICHMOND BOROUGH
HAM

HAM COMMON
North Side

990	† Avenue Cottage (17c.)
991	†† Avenue Lodge (late 18c. and early 19c.)
992	‡ Avenue Lodge Cottage (17c.)
993	†† Garden Cottage (early 19c.)
994	†† Hardwicke House (late 18c.–early 19c.)
995–6	† Orford Hall (formerly Orford House) and stable block (late 18c.)
997	‡ Ormeley Lodge (early 18c.)
998	†† Parkgate Cottage (formerly stable block) (18c.)
999	† Parkgate House (1768)
1000	† Selby House (probably late 17c.)
1001–2	‡ Spur Cottage and South Lodge (early 19c.)
1003	†† Stafford Cottages (late 17c.)
1004	†† Sudbrook Cottages (early 19c.)
1005	†† The Cottage, Ormeley Lodge (late 17c. to Early 18c. and later restored)

South-west side

1006	C.P. Cassell Hospital (formerly Lawrence Hall) (late 18c.)
1007	†† Endsleigh Lodge (early 19c.)
1008	† Gordon House (late 18c. or early 19c.)
1009	† Langham House (late 18c.)
1010	†† The Little House (18c.)

HAM STREET

1011	†† No. 2 Yarrell's Cottages (18c.)
1012	‡ Beaufort House (late 17c.)
1013	† Buckmaster Estate Offices (late 18c.)
1014–5	† Greycourt and Stabling (late 18c.)
1016	†† Stokes Hall (18c.)

UPPER HAM ROAD

1017–8	†† Ivy House and Ivy Cottage (17c. & 18c.)
1019	‡ Sudbrook Lodge (1710)
1020	C.P. Sudbrook Lodge Cottage (18c.)
1021	†† The Rosery (late 18c.)
1022	The Gate House (1771)

Borough or District Civil Parish	No.	Name or Description of Antiquity

KEW

KEW GREEN

1023 †† No. 18 (Hope House) (early 19c.)
1024 † No. 20 (mid 18c.)
1025 †† No. 22 (East Side House) (early 19c.)
1026 †† No. 24 (Barclays Bank) (18c.)
1027 †† Coach and Horses Inn (18c.)
1028–30 †† Nos. 52, 54 and 56 (18c.)
1031–2 † Nos. 59 and 61 (18c.)
1033–5 †† Nos. 62, 64 and 66 (early 19c.)
1036 † No. 63 (18c., altered)
1037 † No. 65 (Warden Youse) (early 18c.)
1038 † No. 67 (White House) (early 19c.)
1039–40 †† Nos. 68 and 70 (early 19c.)
1041 † No. 69 (Ada Villa) (mid 18c.)
1042 † No. 71 (late 18c. & 19c.)
1043 † No. 73 (Danebury House) (late 18c.)
1044 †† No. 77 (early 18c.)
1045 † No. 83 (Capel House) (early 18c.)
1046–54 †† Nos. 90 to 106 (Waterloo Place) (1816)
1055 C.P. Hanover House (early 18c.)
1056 C.P. The Herbarium (18c.)
1057–8 C.P. Nos. 17 and 19 (18c.)
1059 † No. 21 (18c.)
1060–1 † Nos. 23 and 25 (mid 18c.)
1062–4 †† Nos. 27, 29 and 31 (late 18c. and early 19c.)
1065 C.P. No. 35 (King's Cottage) (18c.)
1066 C.P. No. 37 (Museum) (formerly Cambridge Cottage) (early 19c.)
1067 †† No. 49 (Kew Cottage) (early 18c.)
1068 C.P. No. 51 (Royal Cottage) (18c.)
1069 †† No. 53 (mid 19c.)
1070 C.P. No. 55 (Herbarium House) (early 18c.)

KEW ROAD

1071 C.P. No. 199 (Descauso House) (18c.)
1072 †† No. 296 (early 18c.)
1073–5 †† Nos. 338, 340 and 342 (late 18c. or early 19c.)
1076–8 † Nos. 350 (Park House), 352 (Adam House) and 354 (Burnage) (18c.)
1079–80† Nos. 356 (Alaric) and 358 (Denmark House) (early 18c.)
1081 Series of Ha-Ha bordering Old Deer Park (portions *c.* 1760 remainder 1800–1810)

Borough or District Civil Parish	No.	Name or Description of Antiquity

KEW—*contd.*   *RO YAL BOTANICAL GARDENS*

1082   C.P.   Aroid House, No. 1 (19c.)

1083   *C.P. Kew Palace (formerly known as The Dutch House (late 17c.)

1084   C.P.   King William's Temple (19c.)

1085   C.P.   Palm House (1844–1846)

1086   C.P.   Temple of Aeolus (1758–1762)

1087   C.P.   Temple of Arethusa (1758–1762)

1088   C.P.   Temple of Bellona (1758–1762)

1089   C.P.   The Japanese Gateway (1845 and 1866)

1090   C.P.   The Orangery (1761)

1091   C.P.   The Pagoda (1761–1762)

1092   C.P.   Queen's Cottage (19c.)

1093   C.P.   The Temperate House (1860)

PETERSHAM   *GENERAL*

1094   *C.P.   Ham House (1610, enlarged 1672) N.T.

1095   C.P.   Sudbrook Park or House (1726) (Sudbrook Golf Club)

1096   C.P.   Sudbrook Park Lodge (19c.)

PETERSHAM ROAD

1097   †† No. 139 (Church House) (late 18c. and early 19c.)

1098   ‡ No. 141 (late 17c.)

1099–1100 ‡ No. 143 (Petersham House) (*c.* 1680) ‡Stables and Buildings (late 17c.)

1101   ‡ No. 145 (Rutland Lodge) (*c.* 1666)

1102   † No. 147 (The Cottage) (18c.)

1103   † No. 167 (Cecil House) (late 17c. & 18c.)

1104   ‡ No. 186 (Montrose House) (late 17c.)

1105–6 † Nos. 188 (Farm Lodge) and 190 (Avenue Lodge) (17c.)

1107   † No. 216 (Gort House) (early 18c.)

1108   †† No. 230 (Elm Lodge) (17c.)

1109   †† No. 232 (Woodbine Cottage) (17c.)

1110   No. 237 (Park Cottage) (late 18c. or early 19c.)

1111   ‡ Douglas House (Early 18c., enlarged 1766)

1112   †† Manor Farm House (late 17c.)

Borough or District Civil Parish	No.	Name or Description of Antiquity

PETERSHAM—contd.

PETERSHAM ROAD—contd.

1113   C.P. Park Gate (late 18c.)
1114   ††Reston Lodge (18c.)
1115   *The Watchman's Box and Village Lock-up (1782)

RIVER LANE

1116   †Manor House (early 18c.)
1117–8   †Petersham Lodge and summer house in grounds (early 18c.)
1119–20   ††The Glen and Craigmyle (17c.)

SUDBROOK LANE

1121   †Gort Lodge (early 18c.)
1122   ‡Harrington Lodge (late 17c. or early 18c.)
1123   ‡Sudbrook Cottage (late 17c. or early 18c.)
1124   ‡The Red House (late 17c. or early 18c.)

RICHMOND

GENERAL

1125   ††Willoughby House (1830–1840), Bridge Street
1126–7 ††Nos. 12 and 14 (early 18c.), Brewers Lane
1128–9   †Nos. 23 and 24 (Greyhound Hotel) (18c.), George Street
1130   †Grove Road Institution (1786)
1131   †No. 27 (Halford House) (18c.), Halford Road
1132   No. 3 (Maids of Honour Tea Shop) (18c.), Hill Street
1133–5 ††Nos. 1, 2 and 3 (early 18c.), Lancaster Park, Vine Row
1136   C.P. Kew Observatory (1768), Old Deer Park
1137   ††Tudor Cottage (early 19c.), Park Road
1138–9 ††Nos. 1 and 9 (late 18c. & early 19c.), Paved Court
1140   † Richmond Bridge (1777)
1141–5 ††Nos. 1 to 5 (c. 1820) Riverside, St. Helena Terrace
1146   †† Statue of Father Thames (c. 1775), in grounds of Ham House
1147–58 ††Nos. 1 to 12 (early 19c.), Waterloo Place

5

Borough or District Civil Parish	No.	Name or Description of Antiquity

RICHMOND—*contd.*

CHURCH TERRACE

1159–63 †Nos. 1, ‡2 and ‡5 (Seaforth House) (early 18c.) and Nos. 3 and 4 (early 18c.)

1164 ††Bethlehem Chapel (1797)

1165 ‡Houblon's Almshouses, Worple Way (1757–1758)

1166 ††Queen Anne Hotel (formerly Heritage House) early (18c., altered)

CHURCH WALK

1167–8 ††Nos. 3 and 4 (early 18c.)

1169 ††Church Room (late 18c.)

1170 ††Steptoes (18c.)

FRIAR'S LANE

1171 ††No. 1 (Cholmondeley Lodge) (18c.)

1172 ††No. 2 (Cholmondeley Cottage) (18c.)

1173 ††No. 3 (Cholmondeley House) (18c.)

1174 ††St. Helena Cottage (formerly Green Club) (*c.* 1820)

1175–9 ††Nos. 1 to 5 Queensberry Place (early 19c.)

HERON COURT

1180 †Palm Court Hotel (early 18c.) P. 83

1181 †¹Hotham House (early 18c.)

KEW FOOT ROAD

1182–3 ††Nos. 12 (Gothic Cottage) and 14 (Magnolia Cottage) (early 19c.)

1184–6 ‡Nos. 19, 21 and 23 (late 17c. or Early 18c.)

1187 ††No. 39 (Myrtle House) (late 18c.)

1188 ††Richmond Royal Hospital (late 18c.)

KING STREET

1189–90 ††Nos. 15 and 16 (18c.)

1191 †No. 17 (mid-late 18c.)

1192 ††No. 20 (18c.)

LITTLE GREEN

1193–4 ††Nos. 1 (The Willows) and 2 (18c.)

1195 †No. 3 (late 18c. and early 19c.)

¹ Demolished 1960

Borough or District Civil Parish	No.	Name or Description of Antiquity

RICHMOND—*contd.*

OLD PALACE LANE

1196 † "No. 1 The Virginals" (formerly Cedar Grove) (early 19c.)

1197–1214 †† Nos. 8 to 25 (*c.* 1825)

1215 C.P. Asgill House (1760–1770)

1216 †† Asgill Lodge (late 18c.)

OLD PALACE YARD

1217 C.P. [1]The Trumpeters' House (early 18c.)

1218–9 C.P. The Wardrobe (18c.) and walls surrounding

ORMOND ROAD

1220–5 † Nos. 1, 2, 3, 5, ‡6 and 7 (18c.)

1226–7 ‡ Lissoy (18c.) and Ormond House (18c.), Ormond Terrace

1228 †† Ormond Lodge (late 18c. or early 19c.)

1229 † The Hollies (early 19c.)

1230 † The Rosary (early 18c.)

PARADISE ROAD

1231–2 †† Nos. 25 and 27 (early 18c.)

1233–4 †† Nos. 32 and 34 (mid 18c.)

1235–40 †† Nos. 1 to 6 Spring Terrace (late 18c.)

1241 †† No. 8 (Chalom House) Spring Terrace, (early 18c.)

PARKSHOT

1242–4 †† Nos. 4, 5 and 6 (mid 18c.)

1245 †† Parkside Cottage (mid 18c.)

PETERSHAM ROAD

1246–8 † Nos. 43 to 47 (Ivy Hall Hotel) (early 18c.)

1249 †† No. 55 (No. 4 The Paragon) (early 18c.)

1250 † No. 57 (No. 3 The Paragon) (early 18c.)

1251 † No. 59 (No. 2 The Paragon) (early 18c.)

1252 † No. 61 (No. 1 The Paragon) (early 18c.)

1253–6 †† Nos. 136 to 142 (Lansdowne Place) (late 18c. and early 19c.)

[1] Damaged by enemy action, 23rd August, 1944

Borough or District Civil Parish	No.	Name or Description of Antiquity
RICHMOND—contd.		PETERSHAM ROAD—contd.

1257 †† No. 144 (Langholme Lodge) (late 18c. and early 19c.)

1258 No. 191 (Nos. 1, 2 and 3 Vine Cottages (18c.)

1259 † Bingham House (*c.* 1760)

1260 † Boundary Stone inscribed "Richmond 1687", Lower Road

1261 † Northumberland House (1766)

RICHMOND HILL

1262–8 Nos. 34–46 (Lancaster Terrace) (early 19c.)

1269 †† No. 48 (The Old Vicarage School) (mid 18c.)

1270 †† No. 116 (late 18c.)

1271–2 †† Nos. 124 and 126 (early 19c.)

1273 †† No. 142 (Doughty House) (18c.)

1274–6 † Nos. 144, 146 and 148 (Mansfield Place) (late 18c.)

1277–8 † Nos. 150 and 152 (Richmond Hill Hotel) (early 18c.)

1279 †† No. 154 (Stanley Cottage) (late 18c.)

1280 † No. 156 (Syon Cottage) (late 18c.)

1281 † No. 158 (Morshead Hotel) (Late 18c.)

1282 † Ancaster House (Star & Garter Nurses' Home) (1772)

1283 † Cardigan House (late 18c.)

1284 † Cranford Cottage (late 18c.)

1285 ‡ No. 3 (*c.* 1760) The Terrace

1286 †† No. 4 (18c.) The Terrace

1287 φ The Wick (*c.* 1775) and Summerhouse

1288 †† [1] Wick House (18c.)

RICHMOND PARK

1289 C.P. The Lodge at Ham Gate (1742)

1290 †† Pembroke Lodge (late 18c. and early 19c.)

1291 ** King Henry VIII Mount in grounds of Pembroke Lodge

1292–3 C.P. Richmond Gate and Lodges (1798)

1294 C.P. White Ash Lodge (18c.)

[1] Rebuilt as block modern flats

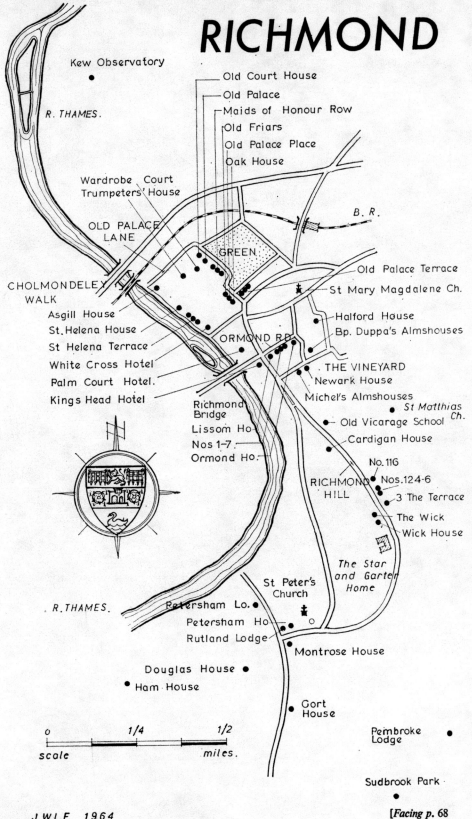

RICHMOND

Kew Observatory

R. THAMES.

Old Court House
Old Palace
Maids of Honour Row
Old Friars
Old Palace Place
Oak House

Wardrobe Court
Trumpeters' House

OLD PALACE
LANE

B. R.

GREEN

Old Palace Terrace
St Mary Magdalene Ch.

CHOLMONDELEY
WALK

Asgill House
St. Helena House
St Helena Terrace
White Cross Hotel
Palm Court Hotel.
Kings Head Hotel

Halford House
Bp. Duppa's Almshouses

ORMOND RD.

THE VINEYARD
Newark House
Michel's Almshouses

Richmond
Bridge
Lissom Ho.
Nos 1–7
Ormond Ho.

St Matthias
Ch.
Old Vicarage School
Cardigan House

No. 116
RICHMOND
HILL
Nos. 124-6
3 The Terrace
The Wick
Wick House

The Star
and Garter
Home

R. THAMES.

St Peter's
Church

Petersham Lo.
Petersham Ho.
Rutland Lodge

Montrose House

Douglas House
Ham House

Gort
House

0	1/4	1/2

scale   miles.

Pembroke
Lodge

Sudbrook Park

J.W.L.F. 1964

[Facing p. 68

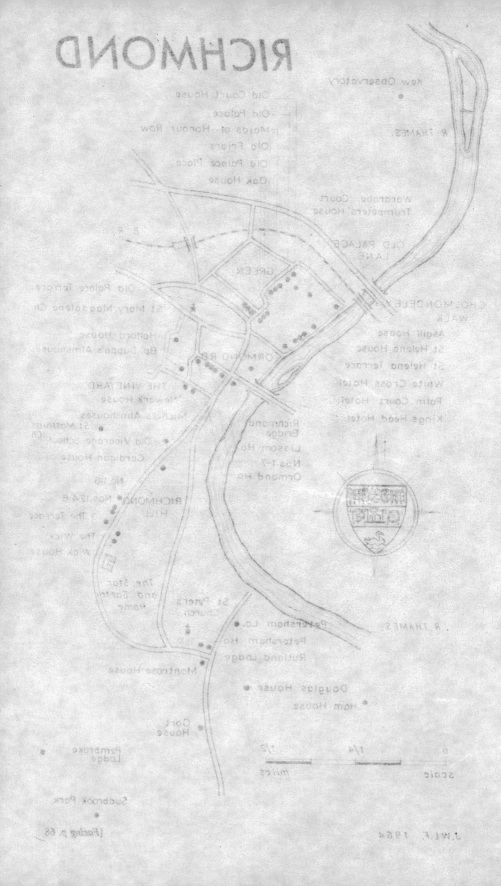

Borough or District Civil Parish	No.	Name or Description of Antiquity

RICHMOND—*contd.*

SHEEN ROAD

1295 † No. 34 (Holly Lodge) (mid-late 18c.)
1296 † No. 36 (Marshgate House) (1702)
1297 †† No. 38 (18c.)
1298 †† No. 39 (Devonshire Lodge) (early 19c.)
1299– †† Nos. 40 to 46 (mid 18c.)
1302
1303 † No. 41 (Court Lodge) (early 18c.)
1304 ‡ No. 43 (early 18c.)
1305 † No. 45 (late 18c.)
1306 † No. 93 (Dunstable House) (*c.* 1770)
1307– †† Nos. 131 to 141 (late 18c. and early 19c.)
12
1313 † Hickey's Almshouses, including chapel (1834)

THE GREEN

1314 † No. 1 (17c.)
1315 † No. 2 (18c.)
1316 † No. 3 (Gothic House) (late 18c.)
1317 † No. 4 (18c.)
1318 † No. 6 (late 18c.)
1319 †† No. 7 (18c., refaced 19c.)
1320–1 † Nos. 8 and 9 (mid 18c.)
1322 ‡ No. 10 (early 18c.)
1323–4 ‡ Nos. 11 and 12 (early 18c.)
1325 † No. 14 (18c.)
1326 † No. 15 (Greenside House) (early 18c.)
1327 † No. 16 (18c.)
1328 † No. 17 (mid 18c.)
1329 † No. 18 (18c.)
1330–1 C.P. Nos. 21 and 22 (Post Office) (early 18 c.)
1332–3 †† Nos. 23 and 24 (early 19c.)
1334 †† No. 25 (late 18c.)
1335 † No. 31 (late 18c.)
1336 ‡ No. 32 (early 18c.)
1337–8 †† No. 44 and Tudor Place (18c., altered early 19c.)
1339– φ Maid of Honour Row, Nos. 1 to 4 (*c.*1720)
42
1343 ‡ Oak House (late 18c.)
1344 C.P. Old Court House (early 18c.)
1345 ‡ Old Friars (17c.)

Borough or District Civil Parish	No.	Name or Description of Antiquity

RICHMOND—*contd.*

THE GREEN

1346   C.P. Old Palace (1500) (small part only remaining)

1347   ‡ Old Palace Place (*c.* 1700)

1348–53   ‡ Old Palace Terrace, Nos. 1 to 6 (Early 18c.)

1354   C.P. The Gatehouse (1500)

THE VINEYARD

1355–61   †† Nos. 1 to 7 (early 19c.)

1362   † No. 2 (Clarence House) (late 17c. or early 18c.)

1363   ‡ No. 9 (Newark House) (*c.* 1760)

1364   † Bishop Duppa's Almshouses (18c.)

1365   †† Michel's Almshouses (1811)

1366   † Queen Elizabeth's Almshouses (1767)

SURBITON BOROUGH

CHESSINGTON

CITY OF LONDON CORPORATION BOUNDARY POST

1367   700 yards S. of Rushett Farm

GENERAL

1368   †† Burnt Stub (Zoological Gardens) (16c., largely rebuilt), Leatherhead Road

1369   * Castle Hill Earthwork, near Epsom (mediaeval moated homestead or farmhouse site)

1370   Chessington Hall (16c. & 19c.) off Leatherhead Road

1371   No. 152 (Pear Tree Cottage), Leatherhead Road

HOOK

HOOK ROAD

1372   †† No. 435 (17c., with later alterations)

1373   †† Orchard Court (early 19c.)

7413   †† The Lucky Rover (P.H.) (18c.)

Borough or District Civil Parish	No.	Name or Description of Antiquity

SURBITON — *GENERAL*

1375 † Southborough House (early 19c.), Ashcombe Avenue

1376–8 † Nos. 124, 126 and 128 Maple Road (early 19c.)

1379 † No. 73 (Horner Cottage) Ewell Road (early 19c.)

TOLWORTH

1380 † Tolworth Court Farm Barn (17c.)

NORTH AND NORTH-EASTERN PLANNING AREA

BANSTEAD URBAN DISTRICT **BANSTEAD**

CITY OF LONDON CORPORATION BOUNDARY POSTS

1381 300 yards S. of Tattenham Corner, W. of Tattenham Corner Railway Station

1382 280 yards S. of above post.

1383 E. side of footpath, ¾ mile S. of Tattenham Corner

1384 S. side of Motts Hill Lane 75 yards W. of its junction with The Avenue

1385 N. side of Chucks Lane, 120 yards from junction with Duffields Lane

1386 E. side of B.2032 Banstead Heath, 360 yards S.E. of above post

1387 E. side of track E of Walton Heath Golf Club, 120 yards S.E. of above post.

1388 E. side of track E of Walton Heath Golf Club, 180 yards S.E. of above post

1389 E. side of track E of Walton Heath Golf Club, 450 yards S.E. of above post

1390 E. side of track E of Walton Heath Golf Club, 475 yards S.E. of above post

1391 E. side of track E of Walton Heath Golf Club, 170 yards S.E. of above post

1392 E. side of track E of Walton Heath Golf Club, 400 yards S.E. of above post

1393 E. side of track E of Walton Heath Golf Club, 80 yards S.E. of above post

1394 E. side of track E of Walton Heath Golf Club, 85 yards S.E. of above post

1395 E. side of track leading to Juniper Hill, 550 yards S.E. of above post

Borough or District *Civil Parish*	*No.*	*Name or Description of Antiquity*
BANSTEAD—*contd.*		*CITY OF LONDON CORPORATION* *BOUNDARY POSTS*—*contd.*
	1396	E. side of track leading to Juniper Hill, 80 yards S. of above post
	1397	E. side of track leading to Juniper Hill, 150 yards S. of above post
	1398	N. of Colley Hill, 165 yards E. of above post
	1399	150 yards S. of The Sportsman (P.H.), Mogador
	1400	150 yards W. of Brighton Road (A.217) opposite Chipstead Lane
	1401	100 yards E. of Brighton Road (A.217) at the Red House
	1402	450 yards S.W. of Perrotts Farm, Banstead Wood
	1403	W. side of Chipstead Valley Road, 430 yards N. of Denehouse Farm
	1404	Junction of Bridge Way, Stagbury Close and Hazelwood Lane

GENERAL

	1405–6	††[1]Flint Cottage and Downsend, High Street (18c.)
	1407	*"Gally Hills" (four barrows), Banstead Downs
	1408	†Rose Hill (18c.)
	1409	*Three quadrangular earthworks, Banstead Heath
	1410	*Tumble Beacon, The Drive
	1411	††Warren Farmhouse (17c., refronted 18c.)
	1412	††Well-cover, N. end of High Street (18c.)
	1413	†Well Farm (15c.–18c.) P. 72

PARK ROAD

	1414–5	††Nos. 1 and 2, Little Woodcote Farm Cottages (early 19c.)
	1416–9	††Nos. 1, 2, 3 and 4, Mint Cottages (early 19c.)
	1420	††Park Cottage (early 18c.) P. 96
	1421	††The Place (early 18c., altered mid 19c.)
	1422	††Woodmans Cottage (18c.)
	1423	††The Mint Farm House (16c.)

[1] Demolished March 1963

Borough or District Civil Parish	No.	Name or Description of Antiquity

BANSTEAD—*contd.*

TADWORTH

1424   Hunter's Hall (16c., with modern additions) P. 82

1425   ††Kyppings (16c. and later)

1426   Meare Close (17c. and later)

1427   **Mound at Preston Hawe

1428   ††Tadworth Cottage, Tadworth Street (1817)

1429–30   C.P. Tadworth Court (18c.) and coach-house (*c.* 1700)

CHIPSTEAD

CITY OF LONDON CORPORATION BOUNDARY POSTS

1431   50 yards N. of Drive Spur, Chipstead Bottom

1432   Centre of Coulsdon Lane at a junction with Hollymead Road

GENERAL

1433–4   †Nos. 1 and 2, (Old School House) Outwood Lane (17c.)

1435   Court Lodge Farm (17c. with later alterations)

1436   ††Denehouse Farm (14c. & 16c.), Outwood Lane

1437–8   †Fair Dene School (Purbright) (17c. and later) and ††Barn, Hogs' Cross Lane

1439   ††Leyfield Farm (17c.), Elmore Road

1440   ††Mill House, Monkswell Lane

1441   ††Pigeonhouse Farm (16c. with later additions)

1442   ††Rumbold's Castle Cottage (formerly Rumbold's Castle Inn) (16c.) Castle Road

1443–4   ††Stables (18c.) and ††Wellhouse (19c.), Shabden Park

1445   ††Thatched Cottage, Markedge Lane (17c.)

1446   ††The Old Mint House, High Road (early 19c.)

1447   †Well House Inn (formerly Old Well House) (16c. and later)

MUGSWELL

1448   †Parson's Cottage (17c.)

1449   ††The Old Rectory (16c. & 17c.)

Borough or District Civil Parish	No.	Name or Description of Antiquity

CHIPSTEAD—*contd.*

SOUTHRENS LANE

1450 †† No. 20 (17c.)
1451 †† Dearings (17c.)

KINGSWOOD

CITY OF LONDON CORPORATION BOUNDARY POSTS

1452   E. side of A.217 opposite Banstead C.P. School

GENERAL

1453   Lovelands Farm (16c.–18c.)

WALTON-ON-THE HILL

CITY OF LONDON CORPORATION BOUNDARY POSTS

1454   S.E. side of Mere Pond, Walton Street

GENERAL

1455 †† Chussex
1456   Ebenezer Cottage (17c.)
1457 †† House at Corner of Ebbisham Lane (late 18c.–early 19c.)
1458 ‡ Manor House (*c.* 1340 and later) P. 99
1459 ** Roman Villa (foundations of), Sandlands Grove
1460 * The Mound (Norman motte), Walton Place
1461 †† Walton Hurst Farmhouse (16c. or early 17c. with later additions)
1462 †† Yeoman House (formerly The Laurels) Walton Street (18c.)

WOODMANSTERNE

CITY OF LONDON CORPORATION BOUNDARY POSTS

1463   W. side of How Lane, 250 yards N. of junction with Coulsdon Lane

Beddington and Wallington Borough

BEDDINGTON

GENERAL

1464   Boundary Wall adjoining Church Path (17c.)
1465 †† Camden House (formerly Brandries Hill House) The Brandries (18c.)

Borough or District Civil Parish	No.	Name or Description of Antiquity

BEDDINGTON——*contd.*

GENERAL—*contd.*

1466 *‡ Dovecote (17c.) Beddington Park

1467 St. Mary's C. of E. School, Croydon Road (early 19c.)

1468-9 † The Banqueting Hall (16c.) and Orangery (17c.) Beddington Hall (Carew Manor S. School

WALLINGTON

GENERAL

1470-7 †† Nos. 1-8, The Green, Hackbridge (18c.)

1478 †† No. 32, Manor Road (early 19c.)

1479-83 † Nos. 8 to 16 Manor Road (early 19c.)

1484 †† Offices of Helm Chocolate Ltd., London Road (early 19c.)

1485 †† Old Red Lion, Hackbridge Road (early 18c.)

1486 †† Woodcote Hall, Woodcote Avenue (early 19c.)

LONDON ROAD

1487 † No. 282, (Bridge House) (18c.)

1488 † No. 284, (Wandle Bank) (18c.)

CARSHALTON URBAN DISTRICT

CARSHALTON

GENERAL

1489-90 †† Nos. 25 and 27, Park Hill (late 18c.–early 19c.)

1491 Butter Hill Bridge (mid 18c.)

1492-6 ‡ Carshalton House (1720) (sometimes called St. Philomena's Convent) and grounds including Water Pavilion, Hermitage and grotto, (early 18c.) Convent Gates and Piers (1710)

1497 Lady Margaret's Stone (1873)

1498-9 Lady Margaret's Well and Pool (1700)

1500 † Leoni Bridge, The Grove (1695)

1501 Manor wall (portion to east of church) (16c.)

1502 †† Premises of S.E.E. Board (early-mid 18c.) The Square

1503 † Road Bridge at The Ponds (early 19c.)

1504 Strawberry Lodge, Strawberry Lane (18c.)

Borough or District Civil Parish	No.	Name or Description of Antiquity

CARSHALTON—*contd.*

GENERAL—*contd.*

1505 † The Grotto well (early 18c.), Carshalton Park

1506 The Grove Gate (18c.)

1507 † The Old Rectory (College of St. Saviour's) (early 18c.)

1508 †† Woodcote House, Wrythe Green (early 18c.)

HIGH STREET

1509 † No. 6 (Late 17c.)

1510 † The Greyhound Hotel (18c.)

1511 Woodman's Shop (Priest's House) (16c.)

NORTH STREET

1512 †† No. 21 (North Lodge) (16c.)

1513 †† Strawberry Cottage (late 16c. and early 17c.)

WEST STREET

1514 †† No. 2 (Waterhouse Cottage) (1700)

1515 †† No. 4 (Waterhouse) (early 19c.)

1516 † No. 6 (The Cottage) (early 18c.)

1517 † No. 8 (Holly Cottage) (early 18c.)

1518 † No. 10 (18c.)

1519 †† No. 12 (early 19c.)

1520 †† Nos. 42 (early 18c.)

1521 † No. 70 (Alton Lodge) (18c.)

1522 †† No. 80 (early-mid 18c.)

1523 Lamorby Cottage (early 18c.)

WESTCROFT ROAD

1524 †† Westcroft (18c.)

1525 †† Westcroft Farm (16c.)

CATERHAM AND WARLINGHAM URBAN DISTRICT

CATERHAM

CITY OF LONDON CORPORATION BOUNDARY POSTS

1526 E. side of Coulsdon Road at junction with The Grove

Borough or District Civil Parish	No.	Name or Description of Antiquity

CATERHAM—*contd.*

GENERAL

1527 *Camp at War Coppice
1528 †The Folly (Whitehill Tower)
1529 ††Grove House (1809)
1530 **New or Wide Ditch near Whyteleafe (16c.)
1531 The Old Cottage, Harestone Lane (16c. & 19c.)
1532 †Upwood Gorse, Tupwood Lane (1868 and later)

CATERHAM-ON-THE-HILL

1533 †No. 7 Town End (*c.* 1640)
1534 ††No. 33 High Street (18c.)
1535–7 Nos. 56, 58 and 60 (Roffey Place) (18c.) High Street

CHALDON

GENERAL

1538–9 ††No. 55 and Forge Cottage (18c.)
1540 †Chaldon Court (early 14c. with 18c. alterations)
1541 ††Fryern (18c. with modern additions)
1542 ††Rook Cottage, Rook Lane (16c.)
1543–4 ††Rook Farmhouse and Barn, Rook Lane (late 17c.)
1545 ††The Rookery (*c.* 1825 on mediaeval foundations)
1546 †Tollsworth Manor House (16c. and later)

WARLINGHAM

CITY OF LONDON CORPORATION BOUNDARY POSTS

1547 N. side of Whyteleafe Road at Public Library
1548 N. side of Woldingham Road at its junction with Stuart Road
1549 E. side of Bug Hill, 80 yards from its junction with Tydcombe Road
1550 Fronting Chelsham Bus Garage
1551 W. side of Chelsham Road at its junction with Sunny Bank
1552 S. side of Harrow Road at its junction with Chelsham Road.

Borough or District Civil Parish	No.	Name or Description of Antiquity
WARLINGHAM—contd.		GENERAL
	1553	†† Court Cottage, Tithe Pit, Shaw Lane
	1554	† Court Farm (16c. with 18c. additions), Tithe Pit, Shaw Lane
	1555	Leather Bottle Inn (17c. and later)
	1556–61	†† The College including Nos. 23 and 25 (The Warlingham Home) No. 27 (The Chelsham Home) No. 29 (The Sanderstead Home) No. 31 (Attwood Cottage) Leas Road (1673)
	1562	† Vicarage (c. 1663)
	1563	† White Lion Inn (17c. and later)
WOLDINGHAM		GENERAL
	1564	†† Marden Park Stables (18c.)
	1565	Upper Court (17c.), North Downs Road
		SLYNES OAK ROAD
	1566	†† Nethern Court (16c., with additions)
	1567	†† Slines Oak (early 19c.)

COULSDON AND PURLEY URBAN DISTRICT

COULSDON		CITY OF LONDON CORPORATION BOUNDARY POSTS
	1568	E. side of Hooley Lane, 130 yards S.W. of Woodfield Hill
	1569	Opposite the Star Inn, Hooley Lane
	1570	E. side of Ditches Lane, Devilsden Wood
	1571	W. side of Stites Hill Road, 400 yards N.E. of The Grove, Caterham
		GENERAL
	1572	†† No. 41 Hayes Lane (formerly Hayes Cottages) (16c. & 17c.)
	1573	Cold Blow, Alderstead Heath (16c.)
	1574	†† Dean's Farm, Dean's Lane (17c.)
	1575	* Earthworks of Surrey Iron Railway
	1576	Bridge over track of Croydon Merstham and Godstone Railway, Dean Lane, Hooley (19c.)
	1577	Milestone on Godstone Road opposite Devon Close, Kenley (19c.)
	1578–9	†† Pair of Cottages, south of Church (18c.)

Borough or District Civil Parish	No.	Name or Description of Antiquity

COULSDON—*cont.*

GENERAL—contd.

1580 **[1]Romano-British Village, Netherne, Woodplace Farm

1581 *Riddlesdown, entrenchment (formerly named New or Wide Ditch)

1582 *Saxon barrow and Celtic field system and fieldway, Farthing Down

1583 ††Taunton Farmhouse (16c. or earlier) Taunton Lane, P. 40

1584–5 †The Barn (16c.) and house to west, Bradmore Green (18c.)

1586 ††The Grange (17c. altered)

1587 ††The Thatched Cottage, Old Lodge Lane (late 16c.)

1588 ††Windmill Cottage, Coulsdon Common (16c. & 17c.)

COULSDON ROAD

1589–90 ††Nos. 214 and 216 (18c.)

1591 ††Cherry Tree Cottage (17c.)

FARLEIGH

CITY OF LONDON CORPORATION BOUNDARY POSTS

1592 E. side of Farleigh Road N. of The Harrow (P.H.)

1593 450 yards E. of The Harrow (P.H.) S.E. of Littlepark Wood

1594 N. side of Featherbed Lane opposite Crab Wood

GENERAL

1595 Elm Tree Farm (17c.)

1596 ††Thatched Cottage, Great Farleigh Green Road (16c. & 17c.)

SANDERSTEAD

GENERAL

1597 *Pit dwellings, Croham Hurst

1598 ††Purley Bury, Downs Road (late 18c.)

1599 ††[2] Sanderstead Court (now Selsdon Court Hotel) (1676)

[1] Surrey Archaeological Collections Vol. L
[2] Severely damaged by fire, 1944.

Borough or District Civil Parish	No.	Name or Description of Antiquity

SANDERSTEAD—*cont.*

GENERAL—contd.

1600 †† Selsdon Park Hotel (15c. with modern additions)

LIMPSFIELD ROAD

1601–3 †† Nos. 44, 46 and 48 (Bellevue Cottages) (18c.)
1604   No. 117 (18c.)
1605   † The White House (16c.)

EPSOM AND EWELL BOROUGH
CUDDINGTON

GENERAL

1606   † Nonsuch House (1802–1806)
1607   Diana's Dyke, Nonsuch Park

EPSOM

CITY OF LONDON CORPORATION BOUNDARY POSTS

1608   675 yards S.W. of Glanmire Farm, Rushett Lane
1609   300 yards S. of Glanmire Farm, Rushett Lane
1610   Entrance to Glanmire Farm, Chessington Road
1611   200 yards E. of Glanmire Farm, Rushett Lane
1612   W. side of Headley Road, 130 yards N. of junction with Chalk Pit Road
1613   S. side of Langley Vale Road at junction with Headley Road
1614   250 yards S.E. of Langley Bottom Farm
1615   150 yards N. of Warren House.
1616   E. side of track to Walton-on-the-Hill, 250 yards S. of Race Course
1617   N. side of Race Course at Mile Post
1618   Fronting Tattenham Corner Hotel

GENERAL

1619   †† No. 16 Waterloo Road (late 17c.–18c.)
1620   ‡ Ashley House (18c.), Ashley Road
1621–3 † Clock House, entrance Lodge and Stables (late 18c.–early 19c.)
1624   † Down Hall, Burgh Heath Road (late 18c. or early 19c.)

Borough or District Civil Parish	No.	Name or Description of Antiquity

EPSOM—*contd.*

GENERAL—*contd.*

1625-7 † Garden wall, gate piers and wrought-iron gates (early 18c.), Madam's Walk

1628 †† Horton Farmhouse, Hook Road (18c.)

1629 †† Longdown Cottage, College Road (early 19c.)

1630 †† Longdown House, Longdown Lane (early 19c.)

1631 †† The Grove House, The Grove (late 18c.)

1632 † Old Well, Epsom Common

1633 †† The Well, Walton Downs

CHALK LANE

1634 † No. 1 (Woodcote Hotel) (1684 or later)

1635-7 †† Nos. 2, 4 and 6 (mid 18c.)

1638- †† Nos. 8, 10, 12 and 14 (early–mid 18c.)
41

1642 †† Chalk Lane Hotel (early 18c.)

1643 † Maidstone House (18c.)

1644 †† The Durdans (mid 18c.) including † entrance gates (17c.)

1645 ‡ Woodcote Grove (*c.* 1680)

CHURCH STREET

1646 † No. 6 (Cromwell Lodge) (mid 18c.)

1647 † No. 14 (The Cedars) (18c.)

1648 †† No. 16 (Cedars Cottage) (late 17c.–early 18c.)

1649- †† Nos. 19 and 21 (18c.)
50

1651 †† No. 24A (garages) (18c.)

1652 † No. 26 (The Old King's Head) (17c.)

1653 †† No. 59 (early 19c.)

1654 † Ebbisham House (*c.* 1720)

1655 †† Hope Lodge (18c.)

1656 † No.18 (Maymaur Nursing Home) (formerly The Old Vicarage) (18c.)

1657 † Parkhurst (*c.* 1700)

1658- † Pitt Place including stables, well-house,
63   dairy and buildings to N.E. garden wall and gate piers (17c. & 18c.)

1664 † Richmond House (18c.)

Borough or District Civil Parish	No.	Name or Description of Antiquity

EPSOM—contd.   *CHURCH STREET*—contd.
1665   †† Stone House (18c.)
1666   †† The Hermitage (17c.–18c.)

DORKING ROAD
1667   †† No. 2 (Convent of the Sacred Heart and Perpetual Adoration) (early 19c.)
1668–   †† Nos. 53, 55, 57, 59 and 61 (*c.* 1700)
72
1673   †† No. 67 (18c.)
1674–5 ‡ No. 71 (The Hylands) including forecourt walls, piers, clairvoyee and gates (18c.) P. 101
1676–8 † Nos. 73A and 73B (P. 106) and †75 (Hylands House and Cottage) (18c.)
1679   The Oaks (early 19c.)

EAST STREET
1680–1 †† Nos. 19 and 21 (early 19c.)
1682–3 †† Nos. 23 and 25 (early 19c.)
1684–5 †† Nos. 24 and 26 (early 19c.)
1686–8 †† Nos. 28, 30 and 32 (18c.)
1689–   †† Nos. 34 and 36 (early-mid 18c.)
90
1691–3 †† Nos. 91, 93 and 95 (early 19c.)

HIGH STREET
1694   † No. 89 (The Spread Eagle Hotel) (17c., much restored) P. 1
1695–6 †† Nos. 94 and 96 (Yew Tree Cottage and Wrights Restaurant) (17c. & 18c.)
1697–8 †† Nos. 102 and 104 (18c.)
1699   †† No. 107 (mid-late 18c.)
1700   †† No. 110 (Perrins) (17c.–18c.)
1701   †† No. 112 (Edwards & Sharp) (late 17c.)
1702–3 †† Nos. 119 and 121 (late 17c.)
1704   †† No. 126 (Unwins) (18c.)
1705   † No. 127 (18c.)
1706   † No. 129 (Late 18c.) (Fullers)
1707   †† No. 130 and 132 (Truelove and Richards) (late 17c.)
1708   †† No. 134 (The Albion P.H.) (early 18c.)
1709–   † Nos. 137A and 139 (Bramshott House) (17c.)
10

Borough or District Civil Parish	No.	Name or Description of Antiquity

EPSOM—*contd.*

HIGH STREET—*contd.*

1711 † No. 141 (Late 18c.)

1712–3 †† Nos. 143 and 145 (18c.)

1714–6 ‡ Nos. 149 to 153 (Waterloo House) (formerly The New Inn) (1716) P. 44

1717 †† Premises of Talbot and Hill (17c.–18c.)

HORTON LANE

1718–9 †† Nos. 1 and 2 (West Farm Cottages) (late 18c.–early 19c.)

1720 †† Long Grove Farmhouse (17c.)

SOUTH STREET

1721 †† No. 6 (18c.)

1722 †† No. 26 (Lovibonds) (17c.–18c.)

1723–4 †† Nos. 37 and 39 (late 17c.–18c.)

1725–6 †† Nos. 60 and 62 (Abell Cottages) (Late 17c.–18c.)

1727 † Nos. 73 and 75 (17c.)

1729 †† The Shrubbery (18c.)

1730–1 † Woodcote Hall including wings and forecourt wall (mid 18c.)

WEST HILL

1732–3 †† Nos. 4 and 6 (early 18c.)

1734 †† West Hill House (early 18c.)

WEST STREET

1735–7 †† Nos. 1, 3 and 5 (*c.* 1700)

1738 †† No. 4 (Marquis of Granby) (18c.)

1739–41 † Nos. 7, 9 and 11 (*c.* 1700)

1742–3 †† Nos. 6 and 8 (18c.)

1744 †† No. 21 (British Legion Club) (late 18c.–early 19c.)

1745 † The Old Manor House (early 18c.)

1746 † The White House (early 18c.)

WOODCOTE GREEN ROAD

1747 †† No. 2 (early 19c.)

1748 † Woodcote Green House (late 17c.)

1749 †† Woodcote House (18c.)

1750 †† York House (early 19c.)

Borough or District *Civil Parish*	*No.*	*Name or Description of Antiquity*

EPSOM—*contd.*

WOODCOTE PARK

1751-6   Entrance Steps, curved colonnades and outer pavilions (18c.) and brick barn, farm buildings and dovecote (17c.)

1757   †† Wellhouse (18c.)

WOODCOTE ROAD

1758–   ‡ No. 7 (Woodcote End) †Garden Walls
60   (18c.) and †Stables (late 18c.) P. 136

1761   †† No. 10 (Early 19c.)

1762   ‡ Queen Anne House (late 17c.–early 18c.)

EWELL

GENERAL

1763   † No. 1, Chessington Road

1764   No. 63 (Hill Cottage), West Street (18c.)

1765   Avenue of lime trees known as The Grove (1688–1689)

1766   † Ewell Castle School (early 19c.)

1767   † Fitznell's Manor House (16c. and later) Chessington Road East

1768   † Old Church Tower in churchyard (15c.) P. 30

1769   †† Pack Horse Bridge (18c.) Ewell Court

1770   † Foundations of Nonsuch Palace (including separate Banqueting House) (16c.)

1771-2 †† The Springs, and Horse Pond (1834) Dipping Place

1773-4   Whipping Trees and Mound (early 19c.)

CHEAM ROAD

1775   † No. 5 (16c. and later)

1776   †† Grove Cottage (early 19c.)

CHURCH STREET

1777   † No. 2 (Roslyn) (18c.)

1778   † No. 4 (Ballards Garden) (18c.) P. 109

1779   † No. 6 (Tabards) (18c.)

1780   No. 7 (18c.)

1781   † No. 8 (Malt End Cottage) (18c.)

1782   † No. 10 (Well House) (18c.)

1783   No. 11 (Rectory Lodge) (formerly King's Head Inn) (late 18c.)

1784   Glyn House (formerly The Rectory) (18c.)

1785   † Matt End Cottage (17th restored)

Borough or District Civil Parish	No.	Name or Description of Antiquity

EWELL—*contd.*

CHURCH STREET—*contd.*
1786   The Old Malthouse (17c., restored)
1787   † The Old Watch and Engine House (*c.* 1780)
      P. 2

EPSOM ROAD
1788   †† Hollycroft (18-c.)
1789   †† Mulberry Cottage (early 19c.)
1790   †† Tayles Hill (early 19c.)
1791   †† The Old House (18c.–19c.)

HIGH STREET
1792   † No. 9 (16c. and later)
1793–5 † Nos. 11 to 15 (17c. & 18c.)
1796   † No. 17 (17c.)
1797   † No. 24 (18c.)
1798   †† No. 26 (17c. & 18c.)
1799– †† Nos. 28 and 30 (Goddard) (18c.)
1800
1801   † No. 31 (17c.)
1802   †† Spring Hotel (early 19c.)

KINGSTON ROAD
1803   † Lower Mill on Hog's Mill River (early 18c.)
1804   †† Upper Mill on Hog's Mill River (18c.)

MILL LANE
1805– †† Nos. 3, 5, 7, 9, 11 and 13 (late 18c.–early
10   19c.)
1811–5 †† Nos. 15, 17, 19, 21 and 23 (early 19c.)
1816–7 †† Nos. 25 and 27 (18c.)

SPRING STREET
1818   † Chessington House (18c.)
1819   †† Chessington Lodge (18c.)
1820   †† Former Stables to Bourne Hall (early 19c.)
1821   † Spring House (*c.* 1740)

MALDEN AND COOMBE BOROUGH
COOMBE

GENERAL
1822   † Coombe Wood House (16c.)
1823   † Coombe Hill Farm (18c. and later)
1824   **†'Tamkin,' Coombe Wood Golf Course

Borough or District *Civil Parish*	*No.*	*Name or Description of Antiquity*

COOMBE—*contd.* · *GENERAL*—*contd.*

1825–7 *†¹Wolsey's three conduit houses (1515 and later) (Ivy Conduit, Coombe Conduit and Gallows Conduit)

1828–9 C.P. Thatched House Lodge (mid 18c.) and Thatched house (reputed to be summer house. 18c.) Richmond Park

MALDEN · *GENERAL*

1830 Old Riding School (18c.), Beverley Lane
1831 † Malden Green Farm (16c. and later)

CHURCH ROAD

1832 † No. 3 (18c.)
1833–40 †† Nos. 16 to 30A (early 18c.)
1841 † Malden Manor House (18c.)
1842 † The Plough Inn (15c.)

MERTON AND MORDEN
URBAN DISTRICT
MERTON · *GENERAL*

1843 †²Ancient Wall surrounding Old Church House (17c.)
1844 Ancient Wall near Manor House (late 18c. or early 19c.)
1845 †³Norman Doorway from Merton Priory (12c.) in Churchyard

KINGSTON ROAD

1846 † No. 120 (formerly Manor House) (17c. & 18c.)
1847–8 †† Nos. 122 and 124 (18c.)
1849 † No. 152 (Dorset Hall) (*c.* 1770)
1850 †† No. 180 (1797)
1851 † No. 269 Long Lodge (late 18c.)
1852 Rowland Wilson Almshouses (1656)

¹ See Surrey Archaeological Collections Vol. LVI
² Old Church House demolished
³ Re-erected in Merton Churchyard in 1935

Borough or District Civil Parish	No.	Name or Description of Antiquity

MERTON—*contd.*
STATION ROAD
1853 †† Colour House at Messrs. Liberty's Print Works (18c.)
1854 Stone gateway and wall to Merton Priory (16c.)
1855 †† Wheelhouse at Messrs. Liberty's Print Works (18c.)

MORDEN
GENERAL
1856 †† Manor House to S. of Church, London Road (early 19c.)
1857 † Morden Cottage (early 19c.)
1858 ‡ Morden Park (Club House) (*c.* 1770)
1859 * Mound (believed Roman Barrow) in Morden Park

CENTRAL ROAD
1860 †† The Grange (late 18c.)
1861 † The Old Schoolhouse (1731)

MORDEN HALL PARK
1862–6 † Entrance gates and piers, garden walls, pedestal and statue of Venus, and Cupid, pedestal and statue of Neptune (18c.)
1867 † Morden Hall (*c.* 1770)
1868 † Morden Lodge (early 19c.)
1869 † Old Snuff Mills (18c.)

MITCHAM BOROUGH
MITCHAM
GENERAL
1870– Nos. 1–15, Prussia Place, near Hall Place,
84 Church Road (*c.* 1810)
1885–7 †† Nos. 3, 4 and 5, Cranmer Road (18c.)
1888 † No. 10 (Wandle House) Riverside Drive (*c.* 1780)
1889– † Nos. 60, 62 and 64, Church Street (early
91 —mid 18c.)
1892 ** Anglo-Saxon Cemetery Site, Morden Road
1893 † Archway entrance to former chapel (*c.* 1400) Hall Place, Church Road
1894 †† Conservative Club, Upper Green (early 18c.)

Borough or District Civil Parish	No.	Name or Description of Antiquity

MITCHAM—*contd.*

GENERAL—contd.

1895 † House at Renshaw's Corner (mid 18c.) Streatham Road and Links Lane

1896 † Mitcham Railway Station (18c.)

1897 C.P. National School House (1788), Lower Green West

1898 Old Workhouse (1759), Windmill Road (now a Cottage)

1899 Remains of Windmill, Windmill Road, Mitcham Common (early 19c.)

1900–2 ‡ The Canons (1730) including Dovecote (17c.) and obelisk (1822)

1903 The Wheel at Ravensbury Mill (mid 18c.)

1904 †† The Tate Almshouses (1829) Lower Green

1905 Water-wheel (rear of Eagle Leather Works) near Beddington Corner

1906 †† White Cottage, Morden Road (18c.)

COMMONSIDE EAST

1907 No. 3 (Clarendon House) (early 18c.)

1908 †† No. 9 (Prospect House) (late 18c.)

1909 No. 17 (18c.)

COMMONSIDE WEST

1910 †† Newton House (early 18c.)

1911 †† Park Place (early 19c.)

1912 †† The Lawn (18c.–19c.)

CRICKET GREEN

1913 † Elm Lodge (early 19c.)

1914 † King's Head Inn (17c. & 18c.)

1915 †† White House (early 19c.)

LONDON ROAD

1916 † No. 224 (Eagle House) (1705) including forecourt wall, railings and gates

1917 †† No. 350 (White Hart Inn) (*c.* 1710)

1918–9 †† No. 475 (Wandle Cottage) No. 477 (The Glen) and No. 479 (Fibre Mills Office) (17c. & 18c.).

Borough or District Civil Parish	No.	Name or Description of Antiquity

MITCHAM—*cont.*

MILESTONES, ETC.

1920   County Boundary stone on Rowe Bridge, Streatham Road (19c.)

1921   †† Milestone in London Road opposite Cricket Green (19c.)

1922   †† Milestone in London Road opposite North corner of Figges Marsh (19c.)

1923   †† The Bidder Memorial (1896), Croydon Road

PHIPPS BRIDGE ROAD

1924   †† Nos. 84–94 (even) (*c.* 1824)

1925   † No. 98 (Wandle Villa) (*c.* 1770)

SUTTON AND CHEAM BOROUGH

CHEAM

SUTTON

GENERAL

1926–7 †† Nos. 1 and 2, Church Road (17c. and later)

1928–9   Nos. 21 and 23 (16c.), High Street

1930   †† No. 740, London Road (late 18c.)

1931   †† Church Farm, Church Farm Lane (early 19c.)

1932   ‡ The Lumley Chapel in churchyard, P. 39

MALDEN ROAD

1933   †† No. 3 (Nonsuch Cottage) (17c.–18c.)

1934–6 †† Nos. 5, 7 and 9 (early 19c.)

1937   † No. 15 (The Rectory) (17c. & 18c.) P. 54

1938   ‡ Whitehall (1520) P. 76

PARK LANE

1939   † No. 5 (18c.)

1940–4   † Nos. 7, 9, 11, 13 and 15 (17c.)

1945–6   † Nos. 17 and 19 (Late 18c.)

1947–8   † Nos. 21 and 23

1949   †† Lodge to Cheam Park (early 19c.)

PARK ROAD

1950   † No. 5 (18c.)

1951–4 †† Nos. 7, 9, 11 and 13 (18c.)

1955   † No. 38 (Cheam Cottage) (18c.)

Borough or District Civil Parish	No.	Name or Description of Antiquity

SUTTON—*contd.*

THE BROADWAY
1956–62 †† Nos. 45 to 57 (1520)
1963 † The Old Cottage (15c.)

SUTTON
GENERAL
1964 † Gibson Mausoleum in Sutton Churchyard (1777)
1965 †† Milestone 13 miles from Standard in Cornhill
1966 † Sutton Lodge, Brighton Road (mid 18c.)

WIMBLEDON BOROUGH
WIMBLEDON

GENERAL
1967–71 †† Nos. 9, 10, 11, 12 and The Aviary (late 18c.) Wandle Bank
1972–85 †† Nos. 10 to 16 (consecutive) and 20 to 26 (consecutive), (18c.), West Place
1986 †† King's College School (Junior) (18c.)

ARTHUR ROAD
1987 † The Well at The Well House (1798)

CHURCH ROAD
1988 † No. 54 (The Old Rectory House) (*c.* 1500)

HIGH STREET
1989 † No. 35 (1760)
1990 † No. 44 (Claremont House) (early 17c. with 18c. additions)
1991–2 † Nos. 45 and 45A (17c. & 18c.)
1993–4 Nos. 50 and 51 (late 18c.)
1995 ‡ Eagle House (*c.* 1613)

WIMBLEDON COMMON
1996 * Caesar's Camp (*c.* 300 B.C.) (Early Iron Age)
1997 † The Windmill (early 19c.)
South Side
1998 †† Rushmere (18c.)

Borough or District Civil Parish	No.	Name or Description of Antiquity

WIMBLEDON—contd.

WIMBLEDON COMMON
West Side

1999 † No. 6 (West Side House) (1750)
2000–5 †† Nos. 14 to 19 (1770) Hanford Row
2006 † No. 24 (The Kier) (early 19c.)
2007 †† Stanford House (18c.)
2008 †† West Side House (stable block, now cottage and garages) (18c.)

WOODHAYES ROAD

2009 † No. 3 (Southside House) (mid 18c.)
2010 † No. 4 (Carfrae House) (mid 18c.)
2011 † No. 6 (Gothic Lodge) (early 19c.)

SOUTH-WESTERN PLANNING AREA

FARNHAM URBAN
DISTRICT

FARNHAM   *GENERAL*

2012–3 † Nos. 1 and 2 (18c.) Abbey Street
2014–5 †† Nos. 2 and 4 Red Lion Lane
2016 †† No. 5 (Vine Cottage) Old Church Lane
2017 † Blue Boy (P.H.) Station Road
2018 † Broomleaf (18c.), Waverley Lane
2019 ** Caesar's Camp
2020–1 **† Earthworks (1070) and buildings south of the Keep (1129 and later), Farnham Castle
2022 * Earthwork south-west of Botany Hill, Crooksbury
2023 ** Five barrows at The Barrows, Charles Hill
2024 Hatch Mill Cottage (17c.) Darvill's Lane
2025 †† Taylor and Anderson's Depositories, Beavers Road
2026 ** The Bishop's Bank
2027 *φ The Keep, Farnham Castle (12c. and later)
2028 φ The Grange, near the Castle (1720) P. 34
2029 †† The Liberal and Albion Clubs, South Street
2030 † The Ranger's House (18c.), Farnham Park
2031 †† "The Maltings" (formerly The Red Lion Brewery), Red Lion Lane

Borough or District Civil Parish	No.	Name or Description of Antiquity

FARNHAM—*contd.*

BADSHOT LEA

2032–3 Badshot Farm and out-buildings (17c.)
2034 Badshot Lea House (17c. & 18c.)
2035 ** Moat, N.W. of Badshot House
2036 The Green Cottage (17c.)

BEAR LANE

2037 †† No. 7
2038 †† Baptist Chapel

BRIDGE SQUARE

2039–43 †† Nos. 6–10 (inclusive) (late 18c.)
2044 † No. 11 (The Old Cottage) (17c. or later)
2045 † No. 13 (formerly No. 6) (16c.)
2046–9 †† Nos. 14–17 (formerly Nos. 2, 3, 4 and 5) (late 18c.)
2050 †† No. 18 (formerly No. 1) (late 18c.)
2051–2 † Jolly Farmers Inn and Bridge Stores (17c.) P. 73

CASTLE STREET

2053 ‡ No. 1 (Coach and Horses Inn) (17c.)
2054 †† No. 3
2055 † No. 4 (early 19c.)
2056 ‡ No. 4A (late 18c.)
2057 ‡ No. 5 (early 19c.)
2058 ‡ No. 7 (late 18c.)
2059 †† No. 8
2060–1 ‡ Nos. 9 and 10 (18c.)
2062–70 † Nos. 11, 12, 13, 14, 15, 16, 17, 18 and 19 (18c. and early 19c.)
2071–7 ‡ Nos. 20, †21, †22, †23, †24, †25 and †26 (late 18c.)
2078–9 † Nos. 27 and 28
2080 † No. 29 (18c.)
2081 † No. 30 (late 18c.)
2082 † No. 31 (mid 19c.)
2083–5 † Nos. 32, 33 and 33A (1840)
2086–90† Nos. 34, 35, 36, 37 and 38 (early 19c.)
2091–3 † Nos. 39, 40 and 41 (19c.)
2094 † No. 42 (late 18c.)
2095 ‡ No. 43 (Castle Hill House) (18c.)

Borough or District Civil Parish	No.	Name or Description of Antiquity

FARNHAM—*contd.*

CASTLE STREET—*contd.*

2096 ‡ No. 44 (Guildford House) (18c.)

2097– ‡ No. 45, †46, †47, †48 and †49 (18c.)
2101

2102–3 † No. 50 (Nelson's Arms (P.H.)) including Cottage at rear (18c.)

2104– ‡ Nos. 53 to 60 (Windsor Almshouses) (1619)
111

2112 ‡ No. 61 (late 18c.)

2113–7 ‡ Nos. 62, †63, 64, 65 and 66 (18c.)

2118–9 ‡ Nos. 67 and 68 (16c. & 17c.)

2120–2 ‡ Nos. 69, ‡70 and ‡71 (18c.)

2123 † No. 72 (late 18c.)

2124 ‡ No. 74 (18c.)

2125 † No. 75 (Lloyds Bank) (18c.)

2126 C.P. No. 76 (late 18c.)

2127– †† Lound's Buildings, Nos. 1 to 9 (early 19c.)
35

2136 † National Provincial Bank (18c.)

CHURCH LANE—LOWER

2137– †† Nos. 3–12 (early 18c.)
46

2147– †† Nos. 13 to 17 (mid 18c.)
51

2152–4 † Nos. 18, 19 and 22 (16c.–18c.)

2155–6 †† Nos. 23 and 24 (early 19c.)

2157– †† Nos. 25, 26, 27 and 28 (*c.* 1840)
60

2161 †† No. 29 (early 19c.)

2162–3 †† Nos. 30 and 31 (adjoining premises) (16c. and later)

2164 †† Mardon and Ball's Yard

CHURCH LANE—MIDDLE

2165–6 † Nos. 1 and 2 (late 18c.)

2167–8 † Nos. 3 and 4 (late 18c.)

2169 † Nos. 5 (early 19c.)

2170–3 † Nos. 6 to 9 (Working Men's Hostel) (18c., altered)

2174–6 † Nos. 10, 11 and 12 (early 19c.)

Borough or District Civil Parish	No.	Name or Description of Antiquity

FARNHAM—*contd.*

CHURCH LANE—UPPER

2177– 80 †† Nos. 1 to 4 (18c.)

2181 † The Rectory (mid 18c., altered)

CHURCHYARD

2182–5 Nos. 1, †2, †3, and †4 (early 18c.)
2186–7 Nos. 5 and 6 (early 17c.)
2188 † No. 7 (early 18c.)
2189 ‡ The Old Vicarage (14c. and later)

COMPTON

2190 † Moor Park House (18c., with traces of late 17c.) P. 125
2191 Mother Ludlam's Cave, Moor Park
2192 Stella Cottage (18c.)
2193 *φ Waverley Abbey Ruins (12c.–14c.)
2194 ‡ Waverley Abbey Mansion (Early Georgian and Regency)

DIPPENHALL

2195 Deans (17c.)
2196 Dippen Hall (18c.)
2197 Halfway House (17c.)

DOWNING STREET

2198 † No. 2 (19c. and earlier)
2199– 2201 ‡ Nos. 3, 4 and 4A (18c.)
2202–5 †† Nos. 8 to 11
2206–7 †† Nos. 15 and 16
2208 † No. 18
2209 †† No. 22 (late 18c. front on earlier building)
2210 No. 27 (18c.)
2211 †† No. 28 (18c.)
2212–3 † Nos. 37 and 38 (18c.)
2214 †† No. 41 (18c.)
2215 No. 42 (18c.)
2216 † No. 45 (18c.)
2217–8 † Nos. 46 and 47 (18c.)
2219 ‡ No. 48 (18c.)
2220–1 ‡ Nos. 49 and 50 (18c.)
2222–3 †† Nos. 51 and 52 (late 18c.)

Borough or District Civil Parish	No.	Name or Description of Antiquity

FARNHAM—*contd.*

DOWNING STREET—contd.

2224–6 †† Nos. 53, 54 and 55 (17c. & 18c.)
2227–8 †† Nos. 56 and †57 (18c.)
2229   ‡ Ivy House (Conservative Club)

EAST STREET

2230–1 †† Nos. 6 and 7
2232   † No. 25
2233   † No. 29 (Still House)
2234–5 †† Nos. 83 and 84 (Heath Bros) (17c.)
2236   †† No. 92
2237–8 †† Nos. 93 and 94
2239– †† Nos. 97 and 98
40
2241–3 †† Nos. 121 to 123 (Southern Gas Service) (17c. & 18c.)
2244–5 †† Bath House and West Meon House
2246–9 †† Elmhyrst, Eastdale, Belfort and Zingari (Terrace of 4 houses)
2250   †† Surrey Knitting Company
2251   No. 8, The County Cinema (front block) (18c.)
2252   No. 4, The Royal Deer (P.H.) (18c.)

FIRGROVE HILL

2253–4   Firgrove Farm and outbuildings (18c.)
2255   † Firgrove House (1688, refronted early 19c.)

GUILDFORD ROAD

2256   Ivy Cottages, Bourne Mill (18c.)
2257–8 †† Nos. 35 and 37 Stanley Villas (18c.)

HALE
GENERAL

2259   Hale Farm House (18c.)
2260   Hill Crest Cottage (18c.)
2261   Patrick's Cottages (17c.) Heath End
2262   * Roman House and Bath buildings, Roman Way Housing Site (now filled in)
2263   The Court House (outbuildings) (18c.)
2264   †† The White Cottage (18c.)

Borough or District Civil Parish	No.	Name or Description of Antiquity

FARNHAM—*contd.*

HALE ROAD
2265 †† Albion Hotel
2266 † Farnham Institution (now Hospital) (18c.)
2267 †† Ravenswood Farm (18c.)

UPPER HALE
2268– †† Nos. 1, 2 and 3 (Court Cottages) (18c.)
70   Upper Hale Road
2271   Beam Cottage (18c.), Alma Road
2272   The Old Cottage (18c.), Hale Laundry

MILLS
2273   † Bourne Mill (17c. and later), Guildford
        Road
2274   † Hatch Mill (late 18c.) Darvill's Lane,
        Farnham By-Pass Road
2275   † High Mill (18c.), Moor Park
2276   † Bourne Place (formerly Mill Place) (18c.),
        Moor Park Lane
2277   † Willey Mill (18c.), Alton Road

PARK ROW
2278– †† Nos. 1, 3, 5, 7, 9, 11, 11A, 15 and 17 (18c.)
86
2287   †† Sherfield's Yard

RUNFOLD
2288   †† Bridge Farm (17c. & 18c.)
2289   †† Hawthorn Cottages (18c.)
2290   †† Runfold Bakery (18c.)
2291–2 †† Runfold House and outbuildings (18c.
        altered)

THE BOROUGH
2293   †† No. 1 (16c., with 19c. front)
2294–5 †† Nos. 4 and 5 (18c.)
2296–98 † No. 6, 6A and No. 7 (18c.)
2299   † No. 10 (c. 1670)
2300–1 †† Nos. 15 and 16 (18c.)
2302   † No. 33 (Midland Bank (18c.)
2303–4 ‡ Nos. 35 and 36 (including buildings at rear
        and stable block (17c. and later)
2305   † No. 37 (16c.)

Borough or District Civil Parish	No.	Name or Description of Antiquity

FARNHAM—contd.

THE BOROUGH

2306 ‡No. 40 (The Spinning Wheel) (16c. & 18c.)
2307–8 †Nos. 41 and 42 (16c. & 17c.)
2309 ‡No. 43 (18c.)
2310– C.P. Bailiff's Hall and Arcade (Old Town Hall)
1 (1674 rebuilt 1930–34)
2312–3††Queen's Head Inn and premises of Speed (tobacconist) (early 19c.)
2314 †The Bush Hotel (17c. & 18c.)

THE BOURNE

2315–6 Caretaker's Cottage and Gymnasium (Old Barn), Farnham Grammar School (18c.)
2317 Twynax Cottage (18c.)

WEST STREET

2318– ††Nos. 2–4
20
2321 ††No. 8 (18c.)
2322 ††No. 9 (18c.)
2323–4††Nos. 10 and 11 (18c.)
2325 †No. 12 (late 18c.)
2326 ††No. 13 (18c.)
2327–8††No. 14 and 15 (18c.)
2329 †No. 19 (Wheatsheaf Inn) (late 18c.)
2330–1 †Nos. 20 and 21 (late 18c.)
2332 ††No. 22 (18c.)
2333–4 ‡Nos. 23 and 24 (18c.)
2335 †No. 26 (18c.)
2336 †No. 27 (Newham House) (18c.)
2337 ‡No. 28 (Vernon House) (16c. altered)
2338– ††Nos. 29, 30 and 31 (17c.)
40
2341 ††No. 32 (early 19c.)
2342–3††Nos. 33 and 33A (18c.)
2344–6††Nos. 34, 35 and 36 (early 19c.)
2347 †No. 38 (Wilmer House) (18c.)
2348 ‡No. 39 (Sandford House) (18c.)
2349 †No. 40 (Wickham House) (18c.)
2350 ‡No. 41 (St. Christopher's School) (Elmer House) (late 18c.)
2351 ††No. 42 (including oast houses)
2352 No. 46A (17c. & 18c.)

Borough or District Civil Parish	No.	Name or Description of Antiquity

FARNHAM—*contd.*   *WEST STREET*—*contd.*

2353   ††No. 60 (18c.)
2354   ††No. 61 (18c.)
2355–6   Nos. 66 and 67 (17c. & 18c.)
2357   ††No. 68 (18c.)
2358   ††No. 69 (early 19c.)
2359–62   ††Nos. 70, 71, 72 and 73 (17c. & 18c.)
2363–5 ††Nos. 80, 81 and Mecca Restaurant (18c.)
2366   ††No. 82 (18c.)
2367   ††No. 84 (18c.)
2368   †No. 85 (The Pilgrim's Way Grocery) (18c.)
2369   †No. 87 (early 19c.)
2370   ‡No. 88 (Bethune House) (late 18c.)
2371   ‡No. 89 (late 18c.)
2372   ‡No. 90 (18c.)
2373–4 ‡Nos. 91 and 92 (late 18c.)
2375–6 †Nos. 93 and 94 (late 18c.)
2377–80 ††Nos. 100, 101, 102 and 103 (early 19c.)
2381–3 ‡Nos. 104, †105 and †106 (18c.)
2384–8 ††Nos. 107–111
2389–91 †Nos. 112, 113 and 113A (formerly The Lion and Lamb Inn) (18c.)
2392–3 †Nos. 114 and 115 (18c.)
2394–9 ††Nos. 116, 117, 118, 119, 120 and 121 (18c. and early 19c. fronts)
2400   ††No. 122
2401   ††The Cosy Cafe (18c.)
2402   ††The Fox & Hounds (P.H.)

WEYBOURNE

2403   Alma Cottage (17c.), Upper Weybourne Lane
2404   †Barling's Farm (16c. & 17c.)
2405   ‡Weybourne House (1724)

WRECCLESHAM
GENERAL

2406–7 †Church of England Schools and School House (1860)
2408   ††The Bear and Ragged Staff (P.H.) (17c.)

FARNHAM

THE BOROUGH
DOWNING STREET

Ranger's House

Mesolithic
Pit Dwellings

HALE ROAD

Six Bells'
Roman Site

GUILDFORD ROAD

St James's Church

The Grange

Farnham Castle

CASTLE HILL

Castle Hill House
Guildford House
Windsor Almshouses
61
62

CASTLE STREET
20

Town Hall
Bailiffs' Hall

Rectory

Spinning Wheel

37-8

EAST STREET

Bush Hotel
Westminster Bank
Liberal Club

Jolly Farmer

FARNHAM BY-PASS

B.R.

R. Wey

R. Wey

Moor Park

WAVERLEY LANE

Waverley Abbey

St Joan's Church

STN

TILFORD ROAD

Lion & Lamb
Vernon House
87-95

13 12

St Andrew's Church

Old Vicarage

20

Elmer House
Sandford House
Willmer House

R Wey

WEST STREET

Mesolithic Site

COX BRIDGE

R Wey

FARNHAM BY-PASS

FRENSHAM ROAD

B.R.

J.W.L.F. 1964

Scale

0   1/4   1/2

Miles

[*Facing p. 98*]

Borough or District Civil Parish	No.	Name or Description of Antiquity

FARNHAM—*contd.*

WRECCLESHAM
GENERAL
2409 †† The Forge (17c.)
2410 †† The Royal Oak (P.H.) (17c.)
2411–2 †† Nos. 1 and 2 Weavers Cottages (17c.)
2413 † Yew Tree Cottage (17c.)
2414 †† The Cricketers Arms (17c.)

ALTON ROAD
2415–6 Cox Bridge Farm and outbuildings (18c.)
2417 †† Cox-Bridge Farm Cottage
2418 † Runwick House (18c.)

GODALMING BOROUGH
GODALMING

GENERAL
2419 †† British Drug House Ltd. (18c.) Westbrook Road
2420 †† Little Fort (18c.) Westbrook Road
2421 †† Meath Home (formerly Westbrook Place) (1770 and later)
2422–7 †† Nos. 51, 52, 56 and 57, 59 and 60 Binscombe (17c.)
2428 Boarden Bridge (medieval) Borough Road
2429 * Tuesley Saxon Church Site

BRIDGE STREET
2430 No. 10 (17c.)
2431 † No. 19 (18c.)
2432 †† No. 20 (18c.)
2433 †† No. 21 (17c.)
2434–7 † Nos. 37 to 40 (16c.)
2438 †† No. 47 (early 17c.)
2439 No. 48 (early 17c.)

BRIGHTON ROAD
2440–1 † Nos. 107 and 109 (16c.)
2442 No. 111 (17c.)
2443 †† Step House (18c.)

CATTESHALL LANE
2444 †† Catteshall Grange (17c.)
2445 †† The Ram (P.H.) (16c.)

Borough or District Civil Parish	No.	Name or Description of Antiquity

GODALMING—*contd.*

CHURCH STREET

2446 † No. 1 (16c.)
2447–8 †† Nos. 3 and 5 (17c.)
2449– †† Nos. 6 and 8 (16c.)
50
2451–2 †† Nos. 7 and 9 (18c.)
2453 †† No. 11 (17c.)
2454 No. 12 (early 17c.)
2455–6 Nos. 16 and 18 (The Old House) (16c.)
2457 No. 20 (16c. & 17c.)
2458 †† No. 22 (early 19c.)
2459 † No. 24 (Deanery House) (mid 19c.)
2460-1 †† Nos. 29 and 31 (16c.)
2462 † No. 33 (18c.)
2463–5 †† Nos. 7, 8 and 9 (17c. & 18c.), Deanery Place
2466 † Church House (16c. and later)
2467 † The Skinner's Arms (P.H.) (18c.)
2468 †† Vicarage (17c. & 18c.)

DEANERY PLACE
(*see Church Street*)

FARNCOMBE STREET

2469 No. 46 (17c.)
2470 †† No. 48 (17c.)
2471–2 †† Nos. 59 and 61 (17c.)

HIGH STREET

2473 †† No. 16 (formerly Nos. 5 (Gas Board) and
5A (Normans)) (18c.)
2474–5 † Nos. 20 and 18 (formerly Nos. 6 and 6A)
(18c.)
2476–7 † Nos. 22 and 24 (formerly Nos. 7 and 8)
(King's Arms Hotel) (18c.) P. 50
2478–1 † Nos. 40, 42, 44 and 46 (formerly Nos. 14A,
15, 15A[1], 15B[1] and 16 Crown Court) (16c.)
P. 42
2482–5 † Nos. 58, 60, 62 and 64 (formerly Nos. 19,
20, 21 and 22) (18c.)
2486 No. 66 (formerly No. 24) (late 17c.)
2487 †† No. 68 (formerly No. 25) (18c.)

[1] Partly demolished 1950 for Public Car Park Access

Borough or District Civil Parish	No.	Name or Description of Antiquity

GODALMING—*contd.*

HIGH STREET—*contd.*

2488–9 †Nos. 74 and 76 (formerly Nos. 28 and 29) (1663)

2490 ††No. 78 (formerly No. 30) (19c.)

2491 †No. 80 (formerly Nos. 31 and 32) (17c.)

2492–6 †Nos. 116, 118, 126, 128 and 130 (formerly Nos. 45 and 48 (C.P.)) (18c.)

2497 †No. 135 (formerly No. 59A) (early 19c.)

2498–9 ††Nos. 111–113 (formerly Nos. 67 and 67A) (18c.)

2500–1 †Nos. 107 and 109 (formerly No. 68) (17c.)

2502–5 †Nos. 103, 105, 101 and 99 (formerly Nos. 69, 69A, 69B, 70 and 71) (formerly Old White Hart) (16c.) P. 70

2506–7 ††Nos. 89 and 91 (formerly No. 73) (18c.)

2508 †No. 77 (16c. & 17c.)

2509–10 †Nos. 71 to 75 (formerly Nos. 78 and 79) (18c.)

2511–3 ††Nos. 65, 61 and 63 (formerly Nos. 82 and 83) (early 19c.)

2514–5 Nos. 59 and 57 (formerly Nos. 84, 85 and 86) (17c.)

2516 ††No. 47 (formerly No. 90) (early 19c.)

2517–26 ††Nos. 45, 43, 41, 39, 37, 33, 31, 29, 27 and 25 (formerly Nos. 91, 92, 93, 94, 95, 96, 97, 98, 99 and 100) (18c.)

2527 ††No. 15 (formerly No. 106) (17c.)

2528–30 ††Nos. 7, 9 and 11 (formerly No. 107) (17c.) The Square

2531 No. 149 (formerly No. 50 Richmond Arms (P.H.)) (17c. & 18c.)

2532 House at rear of Richmond Arms (P.H.) (16c.)

2533 †The Old Town Hall (1815)

2534 †No. 1 Cottage, The Square (16c. & 17c.)

HOLLOWAY HILL

2535–6 Nos. 1 and 3 (17c.)

2537–40 ††Nos. 10, 12, 14 and 16 (early 19c. front on 16c. or 17c. building)

2541–6 ††Nos. 18, 20, 22, 24, 26 and 28 (early 19c.)

2547 Barn (now stables) behind Eashing Farm Dairy (17c.)

Borough or District Civil Parish	No.	Name or Description of Antiquity

GODALMING—*contd.*

MEADROW

2548–9 †† Nos. 28 and 30 (1633)
2550–1 †† Nos. 50 and 52 (17c.)
2552   Mead Cottage (formerly The Firs) (18c.)
2553   φ Wyatt's Almshouses (1622) P. 68

MILL LANE

2554–5 †† Nos. 7 and 9 (16c.)
2556–7   Nos. 12 and 14 (16c.)
2558   Hatch Mill (17c. & 18c.)
2559   † The Mint, Friends' Meeting House (18c.)

MINT STREET

2560   †† Stabling between Nos. 5 and 7 (1835)
2561–2 †† Nos. 7 and 9 (17c.)
2563   † No. 11 (18c.)
2564   †† No. 20 (Brook House) (16c. & 17c.)
2565–6   Nos. 24 and 28 (Whitehall) (16c.)

OCKFORD ROAD

2567–9   Nos. 10, 12 and 16 (17c.)
2570   †† No. 14 (17c.)

2571–3   Nos. 96, 98 and 100 (16c. & 17c. with 18c.
         fronts)
2574–6 †† Nos. 104, 106 and 108 (16c.)
2577–8   Nos. 116 and 118 (16c.)
2579–80 ††Nos. 120 and 122 (16c.) N.T.
2581   † Lake Hotel (early 19c.)
2582   †† The Wagon and Horses (P.H.) (17c.)

WHARF STREET

2583   †† No. 2 (18c.)
2584   †† Sun Hotel (18c.)

GUILDFORD BOROUGH
   GUILDFORD

GENERAL

2585–8   Nos. 1 to 4 Beech Lawn, Epsom Road (19c.)
2589   †† No. 2 Abbott Road (1910)
2590   † No. 13 (Kings Corner) ("neo-late" 17c.)
         Chantry View Road
2591–2 † Nos. 37 and 38 (17c.) Castle Street
2593   Caves (mediaeval), Rack's Close

Borough or District Civil Parish	No.	Name or Description of Antiquity

GUILDFORD—*contd.*

GENERAL—*contd.*

2594–5 † East Lodges (2), Sutton Place (18c., altered 19c.)

2596 ∅ Guildford Castle (early 12c. and later)

2597–8 †† Outbuildings and barn at Guildford Park Farm, Guildford Park (18c. and later)

2599 † Little Croft, Guildown Road

2600 † Littleholme, Upper Guildown Road

2601 Old Wheel (18c.), Guildford Wharf

2602 † Semaphore House (*c.* 1800) Pewley Hill

2603–4 †† Warren Farm (17c. & 18c.) and Barn

2605 †† Yew Tree Cottage (early 19c.), Stoke Fields

BURPHAM

2606–9 † Nos. 1, 3, 5 and 7 (16c.), Burpham Lane

2610 Anchor and Horseshoes (P.H.) (17c. with later additions)

2611 † New Inn Farmhouse (late 17c.)

2612–9 †† Terrace of eight cottages (18c.), Pimm's Row

BURY FIELDS

2620–1 No. 1 and Cottage at rear (18c.)

2622–36 † Nos. 1–15 The Court (20c.)

2637 No. 5 (late 17c.)

2638 †† No. 14 (St. Nicolas Cottage) (18c. with 19c. front)

2639 † No. 15 (Westbury) (17c. & 18c.)

2640–1 †† No. 17 (18c., with modern shop front) and Cottage to south

2642–3 †† No. 19 (*c.* 1800) and Cottage at rear

2644–5 †† Nos. 35 and 37 (1839)

2646–7 †† Nos. 39 and 41 (early 19c.)

BURY FIELDS LANE

2648 †† Bow Cottage (*c.* 1700)

BURY STREET

2649–51 †† Nos. 7 to 9 Caleb Lovejoy Almshouses (1839)

Borough or District Civil Parish	No.	Name or Description of Antiquity

GUILDFORD—*contd.*

BURY STREET—*contd.*

2652–3 ††No. 23 (Wey Cottage) and No. 25 (17c. & 18c.)

2654–6 ††Nos. 27, 29 and 31 (16c. & 17c., refronted 1852)

2657 ††Church View (19c.)

CASTLE HILL

2658 †No. 3 (The Chestnuts) (early 19c.)

2659 ††No. 10 (South Hall) (19c.)

CHAPEL STREET

2660–1 ††Nos. 1 and 2 (16c. & 17c. with 19c. front)

2662–3 ††Nos. 3 and 4 (16c. & 17c. with 19c. front)

2664–5 ††Nos. 8 and 9 (18c. and earlier)

2666–7 †Nos. 10 and 11 (16c. and later)

2668 †No. 21 (16c. & 17c.)

CHERTSEY STREET

2669 ††No. 8 (early 19c.)

2670–5 ††Nos. 13 to 23 (Ivy Place Cottages) (early 19c.)

2676 ††No. 14 (17c. & 18c.)

2677–8 †Nos. 16 and 18 (18c.)

2679 †No. 20 (18c.)

2680 †No. 22 (18c.)

2681 †No. 24 (16c. & 17c.)

2682 †No. 26 (16c. & 17c.)

2683–4 †Nos. 25 and 27 (18c.)

2685–6 †Nos. 28 and 30 (18c.)

2687 †No. 29 (early 19c.)

2688 †No. 32 (17c. & 18c.)

2689–90 ††Nos. 34 and 36 (17c. & 18c.)

2691 ††No. 60 (17c. & 18c.)

2692–3 ††Nos. 70 and 72 (18c.)

2694 ††Vaughan House (mid 18c.)

DAPDUNE

2695 ††St. Saviour's Vicarage (early 19c.), Dapdune Crescent

2696 ††Wharf Cottage (16c. & 17c.), Dapdune Wharf

Borough or District Civil Parish	No.	Name or Description of Antiquity

GUILDFORD—*contd.*

FRIARY STREET

2697 † No. 13 (early 19c. on 17c. front)
2698 † No. 14 (early 19c.)
2699 †† Culpeper House (16c., later rebuilt)
2700 ‡ Gatehouse to wharf (18c.)
2701 † The Bear (P.H.) (16c.–18c.)

HIGH STREET

2702–4 †† Nos. 2, †4 and 6 (formerly 89, 90 and 91) (late 18c. with modern shop fronts)
2705 † Loseley Chapel, St. Nicholas Church (14c.)
2706 †† No. 11 (The Greyhound Inn) (formerly No. 85) (early 18c.)
2707–10† Nos. 23, 25, 27 and 29 (formerly Nos. 79 and 80) (early 18c.)
2711–2 † Nos. 43 and 45 (formerly Nos. 71, 72 and 73) (early 19c.)
2713 †† No. 46 (formerly No. 104) (20c. recently restored)
2714 ‡ No. 56 (formerly No. 108) (early 18c.)
2715–7 † Nos. 61, 63 and 65 (formerly Nos. 62, 63 and 64) (17c., 18c. and early 19c.) (with modern front)
2718 †† No. 64 (formerly No. 111) (early 19c.)
2719– † No. 66 (formerly No. 112) (*c.* 1800) and
20 buildings at rear (15c. & 16c.)
2721 †† No. 68 (formerly No. 113) (late 18c.)
2722–3 †† No. 70 (formerly No. 114) and House to rear (16c. & 17c.)
2724 † No. 71 (formerly No. 60) (18c.)
2725–8 † No. 72, 74, 76 and 78 (formerly Nos. 115 and 116) (mediaeval undercroft) (*c.* 1800)
2729 † No. 73 (formerly No. 59) (late 18c.)
2730 † No. 75 (formerly No. 58) (mid 18c., much altered)
2731–2 †† Nos. 80 and 82 (formerly Nos. 117 and 118) (early 18c.)
2733–5 † Nos. 81, 77 and 79 (formerly Nos. 56 and 57, formerly the old Post Office) (17c. and later)
2736 † No. 83 (formerly No. 55) (*c.* 1800)
2737 ‡ No. 90 (formerly No. 121) (17c. and earlier)

Borough or District Civil Parish	No.	Name or Description of Antiquity

GUILDFORD—*contd.*   *HIGH STREET*—*contd.*

2738   ‡No. 91 (formerly No. 52 The Angel Hotel) (mediaeval undercroft)

2739   ‡No. 92 (formerly No. 122) (16c.–17c.)

2740–1   †Nos. 93 and 95 (formerly No. 51) (early 19c.)

2742–3   †Nos. 97 and 99 (formerly No. 50) (18c.)

2744   No. 101 (formerly No. 49) (18c.)

2745   †No. 103 (formerly No. 48) (17c. & 18c.)

2746   †No. 105 (formerly No. 46) (18c.)

2747   †No. 107 (formerly No. 47) (18c. front)

2748–9   †Nos. 109 and 111 (formerly Nos. 44 and 45) (early 19c.)

2750   †No. 117 (formerly No. 41) (17c.)

2751   †No. 119 (formerly No. 40) (18c. front)

2752–3 ††Nos. 121 and 121A (formerly Nos. 39 and 39A) (early 19c. with modern shop fronts)

2754–6   ‡Nos. 122, 124 and 126 (formerly Nos. 133 and 134) (1536)

2757–8   †Nos. 123 and 125 (formerly Nos. 37 and 38 The Bull's Head Inn) (16c., 17c. and later)

2759   †No. 127 (formerly No. 36) (*c.* 1800)

2760–1   ‡Nos. 128 and 130 (formerly No. 135 Old Corn Exchange Tunsgate) (1818)

2762–3   †Nos. 129 and 131 (formerly No. 35) (The Guildford Arms (P.H.)) (*c.* 1800)

2764   φ The Guildhall (1683)

2765–6   †Nos. 132 and 134 (formerly No. 137) (late 18c.)

2767–8   †Nos. 137 and 139 (formerly No. 32) (18c.)

2769–70 †Nos. 141 and 143 (formerly No. 31) (18c.)

2771   †No. 142 (formerly Nos. 140 and 141) (17c., with modern shop fronts)

2772   †No. 145 (formerly No. 29) (*c.* 1800)

2773–5 ††Nos. 146, 148 and 150 (formerly Nos. 142 and 143) (16c. & 17c. timbers with 20c. brick masking)

2776   ‡No. 147 (formerly No. 30) (mid 18c.)

2777–9   †Nos. 149, 151 and 153 (formerly Nos. 26 to 28 The Crown Inn) (18c.)

2780–4   ‡Nos. 152, 154, 156, 158 and 160 (formerly Nos. 144, 144A and 144B) (18c.)

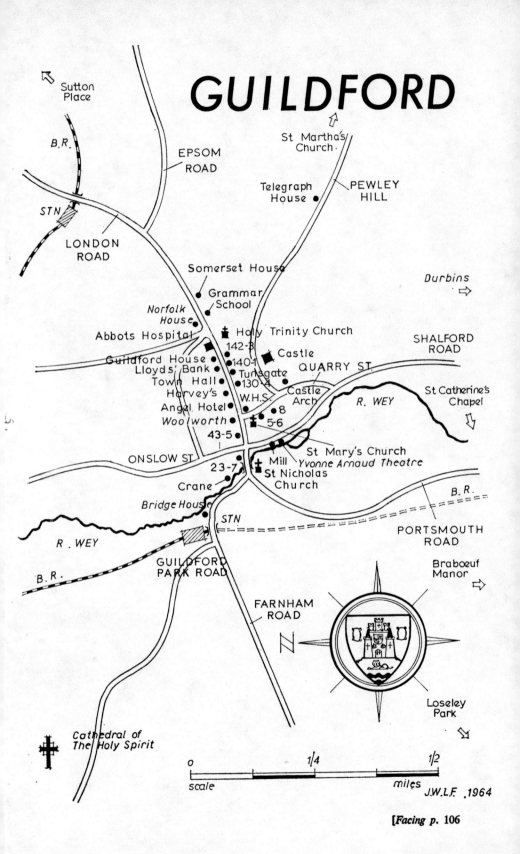

GUILDFORD

Sutton Place

B.R.

STN

EPSOM ROAD

St Martha's Church

Telegraph House

PEWLEY HILL

LONDON ROAD

Somerset House

Grammar School

Norfolk House

Durbins

Abbots Hospital

Holy Trinity Church

142-8

Castle

SHALFORD ROAD

Guildford House

140-1

Lloyds' Bank

Turnsgate

QUARRY ST.

Town Hall

130-4

Castle Arch

St Catherine's Chapel

Harvey's

W.H.S.

R. WEY

Angel Hotel

8

Woolworth

5-6

43-5

St Mary's Church

ONSLOW ST.

23-7

Mill

Yvonne Arnaud Theatre

St Nicholas Church

Crane

B.R.

Bridge House

STN

PORTSMOUTH ROAD

R. WEY

Braboeuf Manor

B.R.

GUILDFORD PARK ROAD

FARNHAM ROAD

Loseley Park

Cathedral of The Holy Spirit

0   1/4   1/2

scale   miles   J.W.L.F. 1964

[Facing p. 106

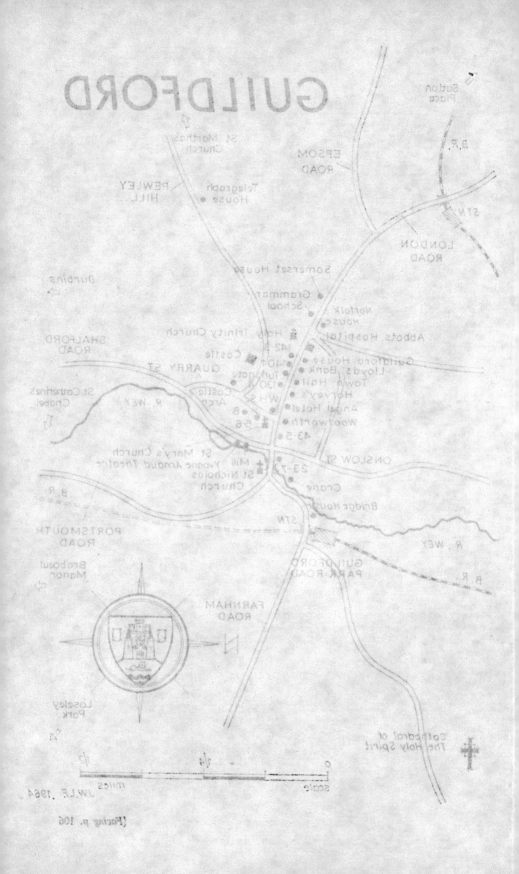

GUILDFORD

Sutton
Place

EPSOM
ROAD

B.R.

STN

LONDON
ROAD

St Matthas
Church

PEWLEY
HILL

Telegraph
House

Somerset House

Durbins

Grammar
School

Norfolk
House

SHALFORD
ROAD

Holy Trinity Church

Abbots Hospital

142 B   Castle

Guildford House

St Catherines
Chapel

QUARRY ST

140 B
Lloyd's Bank

R. WEY

Town Hall

130 K

Castle
Arch

Harvey's
W.H.S.

B

Angel Hotel

Woolworth

56

43 S

St Mary's Church

ONSLOW ST

Mill Yvonne Arnaud Theatre

23-7

St Nicholas
Church

Crane

PORTSMOUTH
ROAD

B.R.

Bridge House

STN

R. WEY

GUILDFORD
PARK ROAD

B.R.

Brabout
Manor

FARNHAM
ROAD

N

Cathedral of
The Holy Spirit

Losley
Park

0   ¼   ½
scale   miles

J.W.L.F. 1964.

[Facing p. 106

Borough or District Civil Parish	No.	Name or Description of Antiquity

GUILDFORD—*contd.*

HIGH STREET—*contd.*

2785   φ No. 155 (Guildford House) (formerly No. 25 Child House) (17c.)

2786–7   † Nos. 157 and 159 (formerly Nos. 24 and 24A) (19c.)

2788–9   † Nos. 161 and 163 (formerly No. 23) (18c.)

2790   † No. 162 (Guildford Club) (formerly No. 145) (late 18c.)

2791   φ Hospital of the Blessed Trinity known as Abbott's Hospital (1619–22)

2792   †† No. 170 (formerly No. 149) (early 19c.)

2793–4 †† Nos. 176 and 178 (formerly Nos. 151 and 152) (17c., framed with modern timbered front)

2795   †† No. 190 (formerly No. 155) (probably 17c., altered)

2796–7   † Nos. 192 and 194 (formerly No. 156) (18c. with modern shop front)

2798   †† No. 196 (formerly Nos. 157 and 158) (Early 19c.)

2799   † No. 202 (formerly No. 160) (18c. front on older house)

2800   †† No. 204 (formerly No. 161) (Late 18c., with modern shop front)

2807–2 †† Nos. 206 and 208 (formerly No. 162) (early 19c. with modern shop front)

2803–6   † Nos. 210, 212, 214 and 216 (formerly No. 163) (early 19c.)

2807   ‡ King Edward VI Grammar School (16c.) and later restored

2808   φ No. 222 (formerly No. 165 Somerset House) (early 18c.)

2809–12 † Nos. 224, 226, 228 and 230 (formerly No. 166) (early 18c. with modern shop front)

2813–8   † Nos. 232, 234, 236, 238, 240 and 242 (formerly No. 167) (18c.)

2819   † No. 244 (formerly No. 168) (18c.)

2820   † No. 246 (formerly No. 169) (18c., with modern shop front)

2821–2 †† Nos. 248 and 250 (formerly No. 170) (19c. with modern shop front)

2823   †† No. 252 (formerly No. 171) (18c.)

Borough or District Civil Parish	No.	Name or Description of Antiquity

GUILDFORD—*contd.*

HIGH STREET—contd.

2824 †† No. 254 (formerly No. 172) (16c. & 17c. altered)

2825–6 † Nos. 274 and 276 (formerly No. 180) (early 19c.)

LEA PALE LANE

2827–8 †† Nos. 1 and 2 (18c.)

2829–31 †† Nos. 3, 4 and 5 (18c.)

2832 C.P. Stoke House (18c.)

LONDON ROAD

2833 †† No. 32 (Delaford) (early 19c.)

2834–5 †† Luss Cottage and The Rowans (early 19c.)

MERROW
GENERAL

2836–7 † Nos. 1 and 2, Old Cottages, near Merrow Siding (16c. & 17c.) Merrow Common

2838 † No. 6 (The Old Cottage) (16c. & 17c.) Trodd's Lane

2839 ‡ Levyl's Dene (16c. & 17c.)

2840 † The Old Farmhouse (17c. and earlier), Leatherhead Road

EPSOM ROAD

2841–2 † Nos. 1 and 2 Park Farm Cottages and Barn, Park Lane (16c.)

2843–4 ††[1] Nos. 217 and 219 (Forge Cottage) (16c. & 17c.)

2845 † No. 221 (16c., with modern shop front)

2846 ‡ Horse and Groom (P.H.) (1615)

2847–8 † House and Barn (16c.) south of Park Lane Farm, Park Lane

MERROW STREET

2849 ††[2] Covey Cottage (early 18c.)

2850 †† Evergreen Cottage (16c. & 17c.)

2851 Merrow House (1802)

2852 †† Yew Tree Cottage (16c. & 17c.)

[1] Demolished 1955
[2] Demolished 1955

Borough or District Civil Parish	No.	Name or Description of Antiquity

GUILDFORD—*contd.*

MILLMEAD

2853–4 †† Nos. 5 and 6 (17c.)

2855–6 † Millmead House (17c. & 18c.) and †† Stables (17c.)

2857 † The Old Water Mill (formerly Town Mills) (late 18c.)

2858 † Weir House (early 19c.)

MOUNT PLEASANT

2859 † No. 2 (18c.)

2860 † Horn Castle (18c. with 16c. & 17c. structure behind)

2861–2 †† Mount Pleasant Cottage and No. 2A (Early 19c.)

NORTH PLACE

2863–4 †† [1]Nos. 10 and 11 (19c.)

NORTH STREET

2865 †† No. 17 (early 19c.)

2866 † Clark's College (formerly Archbishop Abbott's School) (early 17c., altered)

2867 †† Friends' Meeting House (1805 and later)

2868 †† Horse and Groom Inn (17c.–19c.)

PARK STREET
(*including FARNHAM ROAD*)

2869 †† No. 14 (early 19c.)

2870 † No. 17 (16c. & 17c.)

2871 †† Tobacconist's Shop (18c. or earlier)

PORTSMOUTH ROAD

2872–5 †† Nos. 1, 2, 3 and 4 Rectory Place (19c.)

2876 †† No. 28 (late 18c.)

2877 † No. 44 (St. Catherine's Cottage) (17c. with 19c. additions)

2878–9 †† Nos. 61 and 63 (Early 19c.)

2880 † No. 64 (St. Catherine's Stores) (17c.)

2881–2 †† Nos. 65 and 67 (early 19c.)

2883–4 † Nos. 69 and 71 (early 19c.)

2885–6 †† Nos. 73 (The Haven) and 75 (Rockcliffe) (early 19c.)

2887 †† No. 79 (early 19c.)

[1] Demolished 1962

Borough or District Civil Parish	No.	Name or Description of Antiquity

GUILDFORD—*contd.*

PORTSMOUTH ROAD—contd.

2888 †† No. 81 (Fairholme) (early 19c.)

2889 †† No. 97 (Hitherbury House, formerly Astr House) (19c.)

2890 † No. 111 (Priory House) (early 19c.)

2891 †† No. 119 (Braboeuf Cottage) (*c.* 1850)

2892–2900 †† No. 129 and cottages 1 to 4 and 5 to 8 a rear (1881)

2901 † St. Catherine's Priory (18c.)

2902 †† The Cannon Inn (16c. & 17c. with mid 19c front)

2903 † The Ship Inn (early 19c. front on 17c structure)

2904 † Wycliffe Buildings (1894)

QUARRY STREET

2905 †† No. 1 (18c. & 19c. and earlier)

2906 † No. 2 (The Star (P.H.)) (18c.)

2907 † No. 3 (late 18c. and earlier)

2908 † No. 4 (16c.)

2909 † No. 5 (late 17c.)

2910 ‡ No. 6 (late 17c., with earlier structur behind)

2911–2 ‡ Nos. 8 and 8A (late 17c. front)

2913 † No. 9 (Norfolk House) (*c.* 1800)

2914 † No. 10 (early 19c.)

1915 † No. 11 (late 18c. with modern shop front

2916 † No. 12 (17c. & 18c.)

2917 † No. 13 (18c.)

2918 † No. 14 (18c.)

2919 † No. 15 (18c.)

2920 ‡ No. 16 (18c. and earlier)

2921–2 † Nos. 17 and 18 (17c. & 18c.)

2923–4 ‡ Nos. 19 and 20 (Millbrook House) (17c.)

2925 ‡ No. 21 (16c. & 17c.)

2926 †† No. 22 (Millbrook Cottage) (17c. & 18c.)

2927 † No. 28A (Old River Cottage) (16c.)

2928 † No. 43 (Diocesan House) (17c. and later)

2929 † No. 44 (*c.* 1800)

2930 ‡ No. 49 (Castle House (18c.)

2931 †† No. 50 (17c. & 18c.)

2932 †† No. 51 (18c.)

2933 †† No. 52 (The King's Head (P.H.)) (17c.)

Borough or District Civil Parish	No.	Name or Description of Antiquity

GUILDFORD—*contd.*

QUARRY STREET—*contd.*

2934–5 †† Nos. 53 and 53A (early 17c. with early 19c. alterations)

2936   † No. 54 (early 19c.)

2937   ‡ No. 55 (18c.)

2938   † No. 56 (late 18c.)

2939   † No. 57 (*c.* 1800)

2940   † No. 58 (17c., with later front)

2941   †† No. 59 (St. Mary's House) (early 19c.)

2942   †† No. 65 (18c., with modern shop front)

2943   φ Castle Arch (early 17c.)

THE MOUNT
(*formerly MOUNT STREET*)

2944–5 †† Nos. 3 and 5 (17c.)

2946   † No. 4 (17c.)

2947   † No. 12 (mid 18c.)

2948   † Mount Manor House (16c. and later)

2949   †† The Wheatsheaf P.H. (mid 18c.)

SHALFORD
GENERAL

2950   †† Park Cottage (17c. & 18c.) Shalford Road

2951–2 †† Tilehouse Farm (16c., refronted) and outbuildings, East Shalford Lane

PILGRIM'S WAY

2953–4 † Nos. 9 and 11 (formerly the Pest House) (16c. & 17c.)

2955   † East Shalford Manor House (17c. & 18c.)

2956–7 † Half Way Grange (formerly Halfpenny House) (17c.) and outbuildings

SLYFIELD

2958   ‡ Slyfield Farm (16c.)

SOUTH HILL

2959–60 †† Castle Cottage and Warwick Rise (late 18c. & early 19c.)

2961   † Pewley Cottage (17c.)

SOUTH STREET

2962   † No. 1 (Waterworks Cottage) (17c.)

Borough or District Civil Parish	No.	Name or Description of Antiquity

GUILDFORD—*contd.*

ST. CATHERINE'S

2963 †† Ferry Cottage (16c.–18c.) St. Catherine's Ferry

2964–6 ‡ Piccard's Manor (16c. & 17c.) and Barns (2) (18c.) Sandy Lane

ST. MARTHA'S

2967 † Great Halfpenny Farm (16c. restored)

STOKE BY-PASS ROAD

2968 †† Park View (early 19c.)

JOSEPH'S ROAD

2969–71 † Nos. 7, 9 and 11 (1663 and earlier)

2972–4 † Nos. 35, 37 and 39 (16c.)

2975 † Stoke Mill House (18c.)

2976 C.P. Stoke Park (18c. & 19c.)

2977–8 †† Stoke Park Farm (17c.) and outbuildings

STOKE HILL

2979–82 † Stoke Hill, coachhouse, outbuildings and garden wall (early 19c.)

2983 †† Stoke Hill Farm (18c. & 19c.)

STOKE ROAD

2984 † No. 92 (Stoke Hospital) (18c.)

2985–7 †† Nos. 100, 102 and 104 (late 18c.)

2988 †† No. 103 (The Stoke Hotel) (early 19c.)

STOUGHTON

2989 † Tilehouse Farm (15c.–18c.)

SWAN LANE

2990–2 † Nos. 1, 3 and 5 (17c., with modern shop fronts)

2993–4 † Nos. 7 and 9 (17c.)

2995–6 Nos. 11 and 13 (late 17c.)

TRINITY CHURCHYARD

2997–8 †† Nos. 1 and 2 (18c.)

Borough or District Civil Parish	No.	Name or Description of Antiquity

GUILDFORD—*contd.*   *TRINITY CHURCHYARD*—*contd.*

2999–3001 †Nos. 12 (Laburnum Cottage formerly Trinity Cottage) 13 (Willow Cottage) and 14 (Delhi Cottage) (17c.)

3002 †No. 15 The Royal Oak (P.H.) (17c. and later)

3003 †No. 16 (19c.)

3004–6 ††Nos. 17, 18 and 19 (17c. & 18c.)

TUNSGATE

3007 ††No. 7 (17c.)

3008–9 ††Nos. 8 and 9 (17c. & 18c. over modern shop fronts)

WARWICK'S BENCH

3010 †Garden Court (20c.)

3011 †Monks Path (20c.)

3012 †Undershaw (20c.)

NOTE. The undermentioned properties included in *Guildford R.D.*, are (at the date of publication) included in a *Provisional List* of Buildings of Architectural or Historic Interest by the Ministry of Housing and Local Government. It is assumed the grading as annotated (ϕ, ‡, †, ††) indicates that such buildings will be either Statutory listed (owners served with necessary notice) or Supplementary listed under the provisions of the Town and Country Planning Act 1962.

GUILDFORD **R.D.**

    ALBURY   *GENERAL*

3013–5 †Albury Park (18c. & 19c.), †Tunnel entrance and †Bath-house (17c)

3016 †Orange Cottages, Albury Park (early 19c.)

3017 †The Catholic Apostolic Church and Chapter House (1840) (now disused)

3018 ††Cooks Place (formerly The Grange) (19c. and earlier)

3019–21 ††Weston Lodge (16c. and later) and †Dovecote and outbuildings in Weston Yard (17c.)

3022 ††Albury House (17c.–mid 19c.)

3023–4 †Pair of cottages (16c.) at the corner of Church Lane

Borough or District Civil Parish	No.	Name or Description of Antiquity

ALBURY—*contd.*   *GENERAL*—*contd.*

3025   † Premises occupied by Knight and Browne (Builders)

3026   †† The Round House (early 19c.)

3027   † Clive Lodge (early 19c.)

3028   †† The Old Rectory (portion of interior (13c.) altered between 1780–1822)

3029   †† The Cottage

3030   † Ford Farm (formerly Little Ford Farm) (16c.–17c.)

3031   †† Whitelane Farm (formerly Whitelane Cottages) (18c. and earlier) White Lane

3032   † The Old Farmhouse, Newlands Corner (early 19c.)

3033   ** Barrow at Newlands Corner

3034   †† Heath Lodge, Albury Heath (18c. & 19c.)

3035–6 † Elmend and cottage adjoining Little London

BROOK

3037–8 † The Old Cottage and Brook (formerly Northworth)

3039–   †† Chennels East and Chennels West (1636
40   later restored)

3041   †† Atfields Cottage

3042   †† Quillet

3043   †† Brook Farm (18c.)

3044   †† Hull House

FARLEY GREEN

3045   †† Farley Hall Farm House (16c. with modern additions)

3046   † Shophouse Farm

3047   †† Mayorhouse Farm

3048   † Lockhursthatch Farmhouse

3049   * Romano-Celtic Temple on Farley Heath

ARTINGTON   *GENERAL*

3050   φ* St. Catherine's Chapel (14c.)

3051–8 †† Nos. 1–5, 5A, 6 and Cattenhill Cottage, St. Catherine's Hill (18c.)

3059   †† Braboeuf Manor (16c., altered 19c.)

3060   † Shieling (17c.)

Borough or District Civil Parish	No.	Name or Description of Antiquity

ARTINGTON—*contd.*

GENERAL—*contd.*

3061   †Conduit Farm (17c.)

3062–5 ∅Loseley House (1563) †Dovecote (17c.) and gazebos (2) (18c.)

PORTSMOUTH ROAD

3066   †No. 37 (Old Friars) (16c.)

3067–8 ††No. 39–41 Loseley Estate (17c.)

3069   †No. 42 (Little Farmhouse) (18c. or earlier)

3070–1 †Artington Manor Farm (moated) (17c.) and ††Granary

LITTLETON

3072   ††Littleton Farm (17c.)

LITTLETON LANE

3073–4 †Nos. 8 and 9 (17c.)

3075–6 †Nos. 10 and 11 Orange Court Cottages (17c.)

3077–8 ‡Nos. 12 and 13 (17c.)

3079–   ††Nos. 17 and 18 (Pillar Box Cottages) (17c.)
80

3081–2 †Nos. 20 and 21 (cottages next to church on south side) (17c.)

3083–4 ††Nos. 22 and 23 (17c.)

ASH

GENERAL

3085   ††Hartshorn (formerly Hartshorn Inn) (late 17c., restored 1904) Church Road

3086–7 †Old Manor Cottage and Old Moat Cottage (formerly Ash Manor House (moated)) (1657) Ash Green

3088   ††The Grange (early 19c.)

3089   †Ashmead (18c. and earlier)

3090   †The Old Rectory (16c. with later additions)

3091   ††Pratts Farm (18c.) Aldershot Road

ASH STREET

3092   †Lavender Cottage (17c.)

3093   †Ashe Lodge (18c.)

3094–5 ††Post Office (16c.–17c.) and house adjoining

3096   ††The Bricklayers Arms (P.H.) (18c.)

3097   †Merryworth (*c.* 1510)

Borough or District Civil Parish	No.	Name or Description of Antiquity

ASH—cont.

ASH STREET—contd.

3098   The Greyhound (P.H.) (17c., refaced 1930)
3099   † Bricklyn (17c. and later)
3100   †† Tudor House (formerly Bay Cottage) (17c.)
3101   †† Rosedale (formerly Rosewood and Rosewood Cottage)

CLANDON, EAST

GENERAL

3102–3   † Old Manor Farm (17c. & 18c.) and †† Barn
3104   † Queen's Head (P.H.) (17c. and later)
3105–6   † The Old Smithy and house adjoining (formerly The Old Forge Cottage) (17c.)
3107–8   † Nos. 1 and 2 Church Cottages (17c. and later)
3109   † Lamp Cottage (17c.)
3110   † Yew Cottage
3111   † Bay Cottage (late 17c.)
3112–3 †† Nos. 1 and 2, Yew Tree Cottage (18c. or earlier)
3114   †† The Old Rectory (17c. and later)
3115–6   † Nos. 6 and 7, East Clandon or Frogmore Cottages (17c.)
3117   † Tunmore Farmhouse (17c.)
3118–9   † No. 8 East Clandon or Tunmore Cottage (late 17c. or early 18c.)
3120   †† Stuart Cottage (17c.)
3121   Post Office (early or mid 18c.)
3122   White Cottage (17c.), School Lane
3123–4 †† Home Farm and †† Barn (17c.)
3125–6   φ[1] Hatchlands (1759 and later) and † Temple (18c.) N.T.
3127–8   † Nos. 11 and 12 (East Clandon or Whitney's Cottage) (17c.)

BACK LANE

3129   † No. 15 (17c.)
3130   † Daphne Cottage (17c.)
3131–2   † Holmhurst Cottages (two) (17c.)
3133   †† The Old House (17c.)
3134   Briar Cottage (late 17c.)
3135   Chapel Cottage (17c. and later)

[1] See Country Life 17.9.1953 and 1.10.1953

Borough or District Civil Parish	No.	Name or Description of Antiquity

CLANDON, WEST

GENERAL

3136 ϕ [1]Clandon Park House (1731) and:—
3137 †† The Dovecot (18c.)
3138 † The Stables (*c.* 1776)
3139 † Temple (*c.* 1776)
3140–1 † The Lodge and Merrow Gates (1776)
3142 † Grotto in Park (*c.* 1776)
3143 †† Temple Court (17c. and later) Clandon Park
3144 †† Hilliers Cottages opposite Church (17c.)
3145 † Gardener's Cottage (17c.)
3146 †† No. 6 Parkside Cottage (18c.)
3147–8 † West Clandon Post Office with house attached (formerly Goachers Shop) (18c.)

3149 †† Bull's Head Inn (17c. & 18c.)
3150 †† Summers (17c. & 18c.)
3151 † Fludyers Cottages (2) (17c.)
3152 †† Dibbles (16c., restored)
3153 †† No. 1 Old Barn Cottage (17c.)
3154 †† Brownlow Cottage (West Clandon Stores) (17c.)
3155 † Cuckoo Farm (17c.)
3156 †† The Village Pound
3157 †† Pound Cottage (17c.)
3158 † Ellerker Cottage (17c.)
3159–60 † Tudor Cottage and Stoughton Cottage (17c.)
3161 † Hawthorne Cottages (16c. & 17c.)
3162–3 † Nos. 1 and 2, Poyners Cottages (17c.)

COMPTON

GENERAL

3164 †† Westbury Manor (18c.)
3165 Eastbury Manor (early-late 19c.)
3166 † The Dykeries (18c.)
3167 †† Eastbury Farm Cottage (18c., altered 19c.)
3168 Eastbury Manor Farm (17c. and later)
3169 †† Vine Cottage (17c.)
3170 † Compton Coffee House (formerly Moors) (18c.)
3171 † Cypress Farm (17c.)
3172–3 †† Apple Tree and Ross Cottage
3174 †† Mission Cottage

[1] See Country Life 24.11.1960, p.1215

Borough or District Civil Parish	No.	Name or Description of Antiquity

COMPTON—*contd.*

GENERAL—contd.

3175 †† House N. of Church on east side of road (18c. or earlier with later additions)

3176 † White House (formerly White Hart Inn) (16c.)

3177 †† The Limes (early 19c.)

3178 †† Stores Cottage

3179– †† Forge House and Smithy (17c.)
80

3181–2 †† Beech Cottage and Tyrone Cottage (17c.)

3183 †† Watts Gallery (1903–4)

3184–5 † Watts Memorial Chapel (1895) and †Cloister (1911)

3186 † Limnerslease (late 19c.)

3187 †* Roman Villa, north of Limnerslease, nr. Down Lane

3188 †† Coneycroft Barn (17c.)

3189 † Polstead Manor Cottage (16c.)

3190 †† The Withies (P.H.) (18c. and earlier)

3191 †† The Tudor Cottage (formerly Brook Cottage) (16c.)

3192–3 †† Mellersh Farmhouse (17c.) and ††Barn (18c.)

3194 † No. 76, Brickfield Cottage, Loseley Estate (17c.)

3195 †† Rose Tree Cottage (18c. & 19c.)

3196 The Harrow (P.H.) (17c. & 18c.)

3197–8 † Hurtmore Farm (formerly Hurtmore Homestead) (c. 1600) and ††Upland Cottage (formerly Barn) (18c.)

3199 † The Lodge of Flexford House (early 19c.)

3200–1 Rose Cottages (two) (Originally Almshouses) (late 18c.)

COMPTON COMMON

3202–5 Nos. 82–85 (17c.–18c.)

3206 Island Cottage (17c.)

EFFINGHAM

GENERAL

3207–8 Almshouses and weather-boarded Barn (18c.)

3209 † Effingham House (Golf Club) (early 19c.)

3210 The White House (16c. with later additions)

Borough or District Civil Parish	No.	Name or Description of Antiquity

EFFINGHAM—*contd.*

GENERAL—*contd.*

3211 † Browns (formerly Manor Farm), Brown's Lane (17c. & 18c.)
3212 ††¹The Cottage, Lower Road (17c. and earlier)
3213 * Greatlee Wood, moat

CHURCH STREET

3214 †† Dormers
3215 †† Church Cottages (17c. & 18c.)
3216 †† The Old Post Office (18c. and earlier)
3217 ††²The Old Forge (17c.)

ORESTAN LANE

3218 † Old Westmoor Cottage (16c. & 17c.)
3219 †† West Lane Farm (17c.)

THE STREET

3220 † Home Farm (16c. & 17c.)
3221 † Middle Farm (formerly House opposite Sir Douglas Haig (P.H.)) (*c.* 1830)
3222 †† Old Post Office Cottages (18c. or earlier)
3223 †† Vine Cottage (18c.)

THE COMMON

3224 †† Tyrrels (15c. & 16c.)
3225 †† Orchard Cottage (16c. & 17c.)
3226 † Lower Farm (17c.)
3227 †† Flower Cottage (18c. or earlier)
3228–9 † Norwood Farm and Barn (17c.)
3230 Slater's Oak (17c. & 18c.)

HORSLEY, EAST

GENERAL

3231 † The Duke of Wellington P.H. (1861)
3232 ‡ Guildford Lodge (*c.* 1858)
3233 † Horsley Towers (early 19c. and later)
3234–5 †† Two Lodges of Horsley Towers in Ockham Road South (1860)
3236 †† Sartor Resartus, Ockham Road South (1866)
3237 †† Rowbarns Manor, Greendene (early 19c.)

¹ Demolished June 1957
² Demolished May 1962

Borough or District Civil Parish	No.	Name or Description of Antiquity

HORSLEY, EAST—*contd.*   *GENERAL*—*contd.*

3238 **[1]Neolithic Flint-mines at south end of Rowbarns Plantation

3239 ††Old Greendene Cottages, Greendene (17c.)

3240 ††New Marsh Farm (16c. & 18c.)

3241 †Duncombe Farm Cottage (16c.)

HORSLEY, WEST   *GUILDFORD ROAD*

3242–4 φ West Horsley Place (*c.* 1600) with †Gateway and †stables (17c.)

3245 †Place Farm (17c.)

3246–7 †Church House and Church Cottage (16c.)

3248 †Wix Farm (mid 18c.)

THE STREET

3249 †Highbanks (17c.)

3250 †Sumners

3251 ††Swan Court (Tunmore Farm) (17c.)

3252 †Brittain's Farmhouse (16c.)

3253 †The Old School House

3254 Vine Cottage (16c.)

3255 ††The King William IV Inn (18c.)

3256–7 ††Apsley Cottage and Eversley (18c. and earlier)

3258 †Barcombe Farm

3259 ††The Old House (formerly The Old Poor House) (mid 18c.)

3260 ††The Barley Mow Inn (late 18c. and earlier)

3261 †The Old Cottage

3262 †Winterfold (formerly Charlwood) (16c.)

3263 ††Grovelands (17c.)

3264 †Railway Cottages, north side of railway bridge (16c.)

LONG REACH

3265 †Roundtree Farm

EAST LANE

3266 †Lollesworth Farm (18c.)

3267 †Manor Farm

[1] See Surrey County Journal (Jan.–March, 1950), Vol. 2, pp. 71–73

Borough or District Civil Parish	No.	Name or Description of Antiquity

HORSLEY, WEST
—*contd.*

RIPLEY LANE

3268 † The Old Rectory (1819)
3269–71 † Lower Hammonds Farm (formerly Hammonds Farm) and † Barn and Dovecote (17c.)
3272 †† Hammonds Cottage
3273 ††¹Holm Cottage (16c.)

PINCOTT LANE

3274–5 † Helford Farm (formerly Pincott's Farm) and Barn (17c.)

SILKMORE LANE

3276 †† Yew Tree Cottage (17c.)

SILKMORE LANE

3277 †† Silkmore
3278 †† Cripplegate
3279 †† Charles Cottage (17c.)

GENERAL

3280–1 †† Fullers Farm (17c.) (now 2 cottages)
3282 The Soap House (17c.)

NORMANDY

GENERAL

3283 †† No. 9, Guildford Road
3284 †† Stedman's Cottage (17c.)
3285 †† Tatters (1741), Guildford Road
3286 †† Normandy Hill Farm (17c.)
3287 †† Normandy Hill Cottage (formerly Osborne Cottage) (1773)
3288 † Longerend Cottage (16c.)
3289 †† The Manor House (18c.)
3290 †† Hunts Hill Cottage (formerly Lavender Cottage) (17c.)
3291 †† Westwood Farm
3292 † Westwood House (16c. & 18c.)
3293 † Buckhurst (formerly Westwood House Stables) (18c.)
3294 † Glaziers (formerly Glaziers Cottages)
3295–6 † 1 and 2 East Wyke Farm Cottages (18c.) (formerly West Wyke Farm)

¹ Demolished

Borough or District Civil Parish	No.	Name or Description of Antiquity

NORMANDY—*contd.*

GENERAL—*contd.*

3297–8 † Henley Park (1751 with 19c. additions) an† †stables (18c. and later)

3299 †† Chapel Farm

3300 † Bailes Farm (17c. & 18c.)

3301 †† The Homestead (formerly Chandler's Cottage) (17c.)

3302 †† New Cut Cottages (east block)

3303 † New Cut Cottages (west block)

OCKHAM

OCKHAM PARK

3304–6 ¹Ockham Park (*c.* 1638 and later) (par destroyed by fire), ‡Stables (now flats (*c.* 1724 and later), Orangery (now flats (Early 18c.)

3307 †† Park Cottage

3308 †† Church End Lodge (17c.)

GENERAL

3309–11 †† Ashlea, Hautboy Cottage and cottage ad joining (17c.)

3312 †† Apps Tree Farm (17c. and later)

3313 † The Hautboy Hotel (1864)

3314–5 † Bridgefoot Farmhouse and Barns (17c.)

3316–7 † Nos. 1 and 2 Bridgefoot Cottages

3318 †† South End Cottages (17c.)

3319 †† South End Cottage (s. of former) (17c.)

3320 †† Cottage s. of Romer Cottage

3321 †† Batchelor's Farm (17c., 18c. & 19c.)

3322 †† Slade Dairy Farm (formerly Wisley Slade (17c.)

3323 †† Blackmoor Heath Farm (18c.)

3324 † Upton Farmhouse (15c. & 17c.) P.51

3325 †† Poplar House (18c.)

3326 †† The Black Swan (P.H.) (18c.)

3327 †† Bassetts (early 19c.)

3328 †† Pound Farm (18c. and earlier)

3329–30 †† Nos. 1 and 2 Mays Green

3331 †† Millwater (18c. & 19c.)

¹ See Surrey County Journal (Jan.–March 1950), Vol. 2 pp. 71–72

Borough or District *Civil Parish*	*No.*	*Name or Description of Antiquity*

OCKHAM—*contd.*   *GENERAL*—*contd.*

3332–3   1 and 2, Ockham Court, Ockham Mill (*c.* 1700)

3334   †† Bridge End (17c. & 18c.)

3335   †† Bridge End Cottage (18c.)

3336   No. 5, Bridge End (17c.)

3337   Ivy Cottage (18c.), Bridge End

3338   Walnut Tree Cottage, Bridge End (18c.)

3339   ** Barrow near Curries Clump, Ockham Common

PIRBRIGHT   *GENERAL*

3340   † The Old Village School (17c.)

3341   †† Pirbright Green Cottages (18c.)

3342   † Leonards House (18c.)

3343   † Hatchers, on the south-west side of Village Green (16c., restored)

3344   †† The White Hart Inn (17c.)

3345   †† The Cricketer's Inn (18c. and earlier)

3346   †† Tarrens (formerly Grove Farm) (18c.)

3347   † Thorner Cottage (18c. and earlier)

3348   †† Layton House (formerly The Old Pottery House), Chapel Lane (early 17c.)

3349   †† Boro Hill

3350   †† Causeway Bridge Farm (late 16c.) (largely rebuilt)

3351   † Wickham's Farm (16c.), West Heath, P. 93

3352   †† Box Cottage (17c.), Church Lane

3353   † The Manor House (16c. and later) P. 77

3354   † Cowshot Manor (15c. portions reconstructed 17c., enlarged *c.* 1912) P. 53

3355   † Pirbright Lodge (18c. and later)

3356–7 †† Pirbright Mill and Mill House

3358   †† Newmans (early 17c., restored)

3359   †† Hovers Well

3360   †† Fords Farm (17c.)

3361–2 † White's Farm and Tithe Barn (16c.)

3363   †† Stanford Farm (17c.)

3364   †† Baker's Gate Farmhouse (17c.)

3365   †† Heath Mill House (early 19c.)

3366   ** Two earth circles east of Baker's Gate Farm, Bullswater Common

3367   †† Rails Farm

Borough or District *Civil Parish*	*No.*	*Name or Description of Antiquity*

PUTTENHAM

GENERAL

3368   ‡ Puttenham Priory (18c.) P. 24
3369   †† The Old School House (late 17c.)
3370   † Shoelands (1618)
3371   †† Winters Farm Cottage (17c.)
3372   † Heath Cottage (18c.)
3373   Farm Cottage, The Heath (17c.)
3374   †† No. 2 Hook Lane
3375   †† Pilgrims Way Cottage (18c.)
3376   † Rodsall Manor (1680, with 1724 additions) P. 41
3377-8 †† Rose Cot and Briar Cot (18c.), nr. Rodsall Manor
3379   †† Druids (formerly Cutt Corner)
3380   †† Cutt Mill House
3381   ** Earth circle near Frowsbury
3382   * Frowsbury Mound, Puttenham Heath
3383   * Hillbury Camp, Puttenham Common
3384   † Hurlands (1898)

THE STREET

3385   † No. 36 (Greyhome Farm) (18c.)
3386   † No. 48 (Priory Farmhouse) (18c.)
3387   †† No. 56 (formerly No. 1) (adjoining The Good Intent) (1685)
3388   †† No. 62 (The Good Intent P.H.) (18c. or earlier)
3389   † No. 63 (Winters Farmhouse) (18c. or earlier)
3390   †† No. 66 (The Old Cottage) (17c.)
3391   †† No. 68 (Southleigh) (formerly The Post Office) (18c.)
3392-4 †† Nos. 74, 76 and 78 (Wintons Cottages) (18c. or earlier)
3395-6 †† No. 86 (Keston Cottage) and No. 88 (Jasmine Cottage) (18c.)
3397   † No. 129 (Step Cottage) (17c. or earlier with 18c. refacing)
3398   †† No. 139 (Rosemary Cottage) (18c. or earlier)
3399   †† No. 154 (formerly Nos. 17, 18 and 19) (16c., restored)
3400-1 †† Nos. 156 and 158 (formerly Nos. 20 and 22) (17c. & 18c.)

Borough or District Civil Parish	No.	Name or Description of Antiquity

RIPLEY   *HIGH STREET* (*south east side*)

3402   † The Anchor Inn (16c.)
3403   † The Vicarage (late 18c.–early 19c.)
3404–5 † Tudor House and Cedar Hotel (formerly The George Inn) (16c. & 17c.)
3406–7 †† Bassett (Hairdresser) and Cranford Cottage (18c.)
3408–9 †† Ye Olde Sweet Shoppe and The Ship Inn (17c. with later additions)
3410   †† Richardson (Greengrocer and Ironmonger)
3411   † Hurst Park Autos (formerly Blakely Engineering) (Marvelholme) (18c.)
3412   † Cranford (17c.)
3413   †† Cobham Cottages (18c.)
3414   † The Green Cottage
3415   Chemist shop (formerly The White Horse Inn) (16c.)
3416–7 †† Gable cottage and The Gables (16c.)
3418   ‡ The Talbot Hotel (17c. and later)
3419   † Talbot Cottage (*c.* 1630)
3420–1 † Bakers' shop and Estate Office (early 18c.) (formerly Wellers, Bakers and house attached)
3422   † Yew Tree House (early 19c. and earlier)
3423–6 †† No. 1–4, Ripley House (18c. with later additions)
3427   † Bridgefoot House (17c. and later)

HIGH STREET (*north west side*)

3428   † Ryde House (18c.)
3429   †† Elm Tree House
3430   †† No. 100 (18c.)
3431–2 †† The Clocke House and †† stables (18c.)
3433–6 †† Conisbee (Butcher), Jarman, (Confectioner) and two cottages adjoining (17c.)
3437–8 † Pinnock's Cafe and Amberley Cottage (17c.)
3439–40 † Old Manor House, (so-called) (*c.* 1690) P. 80 and Manor Cottage (17c.–18c.)
3441   † The Georgian House (18c.)
3442–3 †† St. George's Farm (2 cottages) (18c.)

Borough or District *Civil Parish*	*No.*	*Name or Description of Antiquity*

RIPLEY—*contd.*

NEWARK LANE
3444 †† Rose Cottage (formerly Nos. 1 and 2, Rose Cottages) (17c.)
3445 †† The Hollies (18c.)
3446 † Homewood Farmhouse (14c. & 16c.)

ROSE LANE (*east side*)
3447–9 †† Rambler Cottage and two cottages adjoining (18c.)
3450 †† Flitress
3451 † Clova Studio (18c.)

3452–3 † Ripley Court Cottage and Barn adjoining (17c.)
3454 † Ripley Court School (1667, 1689 and late 18c.)

ROSE LANE (*west side*)
3455–7 ††[1]Nos. 1, 2 and 3 (18c.)
3458–9 †† Nos. 4 and 5 (18c.)
3460 †† Apple Trees (18c.)
3461 † Chapel Farm (16c.)
3462 †† The Cottage

GROVEHEATH ROAD
3463 † Catherinehams (formerly Groveheath)
3464 † Pipers Hill (formerly The Cottage and cottage adjoining)
3465–6 †† Two cottages to the N.E. of Pipers Hill

GENERAL
3467–8 † Nos. 1 and 2, Paper Court Farm (formerly The Manor House of Papworth) (16c. & 17c.)
3469 † Newark Mill House (early 19c.)
3470 † Newark Mill (17c.)
3471 †* The ruins of Newark Priory (12c. and later)
3472 † Ryde Farmhouse (17c.)
3473 † Jury Farmhouse (17c.)
3474 †† Sussex Farm (16c. and later)
3475 Dunsborough House (18c.) P. 45

[1] Demolished 1962

orough or District Civil Parish	No.	Name or Description of Antiquity

ST. MARTHA'S *GENERAL*

3476   * Barrow near Tyting Farm

3477–8   † Chilworth Manor (16c. and later) and †garden walls (17c. & 18c.)

3479   * Earth circle on St. Martha's Hill

3480   †† Lockners Farm (18c.)

SEALE *GENERAL*

3481   †† The Lyttons (17c.)

3482   † Manor Farm (17c., restored)

3483   † Manor Farm Cottages (17c., restored)

3484–6 †† Nos. 1–3, Seale Lodge Cottages (18c.)

3487   † East End Farm (17c.)

3488   †† Monk's Well (formerly the barn at East End Farm) (17c.)

3489   †† East End

3490   Hampton (18c. & 19c.)

3491   Hampton Lodge (*c.* 1780)

CROOKSBURY

3492   ** Barrow south of Littleworth Clump, Crooksbury Common

3493   * Soldiers Ring Barrow

3494   * Barrow north of Turner's Hill, Crooksbury Common

TONGHAM

3495–7 †† Manor Farm (18c.), Dovecote (17c.) and Barn (18c.)

3498   †† Grange Farm House, Grange Road (18c.)

3499   †† No. 13 Oxenden Road (17c. and later)

3500   †† Oakbeams, Oxenden Road

3501–5 †† Nos. 61, 63, 65, 67 and 69, Poyle Road (formerly Kingston Cottages)

3506–8   † Nos. 71, 73 and 75 Poyle Road

3509–10   † Nos. 85 (Woodville) and 87 (Ivy Cottage)

3511   †† Squillier Cottages, Poyle Road (18c.)

3512   †† Poyle Cottage, Poyle Road (19c. and earlier)

Borough or District Civil Parish	No.	Name or Description of Antiquity

SEND   *GENERAL*

3513–5 †Send Grove and stable block and †Granary (18c.)

3516–7 ††2 Cottages N.E. of Send Grove

3518   †The Lodge, Send Grove

3519   Old Vicarage (15c.)

3520   †Send Court Farmhouse (early 17c.)

3521   ††Fell Hill Farm (17c.)

3522–4 ††Nos. 1–3, Dudswell Manor Cottages

3525   Tithe Barn Cottage (17c.), Tithe Barn Lane

3526   †Hazelhurst Cottage (18c.)

3527   ††Send Barns (formerly The Grange at Newark Priory) (16c. & 17c.)

3528   †Willingham Cottage, Sandy Lane

3529   ††Hillside Farm, Sandy Lane (formerly Stephens Farm)

3530   ††Goodgrove, Sendmarsh Road (early 19c.)

3531   ††Aldertons (formerly Part of Boughton Hall Farm), Sendmarsh Road (15c., restored)

3532–4 †The Manor House (16c. & 17c.) Stable (16c.) and Barn (17c.)

3535   ††Old Manor Cottage, Sendmarsh (formerly Nos. 4 and 5 (16c.)

3536–7 Nos. 2 and 3 (early 18c.), Pullens Cottages, Sendmarsh

3538   ††No. 1 April Cottage, Sendmarsh (16c.)

3539   ††The Corner Cottage (late 15c.), Sendmarsh

3540   ††Saddlers Arms Public House, Sendmarsh (formerly Cooksgreen)

3541   ††Send Lodge (early 19c.)

3542   ††Gosden Hill Farm (17c.)

3543   *Moated site (mediaeval) South of Aldertons

3544   Old Keep House (17c.)

SHACKLEFORD   *GENERAL*

3545   ††Cross Farm (17c. and later)

3546–7 †Dolphin House (formerly The Old Cottage) and garden walls (18c. and earlier)

3548   †Home Farmhouse (18c. and later)

3549–   Aldro School (formerly Hall Place) (16c.–
51   19c.) †stables (1743) and ††Dovecot (18c.)

3552–3 ††Nos. 1 and 2, The Street (17c.)

Borough or District Civil Parish	No.	Name or Description of Antiquity

SHACKLEFORD

—contd.

GENERAL—*contd.*

3554 † The Pump House

3555–7 †† Nos. 1–3, Style Cottages, The Square (late 16c.)

3558– †† Shackleford Post Office with house adjoining and Old Barn Cottage (1690)
60

3561 †† Rokers (18c.)

3562 ‡ Cobblers (early 17c.)

3563–4 † Mitchen Hall (late 17c.) and Cottage adjoining (18c.)

3565 Gatwick End, near Elstead (16c. & 18c.)

NORNEY

3566 †† Norney Farm

3567 † Norney Old House

HURTMORE

3568–9 †† Nos. 1 and 2, Squirrel Cottages (18c.)

3570–2 †† Nos. 1–3, Step Cottages (18c.–19c.)

3573 † Hartsmere Cottage (formerly Hurtmore Farmhouse) (16c., refaced 19c.)

LYDLING

3574 †† Lydling (formerly Lydling Farm) (early 18c.) P. 132

3575–6 †† Nos. 3 and 4 (18c. and earlier)

3577 †† Swallowhill Cottage

LOWER EASHING

3578 † Lower Eashing Farm Cottage

3579 †† Greenways (18c. and earlier)

3580 †† The White House (early 19c.)

3581 † Rose Cottage (18c.)

3582 †† The Old Farm (18c.)

3583 † Tankards (18c.)

3584 †† Post Chaise (formerly The Post Office)

3585–6 *φ Eashing Bridges (2) (N.T.)

3587–8 † Nos. 1 and 2 The Meads (N.T. cottages) (late 16c.)

3589 † The Stag Inn (17c.)

3590 † Style Cottage

3591 †† Wey Cottage

3592 Eashing Mill (17c.)

Borough or District Civil Parish	No.	Name or Description of Antiquity

SHACKLEFORD

UPPER EASHING

—*contd.* 3593–5 †The Brew House (16c. & 18c.)

†† Dovecot ⎫
† Stables ⎬ at Eashing House (18c.)

3596 †Dean Cottage

3597–8 †Jordans and †outbuildings to N. (16c. & 18c.)

3599– †† Eashing Farm and outbuildings (18c.)
600

3601 †† Platt Cottages (18c. and later)

3602 † Eashing Farm Cottages

SHALFORD

THE STREET (west side)

3603–4 † The Stocks and Whipping Post near Parish Church (18c.)

3605 † Stone (base of cross) in Parish Churchyard (17c.)

3606–7 ‡ Shalford House (17c. & 18c.) and †† Icehouse (18c.)

3608–19† Nos. 1 to 12 (17c.)

3620 † Shalford Park Cottage (18c.)

3621 † Beech House (early 19c.)

3622 † The Sea Horse Inn (late 17c., altered 19c.)

THE STREET (east side)

3623 †† Debnersh (18c.)

3624 †† No. 13 (18c.)

3625 † The Cottage (early 19c.)

3626–8 †† Nos. 14, 14A Watermill Cottage and Mill Cottage (17c.)

3629– † Nos. 15 and 15A (17c. altered 19c. and
30 recently renovated)

3631 † Shalford Mill (N.T.) (early 18c.)

3632 † Mill Lane Cottage (17c.)

3633 † The Old House (formerly The Mill House) (17c.)

3634 † Whitnorth (17c. & 18c.)

3635 †† Highway Cottage (formerly stables to Whitnorth)

UNSTED

3636 † Unsted Bridge (19c.)

3637–8 † Unsted Manor House (14c. & 16c.) (now cottages) and †† barn to west

3639 † Upper Unsted Farm (late 15c.) P. 94

Borough or District Civil Parish	No.	Name or Description of Antiquity

SHALFORD—*contd.*   *GENERAL*

3640 †† Tilthams Farm
3641 †† Broadwater Cottage
3642 † Gosden House School (early 19c.)
3643 † Chinthurst Farmhouse (17c.)
3644 †† Chinthurst Farm Cottage (17c.)
3645 †† Hill Cottage, Chinthurst Lane
3646 †† Lantern House (18c. and later)
         Shalford Common
3647 † Bradstone Brook (1791 and later) Shalford
         Common
3648 †† Grove Cottage, Shalford Common
3649 †† Merlins, East Shalford Lane
3650   Lemmon Bridge over Tillingbourne (mid
         18c.)

SHERE   *EWHURST ROAD*

3651 † Cotterels (17c. & 18c.)
3652 † Hound House (17c. & 18c.)

CHURCH LANE

3653 † High House Farmhouse (17c.)

CHURCH SQUARE

3654 †† Sayers (18c.)
3655 † Pantreys Cottage (17c.)
3656 † Pentylla (17c.)
3657   Haven Cottage (17c.)
3658-9 † Rookery Nook Guest House and Grocers
         adjoining (17c.)
3660 †† Vaughan's Cottage (16c. and later)

MIDDLE STREET

3661-2 † Shere Post Office (Forrest's Stores) with
         house adjoining (c. 1600 with later addi-
         tions)
3663-4 † Bodryn and The Forge (17c.)
3665 †† The Pound (18c.)
3666 †† Bridge over the River Tillingbourne (18c.)
3667 †† No. 3 (18c.)
3668 †† Shere Lane Cottage
3669 †† Juden Cottage (1622)
3670 †† White Horse Inn (c. 1600, refronted)

Borough or District Civil Parish	No.	Name or Description of Antiquity

SHERE—*contd.*

LOWER STREET

3671–2 †† Cottage (1705 W.I.D.) and house adjoining

3673–4 † Ash Cottage and Willow Cottage

3675 †† The Forge (formerly a cottage) (17c.)

3676 †¹ The Old Prison House (17c.)

3677–8 † Delmont and cottage adjoining (17c.)

RECTORY LANE

3679 †† The Olde Cottage (formerly Workshop Cottage) (16c. & 17c.)

3680 †† The Cottage (17c.)

UPPER STREET

3681 Burdens (16c.)

3682–3 † Knapps Cottage and Waitlands (formerly Atfields Cottages) (17c.)

3684 †† Lime Cottage (17c.)

3685–6 †† The Old Cottage and The Gables (17c.)

3687 † Denmarke (early 16c. and later)

3688 †† Fernside (17c.)

3689– †† Beulah Cottage and Bignold (17c.)
90

3691–3 Old Manor House Cottages (three) (17c.)

3694 †† June Garden (16c.)

3695 †† Elm Cottage (1620)

3696 † Tudor Cottage (16c. & 17c.)

3697–9 †† Little House, Green Shutters and †cottage adjoining on the east (18c.)

3700 †† Manor Cottage or Freeland (formerly Manor Estate Office)

3701–3 † Vine Cottage (three cottages) (16c.)

3704–5 †† Nos. 1 and 3 (18c.)

3706 †† Seaforth Cottage (17c.)

3707 †† Oak Cottage (17c. and later) P. 63

PONDS LANE

3708 †† Ponds Farm

3709 † Lockhursthatch Farm

¹ Surrey County Journal, July–September, 1949

Borough or District Civil Parish	No.	Name or Description of Antiquity

SHERE—*contd.*

GOMSHALL
Dorking—Guildford Road

3710 † Edmonds Farm (17c.)
3711 †† Craddock Cottages (18c. and earlier)
3712–3 The Tannery and † Packhorse bridge adjacent (16c.)

QUEEN STREET

3714 † King John House (formerly Ivy House) (early 17c.) P. 32
3715–8 †† Nos. 9–12
3719 † Monks House (formerly Gravelpits) (17c.)

STATION ROAD

3720–1 †† The Mill House and the Mill (17c. & 18c.)
3722 †† No. 9
3723–5 † Nos. 1–3, Malthouse Cottages (formerly The Malthouse) (16c. and later)

TOWER HILL

3726 † Tower Hill Manor House (17c.) Tower Hill

COLEKITCHEN LANE

3727 †† Colekitchen Farm (18c.)

ABINGER

3728 † Old Hatch Farmhouse (formerly Hatch Farm) (17c.) P. 48

SUTTON

3729–30 ‡ Fulvens Farm (*c.* 1620) and cottage adjoining (17c.)
3731 † Mutton Farmhouse (formerly Sutton Place Farm) (17c. with 18c. & 19c. additions)
3732 † Sutton Place Cottage (17c. and later)
3733 † The Old Forge (17c.)
3734 † Sutton Cottage, east of The Forge (17c.)
3735 †† Walnut Tree Cottage (17c.)
3736 † The Corner Cottage (17c.)
3737 †† Lavender Ladye, Lower Street (early 19c.)

Borough or District Civil Parish	No.	Name or Description of Antiquity

SHERE—contd.   *HOLMBURY ST. MARY*

3738   † Woodhouse Place (17c.), Holmbury Road
3739   †† Hilda Cottage
3740–1 †† Chapel Cottage and Ivy Cottage
3742   †† Honeysuckle Cottage (17c. restored)
3743   †† Neale Cottage (17c.)
3744   †† Aldermoor Cottage
3745   † Holmdale (1873)
3746   Roman Road, Holmbury Hill
3747   †† White House (18c. or earlier)

PEASLAKE

3748–9 † East View and East View Cottage, Ewhurst
          Road
3750   †† Weston Cottage (formerly Workhouse Cottages) (18c.)
3751   † Lindeth Cottage (17c.)
3752   †† Mackies Hill
3753   † Hollybush Cottage (formerly Trower's
          Cottage) (18c.)
3754   †† The Cottage, Colmans Hill
3755   †† Legion Cottages (formerly Burchett's Hollow) (17c.)
3756–7 † Hazell Hall and Stables (18c.)
3758   †† Jessies Farm (18c.)
3759   † Quakers (formerly Quakers Garth) (18c.)
3760   †† The Old Well Cottage, Hoe Lane (17c.)
3761   † Hoe Farm, Hoe Lane (16c.)
3762   † Keepers (16c. & 17c.)
3763   †† Oak Hill

WANBOROUGH   *GENERAL*

3764–6 †[1] Wanborough Manor House, Tithe Barn to
          S.W. and small barn to west (16c. & 17c.)
3767–8 †† Nos. 1 and 2, Manor Farm Cottages (18c.
          and earlier)
3769   † Wanborough Manor Lodge (early 19c.)
3770   † Octagon, Hogs Back, (early 19c.)
3771–2 †† Two Barns at Inwood Farm
3773   † West Flexford Farmhouse (17c.)
3774   †† Flexford House (c. 1830–40)

[1] See Surrey County Journal, April–June, 1950,
pp. 88–90

Borough or District Civil Parish	No.	Name or Description of Antiquity

WISLEY

GENERAL

3775 † Church Farm (formerly Wisley Farm and Vicarage) (17c. and later)
3776 †† Old School House (two cottages) (17c.)
3777 †† Pheasants Cottages
3778 * Barrows (two) at Cockcrow Hill
3779 ** Barrow west of Cockcrow Hill
3780 ** Barrow near Fox Warren Park

WORPLESDON

PERRY HILL

3781 † Perry Hill Farmhouse
3782 †† Vine Farm (18c.)
3783–4 † Rosedene and The Green (17c.)
3785 † Perry Hill House (17c.)
3786 †† Primmer and Terry, (wheelwrights and farriers) (17c.)
3787 † Crown Cottage (16c. & 17c.)
3788 †† The Old Post House (17c. and modern centre)
3789 † Hollow Trees, near Memorial Hall (1659)
3790–1 †† 1 and 2, Nightingale Cottages
3792–5 † 1–3, Norton Farm Cottages (17c.) and † Barn
3796 † Merrist Wood Hall (1877)

RICKFORD

3797 †† Rickford Mill (18c.)
3798 † The Old Mill House (18c.)
3799 †† Old Rickford (17c.)

GOOSERYE

3800 †† Gooserye

WHITMOOR COMMON

3801 †† Whitmoor Hatch

WHITMOOR COMMON

3802 †† Woodcorner Farm (17c.)
3803 * Barrow west of Mount Pleasant
3804 * Barrow near the Old Cottage

Borough or District Civil Parish	No.	Name or Description of Antiquity

WORPLESDON
—*contd.*

PITCH PLACE

3805–6 †Pitch Place (formerly Cobbetts) with out-buildings (1683)

3807–8 ††Tangley Cottage and Tangley Edge Cottage (formerly The Old Bothy of Tangley Park)

STRINGERS COMMON

3809 ††Stringers Barn (formerly Littlehurst Farm) (late 18c.–early 19c.)

3810 ††Willow Grange (17c. and later additions)

3811 †Burpham Court House (17c.)

3812 ††Gunners Farm

3813 ††Bullens Hill Farm (18c.)

JACOBS WELL

3814 ††Burpham Lodge (early 19c.)

3815 †Watts Cottage

3816 ††Queen Hythe (17c.)

3817–8 ††1 and 2 Farm Cottages (17c.)

3819 ††Burpham Court Farm Cottages

GRAVETTS LANE

3820–1 †Frosbury Farmhouse and Barn adjoining (17c.)

RYDES HILL

3822 Rydes Hill Lodge (17c. & 18c.)

FAIRLANDS

3823 †Fairlands Farm (17c. & 1735)

3824 †White's Cottages (1670)

BROAD STREET COMMON

3825 †Hunts Farmhouse

3826 †Hook Farmhouse

3827–9 †1–3, Springflower Cottages (18c.–19c.)

3830 ††Dunmore Farmhouse (17c. and later)

3831 ††Park Barn Farm (16c., 17c. & 18c.)

PINKS HILL, WOOD STREET

3832 ††Holly Bush Farm (17c. and later)

3833 †Old Gables (Hyde House) (16c., 17c. & 18c.) P. 52

Borough or District Civil Parish	No.	Name or Description of Antiquity

WORPLESDON

WOOD STREET

—*contd.* 3834 Hill Place Farm (17c. with 18c. front)
3835 †† Bracken (18c. and earlier)
3836 †† Nightingale Old Farm (18c.)
3837 † Billhurst Farmhouse (18c.)
3838 †† White Hart Inn (18c.)
3839 † Pound Farmhouse (18c.)
3840 † Wildfield Farmhouse (18c.)
3841 † Passenger's Farmhouse
3842 †† Woodside Cottage
3843 † Comptons Farmhouse, Frog Grove Lane
3844 †† Frog Grove, Frog Grove Lane (17c. with 18c. additions)
3845 †† Frog Grove Cottage, Frog Grove Lane (17c.)

CLASFORD

3846–7 ‡ Littlefield Manor and Barn adjoining (16c. & 17c.)
3848–9 † Whipley Farmhouse and †† Barn (15c., 16c. & 1735)
3850 † Clasford Farmhouse

HAMBLEDON **R.D.**
   ALFOLD

GENERAL

3851 ‡ Alfold House (*c.* 1500) P. 20
3852 †† Brickyard Farm Cottage
3853–5 †† Bridge Farmhouse and †† Barns (2) (17c.)
3856–8 †† Carters Croft (three cottages) (17c.)
3859 †† Cherry Tree Cottage
3860–1 † Church Cottage and Church Hall (17c.)
3862 † Crown Cottage (early 16c.)
3863 †† Eastland Cottage, Horsham Road (17c.)
3864 † Farnhurst Farmhouse
3865 †† Fast Bridge Cottage (17c.), Guildford Park
3866 † Fast Bridge Farmhouse
3867 †† Furzen's Cottage (16c.)
3868 † Glen Grootefontein (formerly Old Park Farm, formerly Alfold Park Farm) (17c.)
3869 †† Great Wildwood Farm (16c.)
3870–2 †† Grocer's Shop, Cottage and Post Office (17c. or earlier)
3873 †† Home Farm, Hall Place (17c.)

Borough or District Civil Parish	No.	Name or Description of Antiquity

ALFOLD—contd.   *GENERAL*—contd.

3874 †† Little Bookerslea (16c.)
3875 †† Little Wildwood Farmhouse
3876 † House attached to Gibb's Hatch Tea Rooms (17c.)
3877 † Males Farmhouse
3878 † Mill Farm (17c.)
3879 † Priorswood Farmhouse
3880 †† Rosemary Cottage (16c., restored), Rosemary Lane
3881 †† Rosemary Croft
3882–3 † Stovolds Hill (17c. and later) and Barn
3884 †† Sydney Farm House (17c.)
3885 † The Crown Inn (18c.)
3886 †† The Pound (18c. or earlier)
3887 †† The Rectory (18c.)

3888 Tickners Heath Farm Cottage (17c.)
3889–
90 †† Velhurst Farm and Barn
3891 † Village Stocks and Whipping Post
3892 †† Waggoner's Cottage

BRAMLEY   *GENERAL*

3893–5 †† East Water House and Barns (2) (17c.)
3896 †† Gatestreet Farm
3897 †† Gatestreet Farm Cottage
3898 Gosden Cottage, Gosden Green (late 18c.)
3899 †† Hurst Hill Farmhouse (18c.)
3900 † Nore (17c.), Guildford–Horsham Road near Cranleigh turning
3901–2 † Nursecombe Farmhouse (early 16c.) and † Barn (17c.) P. 19
3903 † Oak Hatch
3904 †† Old House, Birtley Green
3905 † Orchards (late 19c.)
3906 †† Painshill Farmhouse (early 19c.)
3907 †† Pepper Box Cottage (early 19c.)
3908 † School House (formerly Church House) Station Road (18c.)
3909 † Smithbrook Manor (16c. & 17c.)
3910 †† Smithbrook Manor Cottage (17c.)
3911 †† Snowdenham Cottage

Borough or District Civil Parish	No.	Name or Description of Antiquity

BRAMLEY—*contd.*

GENERAL—*contd.*

3912–3 †Snowdenham House (late 17c., altered 18c.) and ††Mill

3914 †The Corner Cottage (formerly Talskedy Cottage) (16c.), Gosden Common

3915 Tan Yard Cottages (17c. & 18c.)

3916 ††Thatched Farmhouse

3917 †Tillings

3918 ††Thorncombe Park (*c.* 1820)

3919– †Unsted Park (formerly Farley Hill) (*c.* 1780
21 and later), †Stables (18c.) and ††out-buildings (18c.)

3922–3 Wintershall (15c.–17c.) and †Dovecote (17c.)

3924 Woodrough Cottages (16c.)

HIGH STREET

3925 †Bramley Lodge (18c., with alterations *c.* 1840)

3926 ††Bramley Lodge Cottage (18c. and earlier)

3927–8 †East Manor House (mid 16c.) and Cottages adjoining (late 16c.)

3929– †Hollyhocks (17c. and earlier) and House to
30 N. (early 19c.)

3931 †Summerpool House (18c.)

3932 †Summerpool Cottage (17c. & 18c.)

3933 ††The Bakery (*c.* 1780) S.E. of Jolly Farmer Inn

3934 †The Corners (17c.)

3935 ††The Jolly Farmer Inn

3936 ††The Manor House (17c., altered and restored 19c.)

3937 †The Warren (early 19c.)

3938 ††The Wheatsheaf Inn (17c. and earlier)

3938 ††The Store House S. of Stream Cottage
(1) (17 & 18c.)

PALMERS CROSS

3939 †Tanyards (15c.)

3940 ††The Cottage (17c. with later additions)

3941–2 ††Tilsey Manor (17c. and later) and ††Lodge (early 19c.)

Borough or District Civil Parish	No.	Name or Description of Antiquity

BRAMLEY—*contd.*

RUSHET COMMON

3943–6 †† Nos. 3, 4, 5 and 6 Rook Hill Cottages (17c. & 18c.)

3947   †† Old Barns (16c.)

3948   †† Rushetts (formerly Nos. 1 and 2) Cottages (16c. & 17c.)

3949   †† The Old Cottage (17c.)

3950   † The Old Post Office (17c.)

SELHURST COMMON

3951–2 † Nos. 1 and 2 Goose Green Cottages

3953   † Goose Green Farm (formerly Pritchards Farm) (17c.)

3954   †† Magnolia Cottage (17c.)

3955–6 † Scotsland Farm (late 17c.) and ††Barn (17c.)

3957   † The Old Cottage (16c.)

SNOWDENHAM ROAD

3958   †† Bramley Mill (late 17c.)

3959   †† Brighton Cottage (17c.)

3960   †† Millmeadow Cottage (16c.)

3961   †† The Mole Cottage (17c.)

THORNCOMBE STREET

3962–5 †† Nos. 1¹, 2¹, 3 and 4 (16c. Rose Cottages

3966   †† Cobble Cottage (17c.)

3967   Phillamore Cottage (17c.)

3968   †† Raggets Cottage (16c.)

3969   †† Rowe Farm Cottage (18c.)

3970–1 † Slades Farm and †Granary (17c. & 18c.)

3972   † Stoneland (formerly Thorncombe Farm) 15c. & 17c.)

3973   †† Timbers (17c., restored)

3974   † Vanhurst (16c. & 17c.)

BUSBRIDGE   *GENERAL*

3975   † Crowts

3976–7 †† Elm Cottage and cottage adjoining

3978   † Lodkin House (17c.)

3979   † Munstead Wood (1896)

3980   North Munstead (early 16c.) P. 67

¹ Demolished 1961

Borough or District *Civil Parish*	*No.*	*Name or Description of Antiquity*

BUSBRIDGE—*contd.*   *GENERAL*—*contd.*

3981-2 † South Munstead Farm (17c. or earlier) and Garage (17c.)

3983 †† Springfield Farmhouse (now 2 cottages)

3984 Tuesley Manor House (16c. and later)

3985 † Winkworth Farm (16c.)

3986 †† Wood Farm

BUSBRIDGE LAKES HOUSE

3987-9 † Bridge, †Grotto and †Doric Temple, Upper Pond (18c.)

3990-2 † Boathouse (early 19c.), †Bridge and †Doric Temple (18c.), Middle Pond

3993-5 †† Gardens and †Hermits Cave (18c.) †Rooms and ruins, Rustic Pavilion (18c.), New Pond

CHIDDINGFOLD   *GENERAL*

3996 Black Hams, Sydenhurst Lane (early 17c.)

3997 †† Burrell House, Cricket Green (18c.)

3998 †† Catsprey and Pook Cottage (formerly Green Leys) (17c. and later) Pook Hill

3999 †† Coombe Court Farmhouse

4000 † Coombe Farm (17c.)

4001 †† Cherry Tree Cottage

4002 † Church Cottage, Sydenhurst Lane

4003 †† Corner Farmhouse

4004 †† Cottages adjoining Hazel Bridge Court (17c. or earlier)

4005 † Coxcombe Cottages, Coxcombe Lane

4006 †† Elmtree Cottage

4007 †† Fisher Lane Farmhouse

4008 Frillinghurst Cottage (16c.)

4009 †† Greenaway, Hazel Bridge Road (17c. or earlier)

4010 † Hawlands (16c.), West End Lane

4011 † High Prestwick (15c. & 17c.)

4012 † Killinghurst (18c. or earlier)

4013 †† Little Tugley (18c.)

4014 ‡ Lythe Hill Farm House (14c. & 16c.) P. 57

4015 † Mill House (18c.)

4016 †† Misselbrook

4017 †† Northbridge Farmhouse

Borough or District Civil Parish	No.	Name or Description of Antiquity

CHIDDINGFOLD

GENERAL—contd.

	4018	†† Oak Apple Cottage
—contd.	4019	†† Old Dog Kennel Hill House
	4020	Old Cottage, Hascombe Road (*c.* 1670)
	4021	† Old Pickhurst (early-mid 17c.)
	4022	†† Pockford Brook
	4023	† Pockford Farmhouse (1806 with later additions)
	4024	† Prestwick Manor House (early 16c.)
	4025	†† Redlands Farm
	4026	* Roman buildings (site of) 1,700 yards north-east of Rystead House
	4027–8	† Roppeleghs (formerly West End Farm) and †† oubuildings (16c. & 17c.)
	4029	†† Rye Cottage
	4030	†† Rye Street Cottage, Rystead Common (late 16c. & 17c.)
	4031	† Skinners Land Farm (15c.)
	4032	† Tudor Cottage
	4033	†† Tugley Farmhouse (18c. or earlier)
	4034	†† Watlands
	4035	†† White Beech Cottage
	4036	†† Yew Tree Cottage

LINCOLN'S HILL

	4037	†† Hill Cottage (formerly The Limit) (15c. & 17c.)
	4038	† The Old Barn (16c.)
	4039	†† Waterfield (17c. or earlier)

PETWORTH ROAD

	4040–1	†† Nos. 1 and 2 Swan Cottage (16c.)
	4042–3	†† Nos. 1 and 2 Bridge Cottages (16c.)
	4044–5	†† Fairfield (17c.) and Old Barn (16c.)
	4046–7	†† Friargate and Swan Cottage
	4048	†† House attached to Butcher's Shop (Furlonger's) (17c.)
	4049–50	†† Premises of Mann Bros. (Cycle Agents) and Edwards and Wright (Chemists)
	4051	†† The Old Forge (14c. & 18c.)

Borough or District Civil Parish	No.	Name or Description of Antiquity

CHIDDINGFOLD

THE GREEN

—*contd.* 4052 † Beckhams (early 19c.)

4053–4 † Brockhurst and Brook House (18c.)

4055 † Crown Inn (14c., restored) P. 10

4056–7 †† Cottage in grounds of Glebe House and Garden Wall

4058– †† Forest Stores, Bakery and Shop (18c.)
60

4061–2 †† Forest Wine Stores (18c.) and Grove Cottage (19c.)

4063 † Little Beckhams (14c.)

4064 †† Mariners Barn (18c.)

065 † The Glebe House (formerly The Rectory) (1710) P. 11

4066 † The Manor House (17c., with 18c. front)

4067–8 †† Westminster Bank and Toby Jug Restaurant (18c.)

South side

4069– † Lime Cottage and Bow Windows (16c. & 17c.)
70

North side

4071 † Botley House (15c.)

4072 † Hadmans (formerly Orchard Cottage) (late 14c. & 16c.)

4073 † Sandalphon (15c.)

VANN LANE

4074–6 † Pound Cottage and Pound (16c.) with walls of Village Pound adjoining

4077 †† Solars (16c.)

CRANLEIGH

GENERAL

4078–9 † Barhatch Farmhouse and Barn (17c. or earlier)

4080 †† Bridgeham Farmhouse

4081 Bridge Cottage (17c.), Knowles Lane

4082 †† Brooklands Farmhouse

4083 †† Hazelwood Farm (formerly Butcherhouse Farm)

4084 Collins' Farm (18c.)

4085 †† Cranleigh School (late 19c.)

4086 †† Elm Cottages, Ewhurst Road, (17c.)

4087 † Ewhurst Windmill (early 19c.)

Borough or District Civil Parish	No.	Name or Description of Antiquity

CRANLEIGH—*contd.*   *GENERAL*—*contd.*

4088 †† Fair Oaks
4089–90† Great Garson (2 houses) (17c.)
4091 †† Great Inholms
4092 †† Hammer Farmhouse
4093 †† High Canfold Farmhouse
4094 †† High Upfold Farmhouse (early 19c.)
4095 †† Jelleys Hollow, nr. Alderbrook (16c. or 17c.)
4096 † Lapscombe Farmhouse
4097 Little Garson (17c.)
4098 †† Little Inholms
4099 †† Mannings Hill
4100 † N.W. Gateway to Baynards Park (mid 19c.)
4101 † Park Green Cottages (formerly Park House) (16c. & 17c.)
4102 †† Pallinghurst (16c.)
4103 Pollington Mansion (site of) 650 yards east of Collins' Farm
4104–7 † Rye Farm and †† Barns (3) (17c. & 18c.)
4108 †† Ruffold (17c. and later)
4109 † Rydinghurst (early 17c.), Elmbridge Road
4110 †† Snoxhall
4111 * Tumulus (motte), Broomhall Copse
4112 The Old Court (17c.)
4113 † Utworth Farm (late 17c.) Cranleigh-Alfold Road
4114 † Waterbridge Farmhouse (16c.)
4115 †† Waterland Farm Cottage
4116 †† Wykehurst Farmhouse (formerly Wickhurst Farm) (14c.) and †† Barn
4117 †† New Park (15c.–17c.) Cranleigh-Rudgwick Road
4118 † Timbers (formerly New House Farm Cottages) (2) (16c.)
4119 † Wyphurst (formerly Fowls Farmhouse)

THE GREEN

4120 † St. Andrew's House (formerly St. Andrew's Bakery and Cottage) (17c.)
4121 †† Chapel Place (early 19c.)
4122 †† Timbers (formerly St. Andrew's Cottage)
4123 †† Old Tokefield

Borough or District Civil Parish	No.	Name or Description of Antiquity

CRANLEIGH—*contd.*

GENERAL—*contd.*
4124 †† Pear Tree Cottage
4125 †† The White House (early 19c.)

HIGH STREET
4126 †† Belwethers (late 15c. or early 16c.)
4127 Cromwell Cottage (17c.)
4128 †† Fishmongers' Shop (17c.)
4129–30 †† Forest Stores Ltd and house adjoining (18c. or earlier)
4131 †† Oak Room (late 16c.)
4132 †† Obelisk (1794)
4133 †† Oliver House (17c., altered 19c.)
4134 †† The Bookshop (late 16c.)
4135 † The Causey (16c. and later)
4136 †† The Village Hospital (16c.)

HORSHAM ROAD
4137 †† Broadoak (early 19c. and earlier)
4138 †† Rosedene (18c.)

SMITHWOOD COMMON
4139 †† Little Pittance Farm (17c.)
4140 †† Lower House Farm (16c. & 17c.)
4141 †† Manor Cottage (17c.)
4142–4 † Pittance Farmhouse and †Barns (2) (17c.)
4145 †† Smith's Cottage
4146 † Smithwood Farmhouse (15c. & 17c.)
4147–8 † Smithwood House and †Barn (18c.)

DOCKENFIELD

GENERAL
4149 †† Dockenfield Farm (18c.)
4150 † Dockenfield House (17c. & 18c.)
4151 †† Farm Cottage

DUNSFOLD

GENERAL
4152 † Oak Tree Cottages (formerly Nos. 1, 2 and 3), The Green (16c. and later)
4153 † Basket Cottage (16c.)
4154 †† Beverley
4155 † Blacknest Cottage (formerly Farmhouse) (17c. and later)
4156 † Burningfold (16c.)

10

Borough or District Civil Parish	No.	Name or Description of Antiquity

DUNSFOLD—*contd.*   *GENERAL*—*contd.*

4157   †† Chennell's Farmhouse
4158   †† Church Cottages
4159   †† Cobdens Farmhouse
4160–1 †† Cottages (2) Elm Corner
4162   †† Cottage N. of North End (17c. or earlier)
4163   †† Dungate Farmhouse (17c. or earlier)
4164   † Duns Farmhouse
4165–6 † Elm Cottage and †Cottage (Peake)
4167–8 † Fern Cottage and †Gratton Corner Cottage (16c.)
4169   † Field Place
4170   †† Gorebridge Green House (formerly Gorebridge Farm) Loxhill (16c. and later)
4171   † Grattons Corner (16c.)
4172   †† High Billinghurst
4173–4 †† High Loxley and ††Barn (17c.)
4175   †† Hookhouse Farmhouse (17c. or earlier)
4176   †† Hope Cottage (18c.)
4177   † Howicks (16c.)
4178   †† Hurlands (16c.)
4179   † Hurst Hill (early 16c.)
4180   † Knightons (*c.* 1820)
4181   †† Little Hurlands (17c.)
4182–4 †† New Inn, Ivy Cottage and New Inn Cottage (formerly The New Inn)
4185   †† North End (17c.)
4186   †† Old Knightons (16c.)
4187   †† Peartree Green
4188   †† Pond Cottage (formerly Pound Cottage) (18c.)
4189–90 † Pound Farmhouse and ††Granary
4191   †† Ramsnest Cottage (formerly The Cottage) (16c.)
4192   †† Sun Inn (early 19c.)
4193   †† Sun Inn Cottage (18c.)
4194   † The Commons House (16c.) P. 124
4195   † The Forge (17c. or earlier)
4196   †† The Grange (18c. and later)
4197   † The Mill House (17c.)
4198   †† The Mitchell's (17c. and later)
4199   † The Rectory (15c. & 17c.)

Borough or District Civil Parish	No.	Name or Description of Antiquity

DUNSFOLD—*contd.*

GENERAL—*contd.*

4200–1 †† The Stores and house adjoining (18c.)
4202–3 †† Upper Ifold and Annexe (17c.)
4204 † Willards (17c.)
4205 †† Woodside Cottage
4206 †† Wrotham Hill Cottages
4207 † Yonder Lye (16c.)

ELSTEAD

GENERAL

4208 * Barrows (three) in entrenchment north-east of Heatherdene, Crooksbury Common
4209 Alliford Cottage (16c.), Cutmill Road
4210 †† Apple Tree Cottage (17c. or earlier)
4211 † Elstead Bridge (16c.)
4212 †† Elstead Lodge (early 19c.)
4213 †† Fulbrook Cottage (16c.) P. 43
4214 Ingleside (17c.)
4215 †† Lilac Cottage (formerly Post Office Cottage) (16c.)
4216 †† Peat Farm Cottage
4217 † Polshot Manor (15c.)
4218–9 †† Red House Farm and †† Barn (16c. & 17c.)
4220–1 †† The Golden Fleece (P.H.) and Stables adjoining (19c.)
4222–3 † The Mill House and † Mill adjoining (16c. and later)
4224 † The Old Farm House (16c.)
4225 The Old Forge (1686)
4226 †† The White Cottage (17c. or 18c.)
4227 † Turner's Farmhouse
4228 †† Westbrook Farm Cottages (17c. & 18c.)
4229 †† Westbrook Farmhouse (17c. or earlier)
4230 †† Yew Tree Cottage

EWHURST

GENERAL

4231 † Barn in grounds of The Rectory
4232–4 ‡ Baynards Park (16c. & 17c.) † Gatehouse, † Gateway and railings (mid 19c.)
4235 †† Bildens
4236 †† Bramblehurst (early 17c.)
4237 † Coneyhurst (15c.) and †† Barn
4238 †† Coverwood Farm
4239 † Coxland (17c.)

Borough or District Civil Parish	No.	Name or Description of Antiquity

EWHURST—*contd.*   *GENERAL*—*contd.*

	4240	††Crown Inn (19c.)
	4241	††Gadbridge Farm (16c. & 17c.)
	4242	††Greystones (17c., 18c. and later)
	4243–4	†High Edser and ††Barn
	4245	Homecroft (17c., portion)
	4246	†Ivy Cottage (18c. or earlier)
	4247	†Loseley (formerly Loseley Farm (16c.)
	4248	Mapledrakes (16c. & 17c.)
	4249	†Mascalls (17c.)
	4250	††Milk Hall (17c.)
	4251	††Mill Cottage, Pitch Hill (17c. or earlier)
	4252	†Mundys Hill
	4253	††North Breache Manor Farm
	4254	Old Oast (16c. & 17c.)
	4255	††Old Place
	4256–7	††Pitch Gate and Cheapside (18c.)
	4258	††Plough Farm Cottage
	4259	†Sayers Croft Farmhouse (16c.)
	4260	††Slythehurst (formerly Slyhurst) (16c.)
	4261	†Somersbury Manor (16c. restored)
	4262–3	††The Lanterns and Corner House (formerly Nibblets Cottage) (16c.)
	4264	†The Old Cottage (14c. & 16c.)
	4265	†The Old Post Office (formerly The Old House) (16c.)
	4266	†Tudor House (formerly Ewhurst Bookshop) (16c.)
	4267	††Windrums
	4268	††Winton House
	4269	††Woolpit Farm (16c.)
	4270	††Yard Farmhouse

ELLEN'S GREEN

	4271	††Aylwins Cottage
	4272	††Bungtore Cottage
	4273	††Crouchers (18c. or earlier)
	4274	††Dukes Cottage (17c.)
	4275	†Dukes Farm (18c.)
	4276	††Ellen's Farmhouse
	4277	††Hillhouse Farm
	4278	††Little Godlies

orough or District Civil Parish	No.	Name or Description of Antiquity

EWHURST—*contd.*

4279 †† Maybankes (1503 with later additions) and moat 700 yards w.s.w. of
4280 † Pipers Croft
4281 † Pollingfold Farmhouse (formerly Pollingfold Old Farm (16c.)
4282 † Sansoms (18c. or earlier)
4283 †† Tillhouse Farmhouse
4284 †† Trade Winds (17c.)

EWHURST GREEN

4285 † Broadstone Cottages
4286 †† The Corrie (17c. or earlier)
4287 †† Yew Tree Cottage (16c.)

FRENSHAM   *GENERAL*

4288 † No. 1, Priory Lane Cottage (17c.), Priory Lane
4289 †† Broomfield Cottage (17c.)
4290 ** Earthwork on Golf Links, Hindhead
4291 † Frensham Beale Manor (15c. with modern additions)
4292–3 †† Halls Place (17c.) and †Gateway (early 17c.)
4294–5 † Kennel Farm and Kennel Farm Cottages (17c.)
4296 † Kingswood Cottage near Pitthanger (17c.)
4297–8 Pitt Farm and outbuildings (early 18c.)
4299 Pitt Hanger (19c.)
4300 † Spreakley Farm House (16c. and later)
4301 St. Austins (17c., restored)
4302 †† The Burtleys (early 19c.)
4303 †† The Old Post House (formerly Ivy Cottage) (17c.)
4304 †† The Vicarage (18c.)

CHURT

4305–6 †† Nos. 1 and 2, Moorside Cottage
4307 †† Butt's Farm (18c. or earlier)
4308 † Churt Place (Bron-y-de) (1921)
4309 †† Crosswater Farm (18c.)
4310 †† Green Cross
4311 † Hyde Farm (late 16c. and later)
4312 † Marchant Farm (17c. or earlier)

Borough or District Civil Parish	No.	Name or Description of Antiquity

FRENSHAM—*contd.*

CHURT—*contd.*

4313   †† Outmoor
4314   †† Redhearn (17c. and later)

FRENSHAM COMMON

4315   ** Four barrows east of Great Pond
4316   * Group of four barrows west of Lowicks

WEST END

4317   †† Cherry Tree Cottage
4318   † Mill Bridge (16c.)
4319   †† West End Farm Cottage (17c.)
4320–1 †† West End Farm and Oast House (18c. restored)
4322   †† West End House (17c.)
4323–4 †† Westgate (17c.) and Westgate Cottage (18c. Millbridge
4324(1)   Pierrpoint (1876)

HAMBLEDON

GENERAL

4325   †† Admers Cottage (18c. or earlier)
4326–7 †† Lower Farm and Barn (17c.)
4328   †† Beech Cottage (18c.)
4329   †† Bonners (formerly Lower Farm) (18c.)
4330   †[1] Burgate (17c.)
4331–2 †† Cottages (2) at Mervil Bottom
4333   † Court Farm (17c.) and †† Granary
4334   † Hambledon Institution (1730–1786)
4335   † Lower Vann, Vann Lane (16c. with *c.* 1700 additions)
4336   †† Malthouse Cottage (17c.)
4337–9 † Malt House Farm (16c. & 17c.), Barn and Granary
4340   † Mare Pond Farm (17c.)
4341–2 †† Rose Cottage and Hambledon Cottage (late 17c.)
4343   †† Roundhouse (early 19c.)
4344   †† Sandhole Cottages (three) (17c.)
4345   †† School Cottage (16c.)
4346   †† Shaftowes (formerly Raghan)
4347   † The Glebe House (formerly The Old Rectory) (18c.)

[1] Demolished 1959

Borough or District Civil Parish	No.	Name or Description of Antiquity

HAMBLEDON—contd.

GENERAL—contd.

4348 †† The Merry Harriers Inn (18c.)

4349 †† The Old Cottage (17c.)

4350–1 †† Upper Vann Farmhouse (18c.) and ††Cottage to South

4352 †† Walnut Tree Cottage (17c.)

HAMBLEDON COMMON

4353–4 †† Cottages (two) near Cricket Green (16c.)

4355 †† Oakhurst (16c.)

4356 †† Philpot Cottage (17c.)

HYDESTILE ROAD

4357 † Great House Farm (17c. & 18c.) and ††Barn

4358 †† The Pound (17c.)

4359 †† Hydestile Farmhouse (16c.)

HASCOMBE

GENERAL

4360–1 †† Nos. 1 and 2, Pound Cottages (17c.)

4362 † Almshouse Cottages (17c.), Church Lane

4363 †† Ashdale (17c. & 18c.)

4364 Gomers Farmhouse (17c.)

4365 * Hascombe Hill Camp

4366 † Hascombe Place (17c. & 18c.)

4367 † Hoe Farm (16c. & 17c. with 19c. additions)

4368 †† Lambert (17c. & 19c.)

4369 †† Lower House Cottages (two) (17c.)

4370 †† Matthew's Place (17c.)

4371 Olivers (17c.)

4372 †† The Pound (18c.)

4373 †† The White Horse Inn (18c.)

4374 † Upper House Farmhouse (18c.)

LOXHILL

4375 †† Nursery Cottage (formerly Nos. 1 and 2 Loxhill Cottages) (17c.)

4376 Lodge Farm (17c.)

4377 † Markwick Farm (late 17c.)

4378 † The Raswell (19c.)

Borough or District Civil Parish	No.	Name or Description of Antiquity
PEPER HARROW		*GENERAL*
	4379	* Barrow south of Ockley Common
	4380	†† Eashing Lodge (18c.)
	4381	†† Farnham Lodge (18c.)
	4382	†† Glebe Cottage (18c.)
	4383	† Oxenford Bridge (1813)
	4384	† Mulberry House (*c.* 1800)
	4385–7	† Peper Harrow Farmhouse (17c. or earlier) ‡Granary (early 16c. and ††Dovecot (18c.)
	4388–91	‡ Peper Harrow House (1775), †Stables, ††Dairy and ††Dovecot
	4392	†† Shepherds Cottage
	4393	†* Somerset Bridge, near Elstead (central arch 13c.)
	4394	† Somerset Farm, near Elstead (16c.)
THURSLEY		*GENERAL*
	4395	†† Aniker Cottage
	4396	† Badgers (formerly The Old Cottage) (16c.)
	4397	†† Bears Barn
	4398	†† Bedford Farmhouse
	4399–4400	†† Blackhanger Farm and ††Barn (17c.)
	4401	†† Boundless Farmhouse (17c. restored)
	4402	† Boxalls
	4403	†† Boundless Cottage (formerly Creedhole Cottage)
	4404	† Dye House (18c.)
	4405	†† Halls Cottage (17c.)
	4406	†† Hatch Cottages (18c., possibly earlier)
	4407	†† Highcomb
	4408	† Hill Farmhouse (formerly The Manor House) (16c. & 18c.)
	4409	†† Hole Cottage
	4410	†† Horns Cottage (17c.), Church Road
	4411	†† Keeper's Cottage
	4412	† Pitch Place Farmhouse (17c. or earlier)
	4413	† Punchbowl Farmhouse (16c.)
	4414	†† Ridgeway Farmhouse (17c. or earlier)
	4415	†† Smallbrook Farm (17c.)
	4416	† The Lodge (18c.)
	4417	† The Old Parsonage near the church (16c.)

Borough or District Civil Parish	No.	Name or Description of Antiquity

THURSLEY—*contd.*

GENERAL

4418 †Upper Highfield Farm (16c.)
4419 †Vine Cottage
4420 ††Wychmoor (17c.)

BOWLHEAD GREEN

4421 ††Basal Cottage (16c.)
4422 †Timbers (formerly Bowlhead Green Cottages)
4423 ††Corner Cottage (18c.)
4424 †Frith Cottage (17c. or earlier)
4425-7 †Emley Farmhouse, †Barns and Granary (16c.)
4428 ††Heath Hall
4429 ††Homestead
4430 ††Silkmill Cottages
4431 York Cottages (16c.)

HINDHEAD

4432 †The Cross, Gibbet Hill (1851)
4433 †¹The Gibbet Stone on the summit of Hindhead (1787)

THE LANE

4434-7 †Nos. 1 (Oak Cottage), 2 (Pax Cottage), 3 and 4 (Rose Cottage) (16c.) P. 108
4438 Cherry Tree Cottage (16c. & 17c.)
4439 †Oak Cottage (16c.)
4440 †The Olde Hall (16c.)

THE STREET

4441 †Sunset Cottage (16c.)
4442-3 †Wheeler's Cottage and cottage adjoining (16c.)
4444 †Wheelers Farmhouse (16c.)

TILFORD

GENERAL

4445-6 †Nos. 1 and 2 Malthouse Cottages (17c.)
4447 ††Barley Mow (late 17c. and early 18c.) (P.H.)
4448 †Beagleys Cottage (17c. or earlier)
4449 ††Bridge Cottage (18c.)

¹ See Memorials of Old Surrey (J. C. Cox) p. 268

Borough or District Civil Parish	No.	Name or Description of Antiquity

TILFORD—contd.   *GENERAL*—contd.

4450–2 † Bridge Farm and Barn and outbuildings (17c.)

4453 †† Chapel Farmhouse (c. 1830)

4454–5 †† Cottages (2) (18c.) The Green

4456–7 † Sheephatch Farm (16c.) and Barn (17c.)

4458 †† Street Farm (17c.)

4459 † The Mill House (18c.)

4460 † Tilford Cottage (17c.)

4461–4 ‡ Tilford House, † Garden Walls, † Stables and † outbuildings (18c.) (formerly a Chapel)

4465 † Tilford House Farm (15c. & 17c.)

4466–7 ** Two bridges over the River Wey, Tilford Green

4468–9 † Upper Street Farm and †† Barn adjoining (16c.)

WITLEY   *GENERAL*

4470 ** Barrow near London-Portsmouth Road, opposite Half Moon Inn

4471 † Borough Farm Cottage

4472 † Borough Farmhouse (late 18c.)

4473 †† Crossways Cottage (17c.)

4474 †† Damson Cottages, Grayswood

4475 †† White Doves (formerly Lagg Cottage) (formerly Culmer or Colemans Cottage) (late 17c.)

4476 †† Little Shoelands

4477 ** Moat 130 yards north of South Park

4478 †† Old Enton (early 19c.)

4479 †† Tithe Barn at Great Enton

4480 † Rices Farmhouse

4481 †† Sattenham House, Rake Lane (18c.)

4482 †† The Old Cottage

4483 †† The Vicarage, Petworth Road (c. 1830)

4484 †† Wishing Well Cottage

4485 †† Witley Park Farm Cottages

4486 Parish boundary Stone east of Half Moon Inn

BROOK

4487 †† Brook Grange

4488 †† Old Birtley (17c.)

Borough or District Civil Parish	No.	Name or Description of Antiquity

WITLEY—*contd.*

BROOK

4489 †† Sister Cottage (16c. & 17c.)
4490 †† Yew Tree Cottage

CHURCH LANE

4491 † Old Barn Cottage opposite School (17c.)
4492–3 † No. 1 (Step Cottage) (15c. & 16c.)
4494 † No. 2 (The Old Cottage) (15c. & 16c.)

PEPER HARROW

4495 † Oxenford Gate Lodge, Peper Harrow Park (1843–4)
4496–7 † Oxenford Grange Farmhouse (17c.) and Barn (19c.)
4498 †† Oxenford Lodge (*c.* 1763)
4499 † Ruins of Oxenford Grange (13c. & 14c.)

ROKE LANE

4500–2 †† Nos. 1–3, Old Cottage
4503 †† Little Roke (18c.)

SANDHILLS

4504 †† Brook Dene
4505 †† Goose Cottage
4506 †† Institute Cottage (16c.)
4507 † Ivy Cottage (16c.)
4508 †† Meadow Cottage
4509 † Rose Cottage (16c.)
4510 †† Sand Cottage (17c.)
4511 † Step Cottage (16c.)

THE STREET

4512 †† Hillbrow (17c.)
4513–4 †† Lashams (18c.) and Barn adjoining (18c.)
4515–7 † Lloyds Bank Ltd., † Bankside and Ivy Cottage (17c.)
4518 †† Maythorne
4519 † Summerhill Cottage (17c.)
4520–1 † The Donkey Door Antique Shop and † Cottage adjoining (17c.)
4522–5 † The Sun Inn (17c.) and three cottages adjoining
4526 † The White Hart Hotel (14c.–17c.)

Borough or District Civil Parish	No.	Name or Description of Antiquity

WITLEY—*contd.*   *THE STREET*—*contd.*

4527   †† Tilehurst Cottages

4528–   † Witley Manor (18c.) and † Barn on N. side
30   and † garden wall (18c.)

WHEELER STREET

4531–5 †† Nos. 1–5 (18c.)

4536   † Fowl House Farmhouse (15c.)

4537–8 † The Old Manor Hotel and † Tea Barn (16c.)
         P. 90

WHEELER LANE

4539   †† Clematis Cottage

4540   †† Pleck Farm Dairy (18c.)

4541   †† Star Inn (18c. or earlier)

4542   †† Tudor Cottage

WORMLEY

4543   †† Inglewood Cottage

4544–5 †† Tigbourne Court and Little Leat (late 19c.)

MILFORD
AMBERLEY LANE

4546   † Ambergarth (16c. & 17c.)

4547–8 † Ambergarth Farm Cottage and †† Barn
         adjoining on N. (16c. & 17c.)

4549   † Amberley Farm House (16c. & 17c.)

4550   † Low Barbary (16c. & 17c.)

CHURCH ROAD

4551   †† Crossways (early 19c.)

4552   †† Gatton Cottage

4553–4 †† Nine Elms Cottage and Chilston Cottage
         (16c.)

4555   †† The Dormers (16c.)

4556   †† The White House (early 19c.)

GODALMING ROAD

4557   † Dovecot in grounds of The Refectory
         Restaurant (18c.)

Borough or District Civil Parish	No.	Name or Description of Antiquity

WITLEY—*contd.*

GODALMING ROAD—*contd.*

4558–9 † Milford House Hotel (*c.* 1740) and ††Stables (*c.* 1830)

4560 † The Old House

4561 †† The Red House (18c. and later)

4562 † Turnpike Cottage (16c.)

MOUSEHILL DOWN

4563–4 †† Mousehill Manor and Mousehill Court (17c. and later)

4565 † The Chimneys (16c.)

PORTSMOUTH ROAD

4566 † Benacre (16c.)

4567 †† Gothic Cottage (early 19c.)

4568 †† Rodborough Cottage (18c.)

STATION ROAD

4569 † Old Hurst (17c.)

4570–2 †¹Rake Manor (Lake House) (1602) †Dovecot (17c.) and ††Lodge (17c. and earlier)

WONERSH

GENERAL

4573 † Barnett Farm (17c.)

4574 †† Chinthurst Hill (1893–5)

4575 Cottage adjacent to the Corner House (16c.)

4576–8 †† Dahlia Cottage, ††Middle Cot and ††Quill Cottage

4579 †† Darlyn's Brook

4580 †† East Whipley Farmhouse (18c. front on older building)

4581 † Friendly Cottage, Run Common

4582–4 φGreat Tangley Manor (1582), ††Garden Walls and Barn, P. 95

4585 †† Greenlane Farmhouse (17c.)

4586 †† Lavender Cottages

4587 † Lee Crouch (17c. or earlier)

4588 †† Lee Farmhouse (18c. front on older building)

4589 †† Lords Hill Cottage (17c.)

¹ For photograph and article see Country Life, 8th July, 1949, p. 135

Borough or District *Civil Parish*	*No.*	*Name or Description of Antiquity*

WONERSH—*contd.*   *GENERAL*—*contd.*

4590   †† Lostiford House (early 19c.)
4591–2 †¹ Madge Hole Farmhouse and Barn (17c.)
4593–4 † Mill House Cottages (2) (17c.)
4595   †† Norley Farmhouse (1716)
4596   †† Norley House
4597   †† Oriel Cottage
4598   † Pound Land (17c. and later)
4599   †† Reel Hall (15c. & 16c.), Woodhill Lane
4600   †† Smarkham (late 17c.)
4601   † Thames Croft (18c.)
4602   †† The Old Cottage, Wonersh Common (17c. or earlier)
4603   † The Mill House (15c. & 18c.) P. 21
4604   †† The Mill (late 17c. and early 18c.)
4605–6 †† Whipley Manor and Granary
4607   †† Wintersgrace
4608   † Woodhill Farmhouse (17c. or earlier with 18c. additions)
4609   † Woodyers Farmhouse

LONG COMMON

4610   †† Hullhatch (17c.)
4611   Thumbwoods Cottages (17c.)

PALMER'S CROSS

4612   †† Milestone Cottage
4613   † Palmers Cottages (17c.)
4614   †† The Cottage (17c. with later additions)

NORTHCOTE LANE

4615   †† Haldish Farm (17c.)
4616–7 † Northcote Farm and †† Barn (17c.)

SHAMLEY GREEN

4618–   † Nos. 1–5, Malthouse Cottages (formerly
22   The Old Malt House) (late 16c.)
4623   †† No. 1, Red Lion Cottages
4624–5 †† Arthurs Cottage and Arthurs (16c.)
4626   † Barn Cottage (formerly The Old Post Office) (17c.)
4627   †† Briar Cottage (early 19c.)
4628   †† Cherry Tree Cottages (16c. and later)

¹ See Country Life, pp. 438–9, 3.3.1960

Borough or District Civil Parish	No.	Name or Description of Antiquity

WONERSH—*contd.*

SHAMLEY GREEN—*contd.*

4629 †† Dods (17c.)

4630–1 †† Easteds and Easteds Cottage (18c.)

4632 †† ¹Hillyfields (18c. front)

4633–4 † Hyde Farmhouse and Barn (18c. front on older building)

4635 † Lake Cottage (early 17c.)

4636 † Plonk's, near Church (late 16c.)

4637 †† Plonk's Farmhouse

4638 †† Potters (formerly Trabes) (17c.)

4639– †† Tanyard Farm and ††Barns (2) (17c. &
41 18c.)

4642–3 † The Court House (formerly three cottages) and †garage adjoining (17c.)

4644 †† The Old Cottage

4645 † Timbers

4646 †† Yieldhurst (formerly Haddon Cottage) (17c.)

THE STREET

4647 †† Fern Cottage (18c.)

4648 † Grantley Cottages (16c.) P. 78

4649 † Green Place (15c. & 16c.)

4650–1 † Hamshere Cottage and cottage adjoining on the east side (17c.)

4652 † Lawns Mead (18c.)

4653–4 †† Little Stone Cottage and Stone Cottage (18c.)

4655 † Medhouse

4656 †† Mulberry Cottage Garage (18c.)

4657–9 † Park Cottage, †Phlox Cottage and Cottage adjoining (18c.)

4660–1 † Parkside and †Archway adjoining (18c.)

4662 † Tankards (17c.)

4663 †† The Cottage (17c.)

4664 † ²The Dower House (18c.)

4665 † The Grantley Arms Hotel (15c. and later)

4666 † The Green Gateway to Wonersh Park

4667– † The Old House (formerly Three Weaver's
70 Cottages) (16c.) and †2 Cottages adjoining to east and †The Little House (18c.)

¹ Demolished 1962
² See Country Life, p. 1933, 20.6.1953

Borough or District Civil Parish	No.	Name or Description of Antiquity

WONERSH—*contd.*   *THE STREET—contd.*

4671   † The Shielings (17c. on 18c. front)

4672   † Wonersh Yard (formerly stables to Wonersh Park (mid 18c.)

4673   † Woodyers (17c. with 18c. additions)

4674   † Wisteria Cottage (formerly Beeleigh Cottage) (17c. & 18c.)

HASLEMERE URBAN DISTRICT

HASLEMERE   *GENERAL*

4675   † Clammer Hill House, Clammer Hill Road Grayswood

4676   † Foundry Cottage, Kings Road (17c.)

4677   †† Hazelhurst (*c.* 1500, with modern additions) Bunch Lane

4678   †† Tudor Cottage (formerly Henry Court Cottage) in grounds of Courtsmount Courtsmount Road

4679   Imbhams Farm (16c.)

4680   † Little Stoatley Farmhouse, Bunch Lane (17c. or earlier)

4681   †† Puckshott Cottages, Weydown

4682   †† Stedland Farmhouse, Lowder Hill Road

4683–4 †† Sturt Farmhouse and outbuildings, Sturt Road (18c.)

4685   The Boundary Stones (15) of the Ancient Borough

4686   † The Manor House (16c. & 17c.), Three Gates Lane, P. 14

4687   The Town Well, Well Lane

CHURCH LANE

4688   †† Church Hill Cottage (18c.)

4689–
90   ‡ Church Hill House (18c. and earlier) and Church Hill Gate

4691   † Little Barn (formerly Cockescroft) (16c. & 17c.)

HIGH STREET

4692   No. 4 (formerly Macon House) (17c. & 18c.)

4693   †† No. 10 (18c. or earlier)

4694   †† No. 16 (Paris House) (17c. and later)

4695   †† No. 18 (The Old House) (18c.)

Borough or District Civil Parish	No.	Name or Description of Antiquity

HASLEMERE—contd.

HIGH STREET—contd.

4696 †† No. 20 (Kings Arms P.H.)

4697 †† No. 22 (White Horse P.H.) (early 18c.)

4698 †† No. 28 (17c.)

4699 †† No. 30 (15c. & 16c. with modern additions)

4700 †† No. 38 (16c.)

4701 † No. 41 (Tudor Cottage) (16c. & 17c.)

4702–3 † Nos. 66 and 68 (16c.)

4704 †† No. 72

4705 † Haslemere Educational Museum (16c. with 19c. additions)

4706 C.P. Half Moon House (16c.)

4707 † The Georgian Hotel (18c.)

4708–9 †† The Old Bank Pharmacy and premises adjoining to the east

4710 †† The Town Hall (1814)

4711 † Town House (*c*. 1700)

HOLDFAST LANE

4712 † Holdfast Cottage (17c. or earlier)

LOWER STREET

4713–7 † Nos. 29 to 37 (17c.)

4718 †† No. 44 (16c. & 17c.)

4719–21 †† Nos. 50, 54 and 56 (Yew Tree Cottage) (18c.)

4722 † Tudor House (formerly Green Frog Antique Shop)

4723 † Penfolds Corner (16c. & 17c.)

4724 † Verandah Cottage (16c.)

MIDHURST ROAD

4725 † Fleur de Lys (17c.)

4726 †† Houndless Water (17c.)

PETWORTH ROAD
(*formerly East Street*)

4727–9 † Nos. 3 and 5 (17c.) including Old Barn China Shop (1619)

4730–1 †† Nos. 7 and 9

4732–3 † Nos. 10 and 12 (early 18c.) (Riley & Wilshaw, Builders)

4734–9 †† Nos. 13 and 13A, 15, 17, 19 and 21 (18c.)

Borough or District Civil Parish	No.	Name or Description of Antiquity

HASLEMERE—*contd.*

PETWORTH ROAD—contd.

4740 †† No. 14 (17c., refronted)
4741–4 †† Nos. 16, 18, 20 and 22 (18c.)
4745 †† No. 29
4746–7 †† No. 30 (Collards (16c. and later) and outhouse (18c.)
4748–50 † Nos. 31, 33 and 35 (three cottages) (17c.) Thursley End
4751–2 †† Nos. 61 and 61A
4753 †† No. 65 (Fern Cottage) (16c.)
4754–7 † Nos. 68, 70, 72 and 74 (Old Almshouses) (1676)
4758 † No. 82 (Skitreadons)
4759 White Lion (P.H.) (late 17c.)

SHEPHERD'S HILL

4760 †† No. 8 (early 18c.)
4761–5 †† Nos. 11, 13, 17, 19 and 27 (17c.)
4766 †† No. 15 (17c.)
4767–9 21, 23 and 25 (17c.)
4770–1 †† No. 29 (Heath Cottages) and 31 (early 18c.)
4772 †† No. 33 (formerly Nos. 33 and 35 (17c.)

SHOTTERMILL

4773 Boundary Stone, marking boundary between Hampshire, West Sussex and Surrey
4774 †† Sickle Mill House (17c., refronted 18c.)

HINDHEAD ROAD

4775 †† Blossom Cottages
4776 †† Buffbeards (17c. and later)

LIPHOOK ROAD

4777–8 †† Nos. 35 and 37 (Rose Cottage) (17c.)
4779–80 †† Brook Bank and Middlemarsh (18c.)

SOUTH-EASTERN PLANNING AREA

DORKING URBAN DISTRICT

BROCKHAM	*GENERAL*
4781	Brockham Home (19c.)
4782	†† Brockham Warren (*c.* 1830), Box Hill Road, Box Hill
4783	The Pilgrims' Way, Brockham Lime Pits to Duke's Plantation

BROCKHAM GREEN
4784	† Birch Cottage (18c.)
4785	Brick Cottage (early 18c.)
4786	† Brockham Court Farm (18c.)
4787-8 †† Denmark House and Hope House (*c.* 1830)
4789	† Elm Cottage (17c. with additions)
4790	†† Fern Villas (*c.* 1830)
4791	† The Laurels (formerly Laurel Cottage) (19c.)
4792	†† Long Cottage (17c.)
4793	†† North View (17c.)
4794-7 †† Nos. 1 to 4 Church Cottages (18c.)
4798-9	† Nos. 66 and 67 (17c.)
4800	Rose Cottage (17c.)
4801	† Surrey House (15c. and later)
4802	†† The Village Pound (18c.)
4803	† Vicarage Cottage (17c.)
4804	† Vine Cottage (17c.)

MIDDLE STREET
4805	† Brockham House (17c.)
4806	†† The Cottage (17c.)

OLD SCHOOL LANE
4807	†† Brook House (probably 17c.)
4808	†† Dolly House (17c. or earlier)

THE BOROUGH
4809	†† No. 45 (17c.)
4810	†† No. 46 (17c.)
4811-2 †† Nos. 49 and 50 (17c.)
4813-5 †† Nos. 51, 52 and Burnside (17c. and later)

Borough or District Civil Parish	No.	Name or Description of Antiquity

BROCKHAM—*contd.*

WHEELERS LANE

4816–7 † Nos. 4 and 6 (17c.)
4818   † No. 8 (16c. & 17c.)
4819   † No. 10 (16c.)
4820   No. 65 (16c.)
4821   † Moat House (17c.)
4822   † Tumbledown (formerly Cotterstock) (17c.)
4823   †† Wheelwright's Cottage (18c.)

DORKING

GENERAL

4824–5 †† Nos. 1 and 2 (The Tiroler Coffee House, formerly The Gun (P.H.)), North Street (17c. and later)
4826–8   Nos. 3, 4 and 5 (18c. with later additions), Archway Place
4829   No. 7 (early 19c.), Archway Place
4830   No. 3 North Street (see No. 11 High Street) (early 17c.)
4831   ** Barrow on Box Hill
4832   * Barrow on Milton Heath
4833   †† Brookside (18c.), Archway Place
4834   †† Branscombe (early 19c.) London Road
4835   †† Castle Mill, Reigate Road (early 19c.)
4836   † Castle Mill House, Reigate Road (early 19c.)
4837   Cotmandene Almshouses (18c.)
4838   †† Highlands (*c.* 1830) Vincent Lane
4839   † Ladyegate Lodge (*c.* 1804), Ladyegate Road
4840–1 †† Pippbrook Mill (18c.) and †† Pippbrook Mill House, London Road (18c.)
4842   †† Nower Cottages (centre one only), Hampstead Lane (17c.)
4843   The Old House, Rothes Road (17c.)

CHURCH STREET

4844   †† Lesley Cottage (17c. and later)
4845   †† Lesley House (1830)

DEEPDENE AVENUE

4846   † Deepdene Mansion (18c. and 19c.)
4847   †† Glory Farm Cottage (17c. and later)
4848   † Mausoleum, (19c.) Deepdene Mansion (modified and buried to roof level)

Borough or District Civil Parish	No.	Name or Description of Antiquity

DORKING—*contd.*

DENE STREET

4849–50 †† Nos. 27 (Pear Tree Cottage) and 28 (Inglenook) (17c.)

4851–2 † Old Cotmandene Lodge and Cotmandene House (18c.)

HARROW ROAD EAST

4853 †† Harrow Cottage (17c. & 18c.)

4854 †† Kent Cottage (17c. and later)

HIGH STREET

4855–6 † Nos. 11 and 3 North Street (formerly The Old King's Head Inn) (early 17c.)

4857–8 ‡ Nos. 20 and 22 (16c.–18c.)

4859–60   Nos. 24 and 26 (16c.)

4861–2 †† Nos. 37 and 39 (The Wheatsheaf P.H.) (17c., restored)

4863–73 †† Nos. 40 to 60 (early 19c.)

4874–5 †† Nos. 51 and 53 (18c.)

4876–7 †† Nos. 62 and 64 (17c. and later)

4878–81 †† Nos. 100 to 106 (late 18c. and early 19c.)

4882–3 †† Nos. 125 and 127 (The Sun P.H.) (18c.)

4884–8 † Nos. 140 to 148, The White Horse Hotel (16c. and later)

4889–95 †† Nos. 149 to 161 (late 18c. and early 19c.)

4896–9 †† Nos. 150 to 156 (early 19c.)

4900–1 †† Nos. 168 and 170 (18c.)

4902–13 †† Nos. 196 to 218 (early 19c.)

4914–7 †† Nos. 225 to 231 (early 19c.)

ROSE HILL

4918 †† No. 1 (Holly House) (early 19c.)

4919 † No. 15 (Rose Hill Lodge) (early 19c.)

4920–1 † No. 25 (Butter Hill House) and No. 26 (Rose Hill House) (early 18c.)

Borough or District Civil Parish	No.	Name or Description of Antiquity

DORKING—*contd.*

SOUTH STREET

4922–4 †† Nos. 2, 4 and 6 (early 19c.)

4925–6 †† Nos. 8 and 10 (17c.)

4927–8 †† Nos. 16 and 18 (early 19c.)

4929–32 †† Nos. 20, 22, 24 and 26 (early 19c.)

4933 †† No. 64 (formerly Nos. 66 and 68) (Stone-roof) (18c.)

4934 † No. 77 (Little Dudley House) (18c.)

4935–6 † Nos. 80 and 82 (18c.)

4937 † No. 86 (18c.)

4938 †† No. 97 (early 17c.)

4939 † No. 98 (Mount House) (18c.)

4940 †† No. 142 (The Old House) (early 19c.)

4941 Caves (now Kingham's Wine Vaults) (1753)

WEST STREET

4942 †† No. 2 (18c.)

4943 †† No. 7 (18c.)

4944 †† No. 8A (formerly The Rose and Crown P.H.) (17c. & 18c.)

4945–6 †† Nos. 9 and 10 (17c. & 18c.)

4947 †† No. 11 (18c.)

4948 † No. 16 (West Street House (18c.)

4949 †† No. 24 (The Old House at Home) (18c.)

4950–1 † Nos. 32 (West Lodge) and 33 (18c.)

4952–3 †† Nos. 45 (The King's Arm P.H.) and 46 (17c. & 18c.)

4954 No. 54 (17c.)

4955 †† No. 57 (The Bell Inn) (18c.)

4956–9 † Nos. 58 to 61 (17c.)

4960 †† Clarendon House (18c. and earlier)

4961 † The Vicarage (formerly Sondes Place) (17c. & 18c.)

4962 †† The Stables to the Vicarage (17c.)

WESTCOTT ROAD

4963 †† Milton Brook Cottage (formerly Nos. 21 and 22) (early 19c.), Milton Brook

4964 †† Milton Court (1611)

4965 †† Milton Court Mill (19c.)

4966 †† The White Gates (Nutcombe Lane) (late 19c. or early 20c.)

MICKLEHAM

GENERAL

4967 † Burford Corner (formerly West Humble Corner) (early 19c.), West Humble Street

4968 † Flint Cottage (*c.* 1800), The Zig-Zag Box Hill (N.T.)

4969 Mole Cottage (17c. and later)

CHAPEL LANE

4970 Chapel Farm (17c. & 18c.)

4971 †* Ruins of West Humble Chapel (12c.) (N.T.)

LONDON ROAD

4972–3 †† Burford Bridge Hotel (1800) and Stables

4974 †† Burmester House (18c.)

4975 †† Fredley Manor (16c. with modern additions)

4976–8 † Juniper Hall and ††Stables and Cottage to the east (18c.)

4979 † Juniperhill (18c.)

4980 †† Long Cottage (19c.)

4981 † Mickleham Hall (18c.)

4982 †† Rose Cottage (early 19c.)

4983 †† St. Michael's (17c.)

4984 †† The Old Cottage (18c. & 19c.)

4985–6 † The Old House, including the garden gateway (1636)

4987 † The Running Horses Inn (17c.)

NORBURY PARK

4988 †† Lodge Farm (18c.)

4989 †† Lovenden Cottages, Crabtree Lane (17c.)

4990 † The Mansion (*c.* 1775)

SWANWORTH LANE

4991–2 †† Nos. 1 and 2 Hall Farm Cottages (18c.)

4993–4 † Mickleham Post Office and Hall Cottages (18c.)

4995 † Swanworth Farm (16c.)

Borough or District Civil Parish	No.	Name or Description of Antiquity
MILTON		*GENERAL*
	4996– 5001	† Nos. 8, 9, 10, 11, 12 and 14 Castle Gardens, Betchworth Park (19c., restored)
	5002	†* Betchworth Castle Ruins (16c., rebuilt 17c.)
	5003	†† Home Farm (formerly Park Farm) (17c.), Punchbowl Lane
	5004	†† Lodge to Riversdale (early 19c.), London Road
	5005	†† Milehouse Farm (17c.), Coldharbour Lane
		PIXHAM LANE
	5006	†† Pixham Mill (early 19c.)
	5007	† Pixham Mill Cottage (17c.)
		WESTCOTT
	5008	Springfield House (18c.)
	5009	†† Westcott Hill Farm (18c.), Logmore Lane
		BALCHIN'S LANE
	5010	† Churtgate House (16c.) P. 75
	5011	†† Coomb Farm (17c.)
	5012	† Rookery Farm (17c.)
	5013	†† The Old Mill House (17c. restored)
		GUILDFORD ROAD
	5014	†† Bay Tree Cottage (17c.)
	5015	† Regency Cottage (formerly Ellerslie and Heathcote) (early 19c.)
	5016	†† Grocer's Shop (17c.)
	5017	† Ivy Cottage (17c.)
	5018	†† Milton Farm (17c.)
	5019	†† The Springs (formerly Mistress Close) (18c.)
	5020	†† Robin Cottage (17c.)
	5021	†† Sundown Cottage (17c.)
	5022	The Old House (18c.)
	5023	† The Rookery (18c.)
	5024	†† The White House (18c.)
		MILTON STREET
	5025–8	† Nos. 3, 4, 7 and 8 (17c.)
	5029– 30	†† Nos. 13 and 14 (early 19c.)
	5031–4	† Nos. 15, 16, 17 and 18 (17c.) P. 100

Borough or District Civil Parish	No.	Name or Description of Antiquity

MILTON—contd.

MILTON STREET—contd.

5035–7 ‡ Bury Hill Gardens and Stables, including the garden wall (18c.)

5038–9 †† Old Bury Hill House (18c.) and The Observatory (1848 with recent additions and alterations)

WESTCOTT STREET

5040–1 † Nos. 1 and 2 The Barracks (17c.)

5042 † Kingscote (17c.)

5043 † Lower Springfield Farm (17c.)

5044 Rose Cottages (18c.)

5045–6 † Wintershaw (early 19c.) and †† Stables

WORTHING ROAD
NORTH HOLMWOOD

5047 † Redlands Farm (16c.)

5048 †† Rosewood Cottage (c. 1830)

5049 †† Royston (17c.)

5050 †† The Norfolk Arms (P.H.) (c. 1830)

NOTE. The undermentioned properties included in *Dorking and Horley R.D.* are (at the date of publication) included in a *Provisional List* of Buildings of Architectural or Historic Interest by the Minister of Housing and Local Government. It is assumed the grading as annotated (ϕ, ‡, †, ††) indicate that such buildings will be either Statutory listed (owners served with necessary notice) or Supplementary listed under the provisions of the Town and County Planning Act 1962.

DORKING & HORLEY RURAL DISTRICT

ABINGER

GENERAL

5051 Abinger Hatch Hotel, Abinger Hatch (17c. with later additions)

5052 †† Bulmer Farm, Holmbury St. Mary

5053 Chapel Cottage (17c.)

5054 †† Cranes Mill (17c.)

5055 * Holmbury Hill Camp

5056 † Hopedene, Holmbury St. Mary (1873)

5057 Okewood Cottage (18c.)

5058 Old Forge Hole (17c.)

5059 †† Pratsham Grange (16c. & 17c.)

5060 Stocks near Churchyard

Borough or District Civil Parish	No.	Name or Description of Antiquity

ABINGER—*contd.*   *GENERAL*—*contd.*

5061   *[1]The Mound (a Norman motte) west of the
Church in grounds of Abinger Manor
(11c.)

5062   †† The Old Barn
5063   Upfold Farm Cottage (17c.)

ABINGER COMMON

5064   † Abinger Manor (formerly Abinger Manor
Farm) (1872)

5065   †† Glebe House (formerly The Rectory) (17c.
with later alterations)

5066   †† Grovedale (17c.)

5067–9 †† Goddards, Garage and outbuilding to S.E.
(1899, altered 1910)

5070   †† Pasturewood Cottage (17c. and later)

5071–2 †† The Gardener's Cottage (formerly Goddards
Cottage) and outbuildings to S.E.

5073–4 †† The Old Post Office and Old Gate Cottage
(17c.)

ABINGER HAMMER

5075–6 ‡ Crossways Farm (1610) and †† Barn, P. 15

5077   †† Grim's Kitchen (17c.–18c.)

5078   † Hackhurst Farm (16c. with 18c. front)

5079   †† Hackhurst Farm Cottage

5080   †† High Hackhurst (15c. with later alterations)

5081–2 †† Marsh View and Cottage adjoining (17c.)

5083–4 † Paddington Manor Farm (15c. and 17c.)
and †† Barn

FOREST GREEN

5085   †† Bennetts Grove

5086   †† Birkett's Farm (late 16c., with 18c. additions)

5087–8 † Bridgham Farm and †† Barn (1520)

5089   †† Bullcroft Farm (17c.)

5090   †† Cobbett's Farm (17c.)

5091   †† Collin's Farm (17c.)

5092   †† Fishfold Farm (17c.)

5093   †† Ives Farm (17c.)

[1] See *Country Life*, 18th May, 1951, p. 1528

Borough or District Civil Parish	No.	Name or Description of Antiquity

ABINGER—contd.

FOREST GREEN—contd.

5094 †† Lower House (formerly Lower House Farm)
5095 † Lyefield Farm (16c.–18c.)
5096 †† Pisley Farm (17c.)
5097 †† Pondhead Farm (17c.)
5098 †† Redhill Cottage (17c.)
5099 †† Sheepfields (16c. & 17c.)
5100 † Shoes Farm (formerly Joe's Farm) (16c. & 17c.)
5101 †† Tillies Cottage (15c.)
5102 † Volvens Farm (17c.) P. 64
5103 † Wastlands
5104 † Waterland Farm
5105 †† Yard Land (17c., rebuilt 1955)

MOLE STREET

5106 † Castle Cottage (16c. & 17c.)
5107 † Gosterwood Manor Farm (Burchetts Farm) (17c.)

OAKWOOD

5108 † Pollingfold (formerly Pollingfold Farm) (17c.)
5109 †† Standon Homestead (formerly Standon Farm)

OAKWOOD HILL

5110 † Broadstone Farm (18c.)
5111 † Chapelhouse Farm (17c.)
5112 †† Dewest Ride Farm
5113–4 †† Grocers Shop and 2A, Chenies Cottage (17c. or earlier)
5115 † Halehouse (18c.)
5116 † Oakwood Manor (16c.) P. 61
5117–8 †† Pinkhurst Farm (18c.) and Barn
5119– † Ruckmans Farm and ††Barn
20
5121–2 †† Ryders and cottage adjoining
5123 † The Punch Bowl Inn (17c.)
5124 †† Upper Sent (formerly Upper Sent Farm)
5125 †† Woodham's Cottage (16c.–18c.)
5126 †† Woodham Farm (16c.–18c.)

Borough or District Civil Parish	No.	Name or Description of Antiquity

ABINGER—*contd.*   *WALLIS WOOD*

5127 †Abraham's Farm (16c. & 17c.)

5128 ††Froggetts Farm (16c.)

5129 ††Little Meadows (formerly Northbridge Farm) (15c.)

5130 ††Smokejack Farm, Smokejack Hill (17c., altered)

5131 ††The Scarlett Arms (P.H.)

5132 ††Walliswood Farm (17c., altered)

BETCHWORTH   *GENERAL*

5133 ††Ashcroft Farm (18c.)

5134 ††Abbotts (formerly Little Abbotts Farm Cottage)

5135 ††Betchworth Bridge (1843)

5136–8 ‡Betchworth House (1625, with 18c. additions), †Stables and †Garden Gateway (18c.)

5139 †Broome Park (formerly Tranquil Dale) (early 19c.)

5140 ††Coles Hill Farm

5141 ††Cranmer Cottages

5142 †Hall Farm (17c.), Gadbrook Road

5143 †Home Farm (17c. & 18c.)

5144 ††Little Abbots Farm (17c.)

5145 ††Morden Grange Cottages (17c.)

5146–7 †More Place (17c.) and †Stables (18c.)

5148–9 †Old Mill Cottage and Dillon Cottage (17c. & 18c.)

5150 †[1]Johnstons Cottage adjoining The Dolphin Inn (17c. & 18c.)

5151 ††Potters Farm Cottages

5152 †Priest's House, south-east of churchyard (17c.)

5153 ††Noys End (16c.)

5154 ††Ravenleigh Cottages

5155 †Spiders Barn

5156 ††Strood Green Farm (early 17c.)

5157 ‡The Old House (16c. and later)

5158 †The Laurels (18c. and earlier)

5159 ††The Old Vicarage (1715)

[1] Demolished

Borough or District Civil Parish	No.	Name or Description of Antiquity

BETCHWORTH—*contd.*

GENERAL—*contd.*

5160 † The Dolphin Inn (17c. & 18c.)
5161 † Weir Mead (formerly Weir Mead Farm) (17c.)
5162 † Wonham Manor (17c.–19c.), Wonham Lane
5163 † Wonham Mill House (18c.)
5164 †† Woodstock Farm (16c. & 17c.), Gadbrook
5165 †† Yew Tree Cottage (17c.)

CHURCH STREET

5166–7 †† Nos. 1 and 3 (Bylett's Cottages) (17c.)
5168 †† Gardener's Cottage (17c.)

SNOWERHILL ROAD

5169 †† Fryleigh Cottages (two) (17c.)
5170 Orchard Cottage (17c.)
5171 †† Sunny Cottage (17c.)

WELLHOUSE LANE

5172 †† Gadbrook Farm (17c.)
5173 †† Keeper's Cottage (formerly Priest's Cottage) (17c.)
5174 †† Nine Acres Cottages (17c.)

BUCKLAND

GENERAL

5175–9 ‡ Nos. 1–5, Buckland Court (late 18c. or early 19c.)
5180–1 †† Nos. 3–4, Lower Green
5182 †† Dungates Farm
5183 †† Glebe House (formerly The Rectory) (early 19c.)
5184 Old Cottage, Reigate Road (16c. & 17c.)
5185 † Temple in grounds of Broome Park, Betchworth (early 19c.)
5186–7 †† The Buckland Stores & Post Office (formerly the Leg of Mutton and Cauliflower Inn) (early 18c. & 19c.)
5188 †† The Old Cottage (formerly The Old Jolly Farmers Cottages, formerly "Jolly Farmer" Inn) (17c. & 18c.)
5189–90 †† The Round Lodge and Gate House (formerly Lodges to Buckland Court) (early 19c.)

Borough or District Civil Parish	No.	Name or Description of Antiquity

BUCKLAND—*contd.*

GENERAL—contd.

5191 †† The Red Lion Inn (17c. and later)
5192 †† The Stables, Buckland Court (18c.)
5193 †† Yewdells, Dungates Lane (17c.)

RECTORY LANE

5194 †† Oak Cottage (17c.–18c.)
5195 †† Petty's Farm (mid 17c.)
5196   Stonecrop (17c.)

LAWRENCE LANE

5197 †† Lawrence's Farm (17c.)
5198 †† Workhouse Cottages (formerly Orchard Farm or Old Workhouse in 19c.) (Late 15c., with additions)
5199 †† The Harvesters (*c.* 1500) (formerly an Inn on the Pilgrims' Way)

VILLAGE GREEN

East Side

5200–2 † Three timber-framed cottages (formerly The Brew House) (16c.)

West Side

5203–4 † Street Farm and † Barn (formerly The Home Farm) (17c.)

CAPEL

GENERAL

5205   * Anstiebury Camp
5205–7 †† Nos. 2 and 4, Morden Cottages (18c., probably earlier)
5208 †† Bakers Cottages
5209 †† Bay Cottage (17c. or earlier)
5210 †† Bennetts Castle (18c.)
5211   ‡ Bonnetts Farm (late 16c.) P. 8
5212   † Brook House (16c., 18c. & 19c.)
5213 †† Brockholt (17c.)
5214   † Churchgardens Farm (Late 17c.)
5215 †† Clarks Green Farm (18c.)
5216   † Crown Inn (1687 and later)
5217   † Friends Meeting House (1725)
5218–9 † Fylls Cottages or Phyllsbrook Cottage
5220 †† Green's Farm (15c. & 16c.)
5221 †† Homeleigh

Borough or District Civil Parish	No.	Name or Description of Antiquity

CAPEL—*contd.*

GENERAL—*contd.*

5222-3 †† Hoyle Farm and Barn
5224 †† Keepers Cottage, Henfold Lane
5225 †† King's Head (P.H.) (16c. & 18c.)
5226 † Misbrooks (15c.) P. 9
5227 † Osbrook's (formerly Holbrooks and Up-brooks) (17c., restored and enlarged 20c.) P. 69
5228 †† Palmersbeare Farm
5229 † Shiremark Windmill (1774)
5230 Stane Street, Buckinghill Farm, Ockley, to Hollow Way, Dorking
5231 †† The Almshouses (mid 19c.)
5232 †† The Clock House (18c.)
5233 †† The Mill House
5234 † Wattlehurst Farm
5235-7 †† Woodbine Villa, D.E. Carter Tobacconist and The Thrift (18c. and earlier)
5238 †† Yew Tree Cottage (17c. and earlier)

BEARE GREEN

5239 Cherry Tree Cottage (17c.)
5240 † Petersfield Farm (17c.)

RUSPER ROAD

5241 †† Lower Gages Farmhouse (early 17c.)
5242 † Ridge Farm (16c.)
5243 †† Taylor's Farm (14c.–17c.)

TEMPLE LANE

5244 † Aldhurst Farm (16c. with 19c. additions)
5245 †† Copse Cottage (formerly Hatchlands Cottage) (17c.)
5246 † Lodge Farm (15c.)
5247 †† Rushett's Cottages (16c.)
5248 † Temple Elfold (16c.)

CHARLWOOD

GENERAL

5249 †† Bristow Cottage (formerly School Cottage) (17c.)
5250 †† Brook Cottages

Borough or District Civil Parish	No.	Name or Description of Antiquity

CHARLWOOD—*contd.*   *GENERAL*—*contd.*

5251 †† Charlwood Park (formerly Timberham Park) (early 19c.)

5252 ‡ Charlwood Park Farmhouse (formerly Whites Green Farm) (early 16c. & 17c.) P. 7

5253 † Charlwood Place (formerly Saunders Place, later Bullhead Farm) moated (16c.) P. 12

5254 †† Charlwood Place Farm (*c.* 1600) (rebuilt since *c.* 1673)

5255 †† Dormers Cottage (16c.)

5256 †† Edolph's Farm (16c.)

5257 †† Forge Cottage

5258 †† Fulbrook Cottage (18c.)

5259 Glovers Wood (17c., restored)

5260 Half Moon Cottage (17c.)

5261 † Harrow House

5262 † Highworth (16c.)

5263 †† Hillands (late 16c. and early 17c.)

5264 †† Jessamine House (17c., refronted)

5265 †† Laurel Cottage

5266 †† Little Dolby

5267 †† Old Oaks (formerly Lumberwood) (erected 1937)

5268 †† Moors Cottages

5269 †† Oldlands Farm, Tinsley Green

5270 †† Pagewood

5271 †† Pagewood Cottages

5272 †† Poveycross Farm

5273 † Primrose Cottage

5274 †† Ringers Farm (formerly Ringmores Farm) (16c.)

5275 † Robins Farm (17c.)

5276 †† Russ Hill Country Club

5277–8 Spicers Farm and Barn (16c.)

5279 †† Staggers Avon (formerly Mount Pleasant) (18c.)

5280 †† Stanhill (17c.)

5281 †† Street Cottage

5282 †† Swan Cottage

5283 †† Temple Bar House (18c. and earlier)

5284 †† Tifters Farm (formerly Testers) (17c.)

5285 †† The Cottage (16c.), Stanhill

Borough or District Civil Parish	No.	Name or Description of Antiquity

CHARLWOOD—*contd.*   *GENERAL*—*contd.*

5286 † The Greenings

5287 † The Manor House (formerly Taylors Farm) (16c. and later)

5288 †† The Mill (formerly part of Charlwood Windmill) (18c.)

5289 †† The Old Bakehouse (16c.)

5290–2 †† Tudor Cottage and two cottages N.E. of, Rosemary Lane

5293 †† Twin Wells (formerly Spottles Cottages) Spottles Green (17c.)

5294–5 Two Cottages opposite The Halfmoon (P.H.) (16c.)

5296 †† Upper Prestwood Farm

5297 †† Wellingbarn Cottages (erected *c.* 1920)

5298 †† Westfield Farm (17c.)

5299 †† Westlands

5300 †† Westlands Farm

5301 †† Yew Tree Cottage

5302 ** Earthworks, Rectangular Moated Enclosure Meath Green

5303 ** Earthworks, Rectangular Moated Enclosure (nr. Six Bells P.H.)

HOOKWOOD

5304 † Hookwood House (formerly Hooke) (17c.)

5305 †† The Cottage (formerly Hookwood Cottage) (17c.)

5306 †† The Hops (17c., restored)

5307 †† Woodlands Farm (16c.)

LOWFIELD HEATH

5308 ‡ Charlwood House (formerly Ticcaridges) (17c.)

5309 † Gatwick Manor (formerly Hyders) moated, (13c. and later) P. 103

5310 † Rowley Farm (16c. & 17c.)

5311 †† Spikemead (17c. and earlier)

5312–3 †† The Old Post Office and Stores (17c. with later additions)

5314 † The Windmill (18c.) (remains of)

Borough or District Civil Parish	No.	Name or Description of Antiquity

CHARLWOOD—*contd.*   *NORWOOD HILL*
5315   †† Barn at Chantersluer Farm (19c.)
5316   Bo-Peep (18c.)
5317   † Brittleware Farm
5318   †† Fox Cottage
5319   † The Morgans

HEADLEY   *GENERAL*
5320   †† Church Cottage
5321   † Headley Grove (early 19c.)
5322   †† Heather Cottage (17c.)
5323   †† Hurst Farm, Walton-on-the-Hill
5324   † The Old House (17c. portions)
5325   †† Park Corner (early 19c.)
5326   † Remains of Old Church in Parish Church yard
5327   †† Slough Farm
5328   †† Tunbarr or Tumber Cottage (17c.)
5329   †† Vine Cottage

HOLMWOOD   *GENERAL*
5330–1   Anstiebury Farm (two cottages) (17c.) Coldharbour
5332   †† Buckland Cottage (16c.), Betchetts Green
5333   † Collickmoor Farm (16c.)
5334   Ivy Cottage, Ranmore View, Coldharbou (17c.)
5335   †† Stoneheal (17c.)
5336   †† Squires Farm
5337   Stane Street (see also Capel)
5338   †† Waterlands Farm (17c.), Blackbrook Roac

                                      LOGMORE LANE
5339   †† Brook Farm Cottage (17c.)
5340   †† Carolyn Cottage (17c.)
5341   †† Chadhurst Farm (18c.)
5342–3 †† Florence Cottages (two) formerly Florence Farm (17c.)
5344   † Logmore Farm (16c.)
5345   †† Mill Cottage (17c.)

Borough or District Civil Parish	No.	Name or Description of Antiquity

HORLEY

GENERAL

5346   †† The Axes Farm, Axes Lane (16c. and later)

5347   †† Brownslade, New House Lane

5348   †† Bures Manor (18c. with 19c. additions)

5349   †† Collendean Farm, Collendean Lane (17c.)

5350   †† Crutchfield Farm, Crutchfield Lane

5351   †† Dean Farm, Honeycroft Lane (17c. or earlier)

5352   †† Edgeworth House, Balcombe Road (15c. & 17c., with modern additions) P. 92

5353   †† Fishers Farm, Limes Avenue.

5354   †† Horsehills Farm, Horse Hill (18c.)

5355   †† Inholms Farm, Haroldslea Drive (17c. or earlier)

5356   Little Lake Farm (17c.), Hatchersham Lane

5357   Little Meads (16c.), New House Lane, Salfords

5358   †† Mill House (formerly Salfords Farm), Brighton Road

5359   † Old Straddles, Cross Oak Lane

5360   †† Radfords Farm (16c.)

5361   * Thunderfield Castle

5362   †† Stumblehole Farm, Deanoak Lane (17c. or earlier)

BONEHURST ROAD

5363   †† Cambridge Hotel (formerly Cambridge Lodge) (*c.* 1865)

5364   †† Forge Cottage (17c.) and Wailly (18c.)

CHURCH ROAD

5365   † High House (17c.)

5366–7   † Ye Olde Six Bells (P.H.) and †† Barn (15c.) P. 66

HORLEY ROW

5368   †† Benhams (16c., restored)

5369   †† Honeysuckle Cottage (18c.)

5370   †† Lydford (17c.)

5371   †† Monk's Cottage (17c.)

5372   †† The Old Bake House (17c., restored)

5373   † Yew Trees (late 15c., with modern additions)

Borough or District Civil Parish	No.	Name or Description of Antiquity

HORLEY—*contd.*

LEE STREET

5374 †† The Cottage, Sewage Works
5375 †† Fairfield (18c.)
5376 †† The Old Mill House (18c.)
5377 †† Yew Tree Cottage

LONESOME LANE

5378 †† Wyatt's Farm Cottage
5379   York Cottage (early 17c.)

MASSETTS ROAD

5380 †† Vulcan Lodge

MEATH GREEN LANE

5381 †† Cheswick Farm (17c., with modern additions)
5382 †† Cinderfield (early 17c.)
5383 †† Ladylands (formerly Ladylands Farm) (early 17c.)
5384   The Old Cottage (17c., restored)

PICKETTS LANE

5385 †† Picketts Cottage
5386 † Picketts Farmhouse

STAPLEHURST LANE

5387 †† Shocks Green Cottage
5388 †† Staplehurst Farm
5389 †† Staplehurst Farm Cottage

VICTORIA ROAD

5390 †† Birchwood Cottage (18c.)
5391–2 †† The Foresters Arms (P.H.) and Evelyns Snack Bar (mid 19c.)

LEIGH

GENERAL

5393 †† Bunts Farm (17c., restored)
5394 †† Charman's Farm (18c. or earlier)
5395 †† Dawesmead (late 15c. & 17c., restored)
5396 †† Grove Farm
5397 †† Herons Head Farm, moated (15c. & 17c.)
5398 †† Hook Farm (17c., restored)

Borough or District Civil Parish	No.	Name or Description of Antiquity

LEIGH—*contd.*   *GENERAL*—*contd.*

5399– † Leigh Place, moated and †† Barn (12c. and
400   early 17c., exterior rebuilt *c.* 1810) P. 49
5401 †† Little Mynthurst Farm
5402   Orchard Cottage (17c. and later)
5403 †† Park House Farm (17c.)
5404 †† The Plough Inn (18c.)
5405   † Priest's House (formerly Church Cottage)
            (15c., restored)
5406 †† Reeves Cottage (formerly Arnolds Farm),
            Dean Oak Lane (17c.)
5407 †† Shellwood Cross
5408   Shellwood Manor (17c. and later)
5409 †† Sheepcote Cottage
5410 †† Swains Farm (17c., restored)
5411 †† The Chantry (formerly Church Grove Farm)
            (18c.)
5412 †† Thyme Cottage (early 17c.)

NEWDIGATE   *GENERAL*

5413–4 †† Nos. 1 and 2 Lance's Cottages (two) (17c.)
5415   † Ansells Cottages (17c.), Kingsland
5416 †† Blanks
5417 †† Brooklag Farm House (17c.)
5418   † Cudworth Manor House with moat (16c.,
            with later additions)
5419 †† Dean House Farm (16c.)
5420–1 †† Dukes Cottage and cottage adjoining N. of
            Surrey Oaks (18c. and earlier)
5422   † Ewood Farm House (16c. & 17c.)
5423   † Gaterounds Farm (16c.)
5424 †† Goscroft, Henfold Lane (17c.)
5425   † Home Farm (formerly Newdigate Place)
            (early 17c.)
5426 †† Ivyhouse Farm
5427–8 †† Kingsland Farm and Old Kingsland Cot-
            tage (17c. and later)
5429 †† Marelands (16c.)
5430–1 † Mill Cottage and Lodge
5432 †† Nyes Place
5433 †† Oaklands Park Farm Cottage
5434 †† Old Beam Brook

Borough or District Civil Parish	No.	Name or Description of Antiquity

NEWDIGATE—*contd.*

GENERAL—contd.

5435–6   Post Office and ††Cottage adjoining (early 17c.)

5437   †† Reffolds (early 17c.)

5438   †† Rolls Farm

5439   †† Simons (16c.)

5440   † Sturtwood Farm House (17c.)

5441   †† Yew Tree Cottage

PARK GATE ROAD

5442   † Little Trees (17c.)

5443   †† Saplings (18c.)

RUSPER ROAD

5444   †† Chaffolds Farm (16c.)

5445–6 †† Hound House Farm and Barn (16c.)

5447–8 † Hasted Cottage and Northlands (formerly Six Bells Cottages) (early 16c.)

5449   Six Bells (P.H.) (17c.)

5450   †† Tanhurst Farm (16c.)

OCKLEY

GENERAL

5451–4 †† Nos. 1–3 Forge Cottages and The Forge (18c.)

5455   † Boswells Farm

5456–7 † Buckinghill Farm and †† Barn (16c.)

5458   †† Chestnut House (17c. and altered 19c.)

5459–60   † Elderslie and Stables (17c.)

5461   †† Elmer Farm (17c. or earlier)

5462–3 ‡ Eversheds Farm and **Outbuilding**

5464   † Farm Place

5465   † Holbrook's Farm (16c.)

5466   †† House N. of Rallywood (17c. and later)

5467–8 †† Ivy Cottage and Vine Cottage (16c.)

5469   †† Jayes Park (17c. and later)

5470   †† Kings Arms (P.H.)

5471   †† Maple Cottage (17c.)

5472   †† Mill Cottage (early 19c.)

5473   †† Ockley Court (18c. with 19c. additions)

5474   †† Park Cottages (17c.)

5475   †† Park Farm

5476   †† Parkland Farm (17c.)

Borough or District *Civil Parish*	*No.*	*Name or Description of Antiquity*

OCKLEY—*contd.*

GENERAL—*contd.*

5477 †† Rallywood (*c.* 1840)
5478 † Rapleys (17c.)
5479 †† Rectory Cottages
5480–1 † Red Lion Inn (17c.) and Stables (18c.) P. 71
5482 ** Site of Ockley Castle (near church) (probably 12c.)
5483 † Stane House (formerly The Rectory) (1784)
5484 †† Stylehurst (17c.)
5485–6 † Surrey House (Flats A, B and C) (18c.) and House adjoining to N. (17c. or earlier)
5487 † The Tuns (18c.)
5488 † Trouts Farm (1581)
5489   Weavers (16c.)
5490 † Young's Farm (16c.)

THE GREEN

5491–2 † Nos. 10 and 11 (Lime Tree Cottages) (17c.)
5493–4 † Nos. 12 and 13 (17c.)
5495 † No. 17 (Jayes Park Cottage)
5496–8 † Nos. 18, 19 and 20 (18c. & 19c.)
5499– † Nos. 21 and 22 (Tanyard Cottages) (two)
5500   (16c.)
5501–2 †† Nos. 14 and 15 (17c. or earlier)
5503 †† No. 16 (Park Gate Cottage)
5504–5 † The Cottage and ††outbuildings (17c.)
5506–7 † Carpoles Cottages (two) (17c.)

STANE STREET (*ROMAN ROAD*)

5508–9 † Nos. 9 and 9A (The Hatch) (16c.)
5510 †† Carpoles (17c.)
5511 †† Greenside (17c. or later)
5512   Stane Street, Monks Farm to Halehouse Farm, Ockley
5513 † Swiss Cottage
5514 † The Cricketers' Arms (17c.)
5515 † The Old School House (18c.)

WOTTON

GENERAL

5516–7 †† Nos. 3 and 3A, Sheep Green
5518–9   Chandlers Farm (18c.) and The Cottage (17c.), Hollow Lane
5520   Damphurst Farm (17c.)

Borough or District Civil Parish	No.	Name or Description of Antiquity

WOTTON—contd.

GENERAL—contd.

5521 † Leith Hill Tower (1765)
5522 Leylands (17c.)
5523 Leylands Farm (17c.)
5524 †† Mears Farm
5525 * Mound in Deerleap Wood
5526–7 †† Park Farm (18c. and later) and Granary
5528 †† Wotton Hatch Hotel (18c.)
5529– † Wotton House (Fire Services College) (17c.
31   with later alterations) the †Temple (18c.)
     and †Mausoleum (early 19c.)

BROADMOOR

5532 †† Home Farm (17c.)
5533 †† The Old Cottage
5534 †† The Tower (18c.)

FOREST GREEN

5535 †† Birketts Cottage (16c. & 17c.)
5536 † Gosterwood Manor (16c. & 17c.)

FRIDAY STREET

5537 †† Hutchings Cottage (formerly Pug's Corner
     and Gamekeepers Cottage) (17c.)
5538–9 †† Pond Cottage and Mill Pond Cottage (17c.)
5540–1 †† Kempslade Farm (17c.) and Barn (18c.)
5542 †† Fridays Cottages (18c.)

LEITH HILL

5543 †† East Campfield Place (early 19c.)
5544–5 † Forge Cottages and The Stores (17c. & 18c.)
5546–7 † Hartshurst Farm (16c.) and Granary
5548 ‡ Leith Hill Place (16c. and early 18c.)
5549– † Leith Hill Place Farm and ††Barn (17c.)
50
5551 †† Leith Hill Place Cottages (18c. and earlier)
5552 † Tanhurst (late 18c.)

RANMORE COMMON

5553 †† Bagden Farm (16c. & 17c.)
5554 †† Tanners Hatch (16c. & 17c.)
5555 †† Yew Tree Farm (17c.)

GODSTONE RURAL DISTRICT
  BLETCHINGLEY   *GENERAL*

5556	††	Arthur's Seat, War Coppice Road
5557		Barnmoor (early 18c.)
5558	*	Bletchingley Castle (earthworks only) (12c.)
5559–60	††	Brown's Hill Cottages and Harewoods Farm Barn, Brown's Hill (17c.)
5561	††	Chevington Farm, Reigate Road (17c., restored)
5562	††	Church Lane Cottages (17c.), Workhouse Lane
5563–5	†	Court Lodge Farm, ††Barn and outbuildings, Workhouse Lane (17c.)
5566–8	††	Cucksey's Farm and Barns (2) (17c.)
5569	*	Earthwork at Chapel Plat Lodge Farm
5570	††	Gay House, Gayhouse Lane (early 17c. and later)
5571	††	Ivy Mill House (1698 and later)
5572–3	††	Lodge Barn and Farm (17c., with later additions)
5574	††	Lower South Park Farm (formerly Hewletts) (17c.)
5575	††	Lower Tilgates (early 18c.), Little Common Lane
5576		North Park Farm Buildings (17c.)
5577	††	Poundhill Farm, Bletchingley Lane (17c.)
5578		Site of old Windmill, Woolpits
5579		St. Marks Chapel (formerly Stable at South Park Farm) (17c.)

BREWER STREET

5580–1	††	Nos. 1 and 2 (18c.)
5582–3	††	Nos. 3 and 4 (18c.)
5584–6	†	Nos. 6, 7 and 8 (formerly the Brew House) (16c.)
5587	φ	Brewer Street Farm (15c. & 16c.) P. 25
5588	††	Little Hextalls (formerly Whitehill Lane Cottages) (17c.)
5589–90	††	Place Farm Cottages (2) (17c.)

Borough or District Civil Parish	No.	Name or Description of Antiquity

BLETCHINGLEY
—*contd.*

CHURCH WALK
(*Old High Street*)

5591–5 † Nos. 1–5 (inclusive) (16c. and later)

5596 † No. 14 (Butcher's shop) (17c., restored)

5597 †† Legg's Cottages (17c., restored), Middle Row

5598 † Nicholas Wolmer Cottage (1552, restored) P. 59

5599– †† Selmes Barn and Stables
5600

HIGH STREET
North side

5601–7 †† Nos. 1–7, Brittens Cottages (*c.* 1850)

5608–9 † No. 1, Middle Row (17c. & 18c.) and Shop adjoining (late 17c.)

5610 † No. 3 Middle Row (15c. and later)

5611–3 †† Berry House, Elm House and The Limes (18c.)

5614–6 † Bletchingley Garage and †Tunn House and †Tunn Cottage, Middle Row (17c.)

5617 † Camden House (early 19c.)

5618– †† Clive House, cottage adjoining and Bakery
20 (D. Grice) (late 18c.–early 19c.)

5621–2 † King Charles Cottage and †No. 4 (Market House or Cottage) (15c.)

5623 Long Row (formerly The White House) (17c.)

5624 Norfolk House (18c.)

5625–6 †† Poplar House (17c.) and Stable Block (18c.)

5627–8 † Post Office and Post Cottage (17c.), Middle Row

5629 †† The Old Forge (18c.)

5630 †† The Plough Inn (17c., restored)

5631 †† The Clerk's House (16c., restored)

5632 †† The Manse (17c.)

South side

5633–4 † Nos. 1 and 2 Tower House Cottages (late 17c.)

5635–8 † Nos. 3, 4, 5 and 6 Tower House Cottages (17c.)

5639– † Nos. 1, 2 and 3, The Cobbles (formerly Old
41 Leggs House)

Borough or District Civil Parish	No.	Name or Description of Antiquity

BLETCHINGLEY

HIGH STREET—contd.

—*contd.* 5642–3 † Glenfield and outbuildings (early 18c.)

5644 †† Melrose (formerly Coraun) (18c.)

5645 †† The Old Cottage opposite the Red Lion (P.H.) (early 18c.)

5646–8 † Three Gabled cottages (17c.)

5649–51 ‡ White Hart Hotel (16c. & 17c.) and Stables and ††Signpost (18c.)

5652–3 † White Hart Flats (early or mid 17c.) and ††Bakery at rear (18c.)

OUTWOOD LANE

5654 †† Bell Inn (mid 18c.)

5655 † Eddols Cottage (17c.)

5656 † Oxtall (18c.)

5657 † Prince Albert Inn (16c., restored)

5658 † Poundhill Farm (17c.)

5659 †† The Grange (17c.)

PENDELL

5660 †† Cockley Cottage (formerly the Parish Pest House) Mill (17c.) Big Common Lane

5661 †† Mill Cottage (17c.)

5662 †† The Old Cottage (17c.) Little Common Lane

5663–4 ‡ Pendell Court (1624) (extension on east side c. 1880) and Garden House (17c.) P. 22

5665 Pendell Farmhouse (17c.)

5666–8 φ Pendell House (formerly Glyd's House) (1636) Garden Wall (17c. & 18c.) Stable Block (17c.)

5669 ‡ The Manor House (16c. & 18c.)

RABIES HEATH ROAD

5670 †† Brick Kiln Cottage (formerly Prestwell Farm) (17c.)

5671 Coldharbour Farm (16c., restored)

5672 Pound Farm (17c., restored)

5673 Rabbits Cottage (formerly Cacketts) (16c.)

5674 † Raby's (17c.)

5675 Snats (17c., restored)

Borough or District Civil Parish	No.	Name or Description of Antiquity

BLETCHINGLEY

SANDY LANE

—*contd.* 5676 †† Gregorys (formerly Conys) (18c.)

5677 † The Old Rectory (18c.)

WARWICK'S WOLD

5678 †† Stocklands (16c.), Merstham Road

5679 †† Speyns Barn (17c.)

5680 †† Warwicks Wold Farmhouse (late 17c.)

5681 Yew Tree Cottage (17c.)

WHITEHILL

5682 Ancient Trackway known as Pilgrim's Way

5683–4 ‡ Place Farm House (18c.) (formed out of 16c. gatehouse of Bletchingley Place) and Barn (17c.), Place Farm Road

5685 †† The Hermitage (formerly Hextalls) (17c., restored)

BURSTOW

GENERAL

5686 †† Burstow Lodge Cottage

5687 † Doghurst Farm (17c.)

5688 †† Green Meads Farmhouse, Hathersham Lane (17c.)

5689 †† Old House Cafe

5690 †† Old Court (moated, formerly The Manor House) (16c. and later)

5691 †† Stonelands Farm (18c.), Copthorne Bank

5692 †† Teizers Farm (15c.)

5693 †† The Rectory (16c.)

OUTWOOD AREA

5694 †† Bellwether Cottage

5695 † Burstow Park Farm (18c.)

5696 † Cogman's Farm (16c.)

5697 †† Marle Pond Cottage

5698 †† Old Cottage (18c.)

5699 † Outwood Post Mill (1665 and 18c.) P. 16

5700–1 † The Old Farmhouse (formerly Wasp Green Farm) (16c.) and †† Barn, Wasp Green Road

5702 †† Shepherds (18c.)

5703 †† Wasp Well (formerly Red Cottage) (18c.) Miller's Lane, Wasp Green

Borough or District Civil Parish	No.	Name or Description of Antiquity

BURSTOW —contd.

SMALLFIELD AREA

5704–6 †† Nos. 1 and 2 Rough Beech Farm Cottages and ¹Barn (Late 16c.)

5707 ‡ Burstow Lodge (16c.)

5708–9 ‡ Crullings and Smallfield Place (c. 1600) P. 18

5710 †† Forge Cottage (mid or late 18c.)

5711 †† Oldhall Farm (17c.)

5712 †† Plough Inn (mid 18c.)

5713 †† Pagefield Cottage (17c., restored), Scott's Hill

5714–5 †† The Rookery (formerly Rookery Farm) and Barn (16c. and later), Drivers Green

5716 †† Twyners Croft

CHELSHAM

GENERAL

5717 ‡ Beddlestead Farm (15c. and later)

5718 Bull Cottages (17c.)

5719 †† Chelsham Place Farm (16c.)

5720 ** Early pits on Worms Heath near Slines Green

5721 * Earthwork in Henley Wood south of Church Lane

5722 †† Fairchilds Farmhouse, Fickleshole (late 18c.)

5723 † Fickleshole Farm (18c.)

5724–6 † The White Bear (P.H.) and †two adjoining Cottages (late 17c.), Fickleshole

5727–8 †† Two cottages on north side (17c.), Ledgers Road

CROWHURST

GENERAL

5729 †† Altar Cottages (17c. and later)

5730 † Bombers Farm (early 17c.)

5731–2 †† Bowerland Farm and Barn (15c. & 17c., restored)

5733 †† Bowerland Park or Chellows Park (early 18c)

5734 †† Church Farm (late 16c.)

5735 †† Church Farm Cottage (17c.)

5736–8 φ Crowhurst Place (15c.) and two Barns (16c.) P. 46

5739–42 †† Crowhurst Place Cottages (four) (18c.)

¹ Demolished May 1964

Borough or District Civil Parish	No.	Name or Description of Antiquity

CROWHURST   *GENERAL—contd.*
—*contd.* 5743–4 ‡ Mansion House Farm and ††Barn (16c
with 17c. additions)
5745   ** Moated site of Bear Place
5746   † Old Chellows (formerly Chellows Farm)
(early 17c.)
5747   †† Oldhouse Farm (17c. and later)
5748   † Pikes Farm (late 16c.)
5749   †† Stocks (16c. & 17c.)
5750   † Whitehouse Farm (*c.* 1600 and 18c.)
5751   †† Windyridge (early 18c.)
5752–3 † Wintersell Farm (early 16c.) and Granary
(18c.)

GODSTONE   *GODSTONE GREEN*
5754   †† Bankside (18c.)

North side
5755–7 † Nos. 1, 2 and 3 Hope Cottages (18c.)
5758–   † Nos. 1 to 7 and 10, Needle Bank Cottages
65   (16c.–19c.)
5766–8 †† Court View and †Addison's shop and
cottage abutting to N.E. (18c.)
5769   * Earthwork in Castle Hill Wood (motte and
bailey castle)
5770–1 † Hare and Hounds Inn (18c. & 19c.) and
Coachhouse (18c.)
5772–3 †† Pair of cottages N.E. of Hare & Hounds
P.H. (17c.)
5774   †† Rosebank (18c.)
5775   †† White Swan Inn (formerly Godstone Poor
House) (early 18c.)

South side
5776–8 †† North View (3 cottages) (17c.)

HIGH STREET
East side
5779   †† Godstone Place (early 19c., restored) and
† Wall (*c.* 1500)
West side
5780–3 †† Nos. 1, 2, 3 and 4 South View (*c.* 1820)
5784–6 †† Nos. 6, 7 and 8 Burnell's Cottages (early
17c.)

Borough or District Civil Parish	No.	Name or Description of Antiquity

GODSTONE—*contd.*

HIGH STREET—*contd.*

5787   ††Electrecords (formerly Forge Garage) (formerly The Old Forge) (18c.)

5788   Meriden (formerly Nos. 1 and 2 Burnells Cottages (17c.)

5789   ††Stratton (18c. and earlier)

5790   ††The Green Cottage (early 19c.)

5791–3   ‡The Post Office, Tudor Cottage and Highway Cottage (early 18c.)

5794   †Vine Cottage (late 18c.)

BULBEGGARS LANE

5795   ††The Pest House (17c.)

GODSTONE GREEN ROAD
East side

5796–9   †Butchers Shop, The Chestnuts, Green House and Cottages south of the White Hart (P.H.) (18c.)

5800   ††Clayton Cottages (18c.)

5801–3   †Garston Farm (formerly Greyhound Farm) and cottages (2) adjoining (16c.)

5804   †The White Hart (P.H.) (formerly Clayton Arms Hotel) (16c.)

5805   ††The White Hart Barn (Village Hall) (18c.)

West side

5806   ‡The Bell Inn (18c. and earlier)

5807   ††Hillbrow (*c.* 1840)

5808   The Old House (Hall's Stores) (17c. and later)

5809   ††Barnard's Shop (17c.)

CHURCH LANE

5810–2   ††Church Cottages (three) adjoining north-west corner of churchyard (*c.* 1500), with 19c. exterior)

5813   †Church House (18c.)

5814   ††Cottage north of the Old Pack House (*c.* 1800)

5815   †Church End (formerly Stacey's Cottage) (17c. & 18c.)

5816   ††Crossways (17c., enlarged 19c.)

Borough or District Civil Parish	No.	Name or Description of Antiquity

GODSTONE—*contd.*

CHURCH LANE—*contd.*

5817 ‡ The Old Pack House (P.H.) (formerly The Old Pack Horse Inn) (15c. & 16c.) P. 37

5818 †† Pilgrim Cottage (16c., restored)

5819 † Glebe House (formerly The Old Rectory) (*c.* 1800)

5820 † St. Mary's Homes (Almshouses) (1872)

5821 † Cottage opposite St. Mary's Home (16c.)

5822–3 †† Two cottages west of Old Rectory, (17c.)

WALKINGSTEAD

5824 † Leigh Mill House (16c. & 18c.)

5825 † Garden Walls of Leigh Place (17c.)

5826–7 †† Sandpits Cottages (2) (17c.)

5828 †† The Old Pay House, East Grinstead Road (17c.)

BLINDLEY HEATH AREA

5829– †† Nos. 1 and 2, Homers Cottage, Doctor's
30   Corner (17c. with 19c. extension)

5831 †† Bank Farm Cottage (17c.)

5832 †† Barn Gate House (17c.)

5833 † Comforts Place (15c.–17c.), Tandridge Lane, P. 6

5834 †† Elmshade (17c.)

5835 †† Maynards (16c.)

5836   South Cottages (19c.)

5837 † The Blue Anchor Inn (15c., restored)

5838 †† The Elizabethan Cottage (16c., restored)

NEWCHAPEL AREA

5839– †† Cherry Tree Farm and Barn (formerly
40   Youngs Farm) (16c.)

5841 †† Frogit Cottage, Frogit Heath

5842–5 † Gatehouse Farmhouse, †† Barns, †† Granary and †† Stables (16c.)

5846 †† High House Farm (early 17c.)

5847 ‡ Lowlands Farmhouse (15c., with 17c. additions)

5848 †† Raby's House (16c.) and Barn

5849 †† Wire Mill Hotel (19c.)

Borough or District Civil Parish	No.	Name or Description of Antiquity

GODSTONE—*contd.*

NORTHERN AREA OF THE PARISH

5850–3 †† Flinthall Farm (17c.–19c.) and Barns (2) and Granary (18c.)

5854   Nash's Farm (16c. and later)

5855–7 † Quarry Farm (17c.), Barn (18c.) and Quarry Cottage (18c. & 19c.)

5858   ** Two barrows in Hillyfield (prehistoric)

SOUTHERN AREA OF THE PARISH

5859–
62   † Lagham Manor (17c.) with moat (1262),. Brewhouse, Oatshouses and Stable (18c.) P. 27

5863   * Lagham Park, earthworks (prehistoric)

5864   †† North Farmhouse (17c.)

5865   † Posterngate Farm (16c.) P. 55

5866–7 † Yew Tree Farmhouse (15c., restored 17c.) and Barn (17c.)

STANSTED BOROUGH

5868–
72   †† Nos. 1, 2, 3, 4, and 5 (18c. and later)

5873   † Fox & Hounds Inn (16c. & 17c.)

5874–6 † Tilburstow Hill Farm and ††Barn (17c.) and ††Granary (18c.)

FELBRIDGE

GENERAL

5877–8 † Nos. 1 and 2 Hedge Court Cottages (17c.)

5879   † Lake Cottage (early 17c.)

5880   †† Starr Inn (18c., restored)

5881–2 †† White Duchess Hotel (formerly Felbridge Place Hotel) including stable block (18c., refaced *c.* 1860)

HORNE

GENERAL

5883   †† Bakers Barn Farmhouse (15c. and later)

5884   †† Barns Branford (15c.), Brickhouse Lane

5885–6 † Chithurst Farm and ††Barn (17c.)

5887   Church Farm (17c.)

5888   †† East Bysshe Farmhouse (17c.)

5889–
90   †† Hedge Court Farm and Barn (17c.), Felbridge

5891   †† Highfield Farm (18c.), Clay Lane

5892   †† Hornehouse Farm (early 17c.)

Borough or District Civil Parish	No.	Name or Description of Antiquity

HORNE—*contd.*

GENERAL—*contd.*

5893   Paradise Cottage (15c. & 16c.), Wilmot's Lane
5894 †† Perry Farm (18c.)
5895 †† Stanton's Hall (mid 18c.), Blindley Heath
5896 †† The Glen Farm (17c. and later), Bones Lane
5897   Wilmot's Farm (15c. and later)

BYERS LANE

5898 †† Horne Park Cottage (early 17c.)
5899 †† Pond Lake Cottage (mid 18c. and later)

HARE LANE

5900–1 †† Colboys (15c.) and Barn (17c.) P. 13
5902   Goulds Farm (16c., restored)

HORNECOURT HILL

5903 †† Hornecourt Hill Cottages (late 18c.)
5904–5 †† Hornecourt Manor Farm and †† Barn (17c.)

NEWCHAPEL

5906 †† Little Brook Farm (formerly Lowlands Cottages) (17c.)
5907   Kingswood Farmhouse (18c.)
5908 †† Parish Council Cottage (mid 18c.)

WHITEWOOD

5909–10 † Jarves Farmhouse (15c.) and Barn, P. 104
5911 †† The Old Cottage (16c.)
5912 †† The Jolly Farm (P.H.) (1788)
5913   Whitewood House Farm (16c.)

LIMPSFIELD

GENERAL

5914–23 †† Nos. 1–10 Wolf's Row (18c. & 19c.)
5924   High Ridge Farm, Merle Common (17c.)
5925–6 ‡ Court House and Little Court Cottage (formerly The Old Court Cottage) (14c. and later), Titsey Road
5927 † Limpsfield Lodge Farm (*c.* 1600)
5928 †† Mill House (17c.), Tally Road, Limpsfield Chart

Borough or District *Civil Parish*	*No.*	*Name or Description of Antiquity*

IMPSFIELD—*contd.*

GENERAL—*contd.*

5929–30 ‡ Moat Farm House and Barn (15c., 16c. and later)

5931–3 † Park Farm (early 18c.), †† Barn and outbuildings (18c.), Bluehouse Lane

5934–5 † Trevereux (*c.* 1736, with late 19c. additions) and Stable range (18c.)

5936 Village Pound (18c.)

GRANTS LANE

5937–8 † Black Robins Farm House (early 17c.) added to later, *c.* 1934) and Barn (17c.)

5939–41 †† Bolthurst Farm House (15c., altered *c.* 1850), outbuildings and Barn (17c.–19c.)

5942 †† Comforts Cottage (early 17c.)

5943 † Doghurst (16c. & 19c., enlarged *c.* 1920)

5944–6 φ Grants (formerly Whitegates Farmhouse) and Barns (two) (15c.)

5947–8 † Stockenden Farm (15c. and additions of 1604) and Granary (18c.)

5949–50 †† The Horns (two cottages) (18c.)

GUILDABLES LANE

5951 †† Couldens Farm (17c.)

5952–3 † Nos. 1 and 2 Guildables Cottages (formerly Privett Cottages) (three) (16c.)

5954 †† Guillvers Farm (formerly Guidables) (18c. and earlier)

HIGH STREET

East side

5955 † Brasier's Cottage (17c.)

5956 †† Bull Inn (17c., with 19c. additions)

5957 †† Lilac Cottages (17c.)

5958–9 †† Jessamine Cottage and Sandridge (early 19c.)

5960 † Manor House (late 18c. with 19c. additions)

5961–3 ‡ Old Court House, Osterley and adjoining shop (originally one house (15c.))

5964 †† Rodney House (15c.)

5965–70 † Fern Cottage, Registry Cottage, White Hart Cottage, April Cottage and Nos. 1 and 2

5971 †† Rose Cottage (17c. & 18c.)

Borough or District Civil Parish	No.	Name or Description of Antiquity

LIMPSFIELD—*contd.*

HIGH STREET—*contd.*

East side—*contd.*

5972–3 ††Rosewell Cottages and premises N.W riding school (18c.)

5974 ††The Stores (early 19c.)

5975 ††Vine Cottage (18c.)

West side

5976–7 †Nos. 1 and 2 Chapel Cottages (17c. an later)

5978–82 ‡Nos. 1, 2, 4, 5 and 6 (16c. and later) P. 11

5983–6 †Nos. 1 to 4 Forge Cottages (17c. and later

5987 †Butcher's shop (16c. & 17c.)

5988 ‡Detillens House (15c.) P. 86

5989 †Hookwood (early 19c.)

5990 ††Hookwood Cottage (17c. or 18c.)

5991 †Jarrett's (16c.)

5992 ††Loveland Cottage (17c.)

5993 ‡Pebble Hill House (late 18c.)

5994 ††Plumbers Arms (P.H.) Wolfs Corner (portion 17c.)

5995 †Ridlands Farm (16c.–19c.), Ridlands Lane

5996 †The Bower (17c.)

5997 †The Rectory (18c., with *c.* 1800 additions)

5998–9 ††Two Cottages (late 17c.), Grub Street

6000 ††Ratcatcher's Cottage (late 16c.), Tidy's Green

6001 †Whinchat Cottage (17c.)

6002 †White Hart Lodge (16c.)

6003 †Whitehouse (late 18c., with *c.* 1800 additions)

ITCHINGWOOD COMMON

6004 †Comforts Cottage (17c.)

6005 ‡Tenchley Manor (*c.* 1600, with 19c. additions), Tenchley's Lane

LIMPSFIELD COMMON

6006 †Lombarden Cottage (15c.)

6007 ††The Salt Box (17c., with 1878 additions), Little Heath

Borough or District Civil Parish	No.	Name or Description of Antiquity

LIMPSFIELD—*contd.*

MONK'S LANE

6008 ‡ Batchelor's Farm (15c.–19c.)
6009 †† Capers Farm (early 17c.)

MOORHOUSE BANK

6010– †† Nos. 4 and 5 Moorhouse Farm Cottages (2)
12 (17c.–19c.) and Oasthouse (19c.)
6013–4 †† Nos. 9 and 11 Moorhouse Bank Cottages (early 19c.)
6014 Nos. 12 & 14 Moorhouse Bank Cottages
(1)(2) (early 19c.)
6015–6 † Moorhouse Farmhouse and Barn (16c.– 19c.)
6017–9 †† 1, 2 and 3 Moorhouse Farm Cottages (17c.–19c.)
6020 * Linear Earthwork, Covers Farm
6021
6022

PAINES HILL

6023–5 ‡ Nos. 4, 5 and 6 (Friars Cottage) (16c., with 19c. additions), Paines Hill Cottages
6026 †† Cottage south of Lock Cottage (early 18c.)
6027 †† Lock's Cottage on east side (18c.)
6028 † Strange Cottage (formerly Nos. 1 and 2) (17c.)
6029 †† Weald Cottage (formerly Gibbs Farm) (15c., with 1918 additions)

RED LANE

6030 †† Grub's Farm (early 17c.)
6031 † Old School House (16c., restored)
6032 †† Red Lane Farm (17c., with modern additions)
6033 †† Una Cottage (formerly Whitehouse Farm Cottage) (early 17c.)

LINGFIELD

GENERAL

6034 †† No. 3 Jacksbridge Manor, Jacksbridge (16c. & 17c., with modern additions)
6035 †† Chartham Park (*c.* 1830)
6036 †† Church Cottage (18c.), Church Road
6037 † Church Gate Cottage (17c. or 18c.)

Borough or District Civil Parish	No.	Name or Description of Antiquity

LINGFIELD—*contd.*

GENERAL—contd.

6038   * Dry Hill Camp

6039   ‡ Guest House (formerly Church Stile House (late 15c., restored) Vicarage Road

6040–1 † Old Town House (formerly Old Town Stores (grocer's shop)) and Cottage opposite churchyard (16c., restored)

6042–3 ⌀ Pollard Cottage (formerly Butcher's shop and ††Barn (early 15c. with 16c. additions) P. 23

6044–5 ‡ Star Inn Cottages and former †Star Inn (16c. & 18c.)

6046–8 ‡ The College House, Bakehouse and stone walls of forecourt at west end of church yard (early 18c.)

BALDWINS HILL

6049   †† Cromwell Hall (17c. and later)

6050   † Frith Manor (formerly Frith Farm) (early 17c., restored 1930)

BLACKBERRY LANE

6051–2 †† Nos. 1 and 2 Doggets Cottages (17c.)

6053   †† No. 4 (formerly Nos. 4 and 5) Doggets Cottages (17c.)

6054   †† Dormans Riding Stables (18c.)

6055   †† Cottage beside Railway (17c. & 18c.)

6056   †† Weir Courteney (15c.–18c.)

DORMANSLAND
HIGH STREET

East side

6057   †† Farthingdale Cottage (17c.)

6058   Farthingdale House (17c.)

6059   †† Hillside (early-mid 19c.)

6060   †† Hillside Cottage (17c.)

6061   †† Dormansland Baptist Chapel (1817)

6062   †† The Holly Bush (early 17c., restored)

West side

6063   †† Bassets Field Cottages (17c.)

6064–5 †† Butcher's shop and House (mid 18c.)

6066   †† Grocer's shop (17c., with later additions)

6067   Lindfield Cottages (17c.)

Borough or District Civil Parish	No.	Name or Description of Antiquity

LINGFIELD—*contd.*

DORMANSLAND
HIGH STREET—contd.

East side

6068–9 †† Lock's Cottage (two) (late 17c.)

6070 † Wall's Cottage (17c.)

6071–2 †† Cherry Cottages (two) (17c.), West Street

DORMANSLAND AREA

6073 †† Dormans Cottage (17c., restored, with additions)

6074 †† Ford Cottage (early 17c., with 19c. additions)

6075 †† Frys Cottage, West Street (late 18c.)

6076 †† Morven Lodge (*c.* 1840)

6077 †† Old Mousers (formerly Boxcote) (late 16c. or early 17c.), Lingfield-Edenbridge Road

6078 The Hidden Hut (rear of Post Office) (17c.)

6079 †† The Old Post House (early 18c.)

6080–1 †† Woodgate Cottages (two) on north side to Ford Manor

DORMANSLAND—COWDEN ROAD

6082 †† Burnt Pit (18c., with 19c. additions), Moon's Lane

6083–4 ‡ Lullenden (15c., and later restored) and ††House (formerly barn) (16c.)

6085 † Lower Stonehurst Farm (early 17c.)

6086 †† Old Lodge Farm (16c., with later alterations)

6087 † Smithers Farm (16c.)

DORMANSLAND
EAST GRINSTEAD ROAD

6088 †† Apsley Farm Barn (1765)

6089 †† Moor Hawes (17c.)

DORMANSLAND
EDENBRIDGE ROAD

6090–2 ‡ Hoopers Farm (16c. and later), ††outbuildings and Oasthouse

6093–5 † Lingfield Lodge Farmhouse, ††Barn and ††Oasthouse (17c. restored)

6096 † Moor Farm (17c.), Moor Lane

Borough or District Civil Parish	No.	Name or Description of Antiquity

LINGFIELD—contd.

DORMANSLAND
EDENBRIDGE ROAD—contd.

6097 † Old Forge Farm (16c. and mid 18c.)

6098– ‡* Starborough Castle (remains of). Walls
101   (c. 1341), Garden house (1754) within the
   moat and Stable range (mid 18c.)

6102 †† The Plough Inn (18c. with 19c. additions)

GODSTONE ROAD

6103–6 † Lynehouse Farm (16c. & 17c.), †timber
   Barn to South-west (17c.), †Granary
   (1738) and †Barn north-west of house
   (18c.)

6107 †† Porter's Hall (late 17c.)

6108   Ray Lodge (16c. & 17c.)

6109 †† Thatched Cottage (16c.)

6110 † The Old House (formerly Wheelwright's
   Cottage) (16c., restored)

6111 †† Tower Cottage (17c.)

6112 †† Wheelwright's shop (17c.)

HOLLOW LANE

6113–6 †† Nos. 1–4, Ford Estate Cottages (1920)

6117 †† Yew Tree Cottage (18c.)

6118   φ Old Surrey Hall (formerly Blockfield),
   moated (15c. and later) P. 58

LINGFIELD COMMON AREA

6119 †† Coldharbour (16c., with alterations)

6120–2 †† Paris Farmhouse and Barns (two) (15c.)
6123

LINGFIELD COMMON
Edenbridge Road

6124–6 †† Nos 1, 2 and 3 Haxted Cottages (early 19c.)

6127–8 ‡ Dwelly (15c. and early 18c.), and Barn
   (16c.), Dwelly Lane

6129   ‡ Old East Haxted (15c., 17c. and later)

6130–1 †† East Haxted Farmhouse (17c.) and Barn

6132   † Haxted House (17c., with additions 1805)

6133–4 † Haxted Mill with Stable Range (late 18c.)

6135 †† Haxted Mill House (17c.)

6136   ‡ Puttenden Manor (15c. & 16c.) P. 5

Borough or District Civil Parish	No.	Name or Description of Antiquity

LINGFIELD—*contd.*

LINGFIELD-CROWHURST ROAD

6137 †† Arden Green (formerly Bowerland Cottage) (17c.), Arden Green

6138 Arden Green Cottage (16c., restored)

6139 †† Arden Run Cottage (early 18c.), Crowhurst Road

LINGFIELD-DORMANSLAND ROAD

6140–1 † Notre Dame Convent School (formerly Batnor's Hall) (1589–1718) and wall (18c.)

6142–4 † St. Pier's Farmhouse (16c.–18c.) with converted Barn and Granary (18c.)

LINGFIELD-EAST GRINSTEAD ROAD

6145–7 †† Driver's Cottages (three) (16c., restored)

6148 †† Oaklands (formerly Felcourt) (17c. & 18c. with later additions)

6149 † Old Felcourt (formerly Felcourt House Farm) (15c., later restored)

MUTTON HILL

6150 † Apsley Town Country Hotel (15c. and 16c. with 19c. additions)

6151 †† Barn at Nobles (17c.)

6152 †† Charlock's (formerly Gardener's Cottage) (17c. and later)

6153 †† Farindons (*c.* 1820)

6154 † The Beacon (*c.* 1820)

NEWCHAPEL ROAD

6155–6 † Bricklands (16c., restored), and †† Barn (18c.)

6157 †† Crooked Cottage (17c., later restored)

6158 †† Oat Barns (early 17c.)

6159– † Rowlands Farmhouse (17c., restored),
61   †† Barn and Oasthouse (18c.)

6162 ‡ The Garth (Old Parish Workhouse) (1729)

PLAISTOW STREET

6163–7 † Nos. 1, 2, 3, 4 and 5 Billhurst Cottage (formerly Billhurst Farm) (16c., restored)

6168 ‡ Magnus Deo Farm (17c.)

Borough or District Civil Parish	No.	Name or Description of Antiquity

LINGFIELD—*contd.*

PLAISTOW STREET—*contd.*

6169–71 † Rose Cottages (three) (16c.)

6172 φ* St. Peter's Cross (*c.* 1437) and Village Cage (1773)

6173 †† The Greyhound Inn (17c., restored)

6174 †† The Little Shop (18c., restored)

6175 †† The Old Cage Café (late 16c., restored)

6176–7 The Shoe Shop (formerly Castle Stores) and ††Warehouse (18c.)

SAXBY'S LANE

6178 †† Lullenden Cottage (17c.)

STATION ROAD

6179 † The Old Cottage (18c., restored) adjoining New Place

6180–1 ‡ New Place (1617) and stone wall of garden, P. 28

6182–3 †† Old Oasthouse (18c.) and Farm buildings, New Place Farm

6184 †† Rushford Cottage (early 17c.)

6185 †† The Hatch (early 17c.)

NUTFIELD

GENERAL

6186–7 †† Nos. 30–32, High Street (17c., 18c. or early 19c.)

6188 †† Queen's Head Inn (16c.), High Street

6189–90 †† Laundry & Hawthorne Cottages (formerly Philanthropic Society's School Cottages) (17c.)

BLETCHINGLEY ROAD

6191 †† Halfway House (or Dellcroft) (late 17c.)

6192 †† The Glebe House (18c.)

COOPER'S HILL ROAD

6193 †† Kentwyns (15c. with late 16c. alterations)

6194–5 †† Porter's Lodge and Barn (17c., later restored)

Borough or District Civil Parish	No.	Name or Description of Antiquity

NUTFIELD—*contd.*

KING'S MILL LANE

6196 †† King's Mill (18c. & 19c.)
6197 †† Kings Mill House (16c. & 17c.)
6198–9 † Hamme House including garden wall (16c., altered early 19c.)

MARSH LANE

6200 †† Hall Lands (18c.)
6201 † Leather Bottle Cottage (17c.)
6202–3 †† Mercer's Farm and †† Marsh Barn (17c.)
6204–7 Marchants Place (block of four cottages) (1805)

OUTWOOD

6208 †† Little Woolborough Farm, Green Lane early 18c., restored)
6209 †† Woolborough, Hatch Lane (17c.–19c.) P. 84

RIDGE GREEN

6210 †† Crabhil Farm (16c. & 17c.)
6211–4 † Hale Farmhouse and †† Barn (16c.), †† Coachhouse and †† Granary (now a cottage) (18c.)
6215 †† Ridge Green Farmhouse (16c.–18c.)

SOUTH NUTFIELD

6216 † South Hale Farm (16c. and later), Green Lane

OXTED

GENERAL

6217– †† Nos. 1–9, Shorters Row and Cottages (2)
27 adjoining (early 19c.)
6228 †† Barn Theatre, Bluehouse Lane (1924)
6229– φ Barrow Green Court (early 17c.), Garden
31 Wall (17c., Garden House (18c.)
6232–4 ‡ Barrow Green Farm, Barn and Oasthouse (16c.)
6235 Hall Hill (18c., with later additions)
6236 * The Mount, Barrow Green
6237 †† Oxted Court (16c.–19c.)
6238–9 †† South House and Dovecot
6240 †† Village Pound (18c.), Sandy Lane
6241–2 †† Stable Block (2 cottages) at Stone Hall (1750–1760)

Borough or District Civil Parish	No.	Name or Description of Antiquity

OXTED—*contd.*

BEADLES LANE

6243 †† Oxted Mill (19c.)
6244 †† Oxted Mill Cottage (early 18c.)
6245 †† Standwell House (late 18c.)
6246–8 †† Yew Tree Cottage, Orchard and Rose Cottage (late 18c.)

BROADHAM GREEN

6249– †† Nos. 6 and 7 Harlin's Row (17c.), Tanhouse
50   Road
6251–2 ‡ Mayflower Cottages (two) (15c.)
6253 †† Oxted Place (formerly The Rectory) (early 19c., with later additions)
6254–6 †† Perrysfield Farmhouse, Barn and Granary (17c. & 18c.)
6257   Roundhurst House (18c.)
6258 ‡ Stocketts Manor House (15c., refaced early 17c.)
6259– †† Stocketts Manor Barn (17c.) and Oast-
60   house (18c.)
6261 †† The Old Rectory Cottage (formerly the Rectory) (17c., with later additions), Oxted Place
6262 ‡ The Old Cottage (early 16c.) (later restored, with additions)

BROOK HILL

6263–4 † Nos. 1 and 2 (formerly Best's Cottages) (18c.)
6265 †† Brook House (17c.)

GIBBS BROOK LANE

6266 †† Perryfield (early 19c.)
6267 †† Rose Farm (late 16c.)

HIGH STREET

6268–9 † Nos. 1 and 2 Berry's Cottages (18c.)
6270–3 † Nos. 1, 2, 3 and 4 (15c.–18c.) Crown Hill
6274–5 †† Nos. 1 and 2 (18c.), Dairy Cottages
6276–8 ‡ Beam Cottage and † No. 2 and Forge Cottage (15c.–18c.)
6279 ‡ The Old Bell Inn (16c., with later additions)

OXTED—*contd.*

HIGH STREET—*contd.*

6280-2 † Bennetts (two Cottages east of approach to Shorter's Row) and †Old Lock-up (16c.–18c.)

6283-5 † Butcher's shop, ††Stable and ††slaughterhouse, (disused) (R.P. Smith) (17c.)

6286 †† Crown Inn (17c. and earlier)

6287-9 † Flaxman Cottages and two adjacent cottages (17c.)

6290 †† George Inn (16c.–18c. and later)

6291 † London Stores (early 18c.)

6292-4 † Lenton's Dairy and Ivy Cottage and adjoining Cottage (18c.)

6295 †† Post Office (north wing) (17c.)

6296– ‡ Shrine Cottage, Shrine Terrace, Terrace
300 Cottage, Streeters Cottage, Crown Hill (15c. and later)

6301-2 † The Old Cottage and adjoining premises (16c.)

HURST GREEN

6303 †† Colstford Mill (17c.), Mill Lane

6304 †† Comforts Farm Cottage (18c.)

6305 †† Holly Cottage (18c., with 19c. addition)

6306 †† Old Meldrum (formerly Ramshack) (early 17c.)

6307 * Packhorse Bridge, Home Farm (17c.)

6308-9 †† Foyle Riding and Barn (17c., restored), Red Lane

6310 †† Sheppards Barn (early 16c.)

6311-2 † Sunt Farmhouse (early 17c.) and Barn (16c.), Caterfield Lane

6313 †† The Home Farm (early 18c.)

6314 The Pound (18c.)

POPES LANE

6315 † Foyle Farm (late 16c. & 17c.)

6316 † Gincocks Farm (formerly Janecocks) (17c.)

6317 †† Merle Common Cottages (18c.)

6318 † Merle Common House (formerly Old Foyle) (16c., restored)

Borough or District Civil Parish	No.	Name or Description of Antiquity

OXTED—*contd.*

WOODHURST PARK

6319–20 †† Flint House (now 2 cottages) Whistler's Wood (17c. & 19c.)

6321–2 †† Hoders & Hoders Cottage (formerly Stables) (18c.)

TANDRIDGE

GENERAL

6323–7 †† Newhouse Farmhouse, Two Barns, Granary and Stables (18c.)

6328   † Oldhall Farm (16c. with 17c. additions)

6329   † Ouborough (formerly Rooksnest), Moot Hill (1775–1781 and early 19c.)

6330   †† The Priory (18c. and early 19c.)

BLINDSLEY HEATH

6331   †† Clacks Cottages, east side of Heath (early 18c.)

6332   Martyn's Platt (16c., with later additions)

6333   † Moat Farm (*c.* 1800)

6334–5 ‡ The Red Barn (formerly Snouts Farm) (15c. with 17c. and modern additions) and Barn (late 17c.)

SOUTHLANDS LANE

6336   †† Southlands (early 19c.)

TANDRIDGE LANE

6337   The Barley Mow (P.H.) (*c.* 1820)

6338   †† Brook Cottage on the west side of the lane near Gibbs Brook (16c. with later additions)

6339   Brook Farm (*c.* 1750)

6340   †† Flagpole Cottage (probably 1743)

6341   ‡ Hobbs Farm (15c. with 17c. additions)

6342   †† Tandridge Court (1926–7)

6343   †† Tandridge Court Lodge (early 19c.)

6344   †† Tandridge Hill Farm (formerly Laundry Cottages) (17c. and later)

6345–8 †† Nos. 1–4 Step Arbour Cottages at rear of the Barley Mow (P.H.) (17c. & 18c.)

Borough or District Civil Parish	No.	Name or Description of Antiquity
TATSFIELD		*GENERAL*
	6349	† Colegates (formerly Calcotts and Ken Court) (15c. with 17c. and modern additions)
	6350	†† Grasshopper Inn (17c. with 19c. additions), Moorhouse Bank
	6351	†† Manor House (formerly Godards Farm and Bucklands Farm) (17c. with modern additions)
	6352	†† Tatsfield Court Farm (late 18c.)
	6353	†† Westwood Farm, Clacket Lane (late 18c.)
	6354	* Linear Earthwork, Cover's Farm
TITSEY		*GENERAL*
	6355	†† Broomlands Farm (17c., refaced late 18c. or early 19c.)
	6356	†† Cheverell's Farm (formerly Chevelers Manor House) (16c. and later)
	6357–60	† Nos. 1–4 Church Cottages (four) (16c. and later)
	6361	† Botley Hill Farm (late 16c., with modern additions), Limpsfield Road
	6362	** Foundation of a Romano-Celtic Temple in Church Field, Pilgrims' Lodge Farm
	6363	†† Pitchfont, Pitchfont Lane (18c.)
	6364	* Remains of Roman Villa in Titsey Park
	6365	†† Titsey Court (early 18c.)
	6366	†† Titsey Place (1770–1780, with remains of 17c. house)
		SOUTH GREEN
	6367–8	Cottages (two) on west side (17c., with 19c. additions)

LEATHERHEAD URBAN DISTRICT

ASHTEAD

		CITY OF LONDON CORPORATION BOUNDARY POSTS
	6369	500 yards N.W. of Highfield Farm, Dorking Road

Borough or District Civil Parish	No.	Name or Description of Antiquity

ASHTEAD—*contd.*

GENERAL

6370   Ashtead Lodge, Parkers Hill (late 18c.)

6371–2 †Ashtead Park House (City of London Freemen's School) (1790) and Headmaster's House (1734), Ashtead Park, P. 79

6373   † The Old Bakery (17c.), Crampshaw Lane

6374   †† The Old Cottage (16c. & 17c.), Ottway's Lane

6375–6 †† Nos. 33 and 35 (The Cottage) (17c. & 18c.), Woodfield Lane

6377   *Mediaeval sunk trackway at north end of churchyard (St. Giles Church) (date 13c.) by excavation 1933, this trackway led to the early mediaeval Manor House)

6378   *Roman Villa in Ashtead Forest

6379   *Stane Street (Roman road)

6380   *Triangular enclosure in Ashtead Forest (probably of Roman date as similar enclosures elsewhere, and connected with the nearby Roman villa and brickworks)

AGATES LANE

6381–2 †† Nos. 60 and 62 (16c. & 17c.)

6383   † Merry Hall (18c.)

FARM LANE

6384   † Ashtead House (*c.* 1740)

6385   ‡ Ashtead Park Farm House (early 18c.) P. 65

RECTORY LANE

6386   †† No. 12, Fowler's Cottage (16c. & 17c.) P. 115

6387–8 †† ¹No. 18 Applebough (formerly Barons' Cottages) and No. 20 (16c. & 17c.) P. 126

6389–90 †† No. 24, Old Forge Cottage, and No. 26, Wistaria Cottage (formerly Forge Cottage) (16c.)

6391   † The Old Rectory (18c.)

THE STREET

6392–3 † Nos. 44 and 46 (17c.)

6394–5   Nos. 55 and 57 (17c.)

¹ See Homes & Gardens, November 1960

Borough or District Civil Parish	No.	Name or Description of Antiquity

GREAT BOOKHAM

GENERAL

6396–8 † Bookham Grove (1750), Stables and House to east (18c.)

6399 †† Old Pound Cottages (16c.), The Street

6400 † Foxglove Cottage (17c.), Station Road

6401 † Polesden Lacey (1824) (N.T.)

6402–3 † Sheepbell Farm and Barn (17c.), Cobham Road

6404 φ Slyfield House (1614)

6405–6 φ The Barn (formerly Slyfield Farm) and outbuilding to S.W.

6407 †† Walnut Tree Cottages (1750), Townshot Close

6408–9 †† Nos. 1 and 2 Grove Cottages, Guildford Road (formerly Saracen & Ring Hotel) (16c. & 17c.)

CHURCH ROAD

East side

6410 †† Dawnay Cottage (formerly The Old Almshouse) (early 19c.)

West side

6411–4 † Nos. 1–4 (15c. with 17c. additions)

6415–7 Nos. 5–7 Church Cottages (17c. & 18c.)

6418–9 † Nos. 1 and 2 Gables Cottage (16c. and later)

6420 † Corner House (formerly the King's Arms (P.H.) (16c.–18c.)

6421–2 †† Gothic House and Post Office (early 19c.)

6423 †† The Tyrells (17c.)

HIGH STREET

East side

6424–6 †† Nos. 5, 7 and 9 (Donaldson, Clothier) and (Eatons and Heathers) (16c. & 17c.)

6427 † No. 19 (Old Forge Cottage) (17c.)

6428–9 † Nos. 27 and 33 (Warrell & Sons and M. A. Perry) (16c.)

6430 † Jackson's (Granaries) and outbuildings (16c.–19c.)

6431 †† Vine Cottage (*c.* 1800)

West side

6432–4 † Nos. 18, 20 and 22 (Royal Oak Cottages) (mid 18c.)

14

Borough or District Civil Parish	No.	Name or Description of Antiquity

GREAT BOOKHAM
—contd.

HIGH STREET—contd.
West side

6435–6 ‡ Nos. 28 and 30 (Englands) (16c.), Victoria Cottages, P. 116
6437 †† Burpham (formerly Franton's) (early 19c.)
6438 † The Royal Oak (P.H.) (17c.)
6439 † Fairfield House (early 18c.) (with modern additions)
6440-2 † Nos. 18, 20 and 22, Royal Oak Cottages (mid 18c.)

LOWER ROAD

6443 † Anchor Inn (formerly The Red Lion) (17c.)
6444 †† Eastwick Cottage (17c. & 18c.)
6445 † Halfway (corner of Child's Hall Road) (16c., 17c. and later)
6446 †† Hop Garden Cottage (17c. & 18c.)
6447 † The Hermitage (formerly Fairfield House) (18c. with later additions)
6448 † Woodcote (16c. & 17c.)

LITTLE BOOKHAM

GENERAL

6449 † Half Moon Cottage (formerly "Rolts") Preston Cross (16c.), P. 122
6450–1 †† Maddox Farm and †† Barn, Little Bookham Street (18c.)
6452–3 Manor Farm and † Tithe Barn (near church) (probably 17c.)
6454 ‡ The Manor House (near church) (early 18c.)
6455 †† The Old Rectory (18c., with additions), Rectory Lane

STATION ROAD

6456 † Dawes Cottage (16c.)
6457 †† Post Cottage (17c. & 18c.)
6458 †† Rose Cottage (late 18c.)
6459 † The Windsor Castle (P.H.) (formerly Potter's) (16c., with modern alterations) P. 117

orough or District *Civil Parish*	*No.*	*Name or Description of Antiquity*

FETCHAM

GENERAL

6460 † Fetcham Cottage (18c.), Bell Lane

6461–2 Highwayman's Cottage (Old Cottage) (16c.) and Rose Cottage (17c.), Fetcham Common Lane (formerly Kennel Lane)

6463–5 †Roaring House Farm, Barn and outbuildings (16c. & 17c.)

6466 †The Old Rising Sun (formerly P.H. now restaurant) (15c. and later)

COBHAM ROAD

6467 †Orchard Cottage (late 17c.) P. 118

LOWER ROAD

6468 †Badingham College (formerly Fetcham Park) (1740–1770, with later alterations)

6469 ††The Salt Box (18c.) P. 119

THE STREET

6470–1 †Nos. 75 (Yew Tree Cottage) and 77 (Tea Tree Cottage) (17c.)

6472–3 Ballands Hall and Little Ballands (17c. and early 19c.)

6474–5 †Home Farm and outbuildings (17c. & 18c.)

LEATHERHEAD

CITY OF LONDON CORPORATION BOUNDARY POSTS

6476 The Star (P.H.), Telegraph Hill

GENERAL

6477 † Barnett Wood Farm (17c. and 18c.), Barnett Wood Lane

6478 * Barrows north-east of Cherkley Court, Leatherhead Downs

6479–80 Bockett's Farm and Great Barn (18c.), Norbury Park Estate

6481 †The Cottage (17c.), Bull Hill

6482–4 †Highlands Farm (*c.* 1800), ††Barns (17c.) and ††Well house (18c.), Headley Road

6485 † Leatherhead Bridge (1783)

6486 *Moated Manor House, site known as "The Mounts" (*c.* 1200–1350), (the moat dug 1290–1291) (site excavated 1947–1949)

Borough or District Civil Parish	No.	Name or Description of Antiquity

LEATHERHEAD   *GENERAL—contd.*

—contd. 6487–8   †Pachesham Farm and ††cottage to N.W (16c. & 17c.), Randall's Road

      6489   ‡Rowhurst (16c. & 17c.), Oxshott Road

      6490   *Stane Street (Roman road) on Leatherhead Downs from Millway to Micklehan Downs

BRIDGE STREET

      6491   †No. 5 (early 19c.)

      6492   †No. 15 (17c.)

      6493   †No. 26 (Newbridge Restaurant), (19c.)

      6494–7   †Nos. 28, 30, 32 and 34 (early 19c.)

      6498   ‡The Running Horse (P.H.) (1520) P. 120

      6499   †No. 17 (17c.)

      6500–1   †No. 25 and 27 (17c. & 18c.)

      6502   †No. 31 (early 19c.)

      6503–4   †Nos. 39 and 41 (17c.)

      6505   ††No. 37 (Yardleys) (late 18c.)

      6506   †No. 43 (early 19c.)

CHURCH ROAD

      6507   †No. 18 (early 18c.)

      6508–9   ††Nos. 25 and 27 (early 19c.)

CHURCH STREET

      6510–1   †Nos. 1 and 3 (late 17c.) (see also High Street, No. 2)

      6512–4   †No. 17 and Cottages, Nos. 1 and 2 at rear (16c. & 17c.)

      6515   ‡No. 33 (The Cottage) (16c. & 17c. with 18c. front) P. 121

      6516   †No. 35 (formerly Moss Cottage) (probably 16c.)

      6517   †No. 64 (formerly No. 28) (16c. & 17c.)

      6518   †No. 66 (formerly No. 30, Devonshire Cottage) (16c. and later)

      6519–20   ‡The Mansion and outbuildings (*c.* 1739)

DORKING ROAD

      6521–2   †Thorncroft Manor House and Lodge (1772)

      6523–4   †Vale Lodge and Stable Block (18c.)

Borough or District Civil Parish	No.	Name or Description of Antiquity

LEATHERHEAD

GRAVEL HILL

—*contd.* 6525-7 † Nos. 2, 4 and 6 (formerly Sweech Farm now Sweech House) (16c., later restored) P. 97

6528-9 † Nos. 16 and 18 (1799)

HIGH STREET

6530 † No. 2 (late 17c.) (See also Church Street Nos. 1 and 3)

6531 † No. 8 (18c.)

6532 † No. 10 (18c.)

6533-5 † Nos. 27, 29, and 31 (late 17c. & 18c.)

6536-7 † Nos. 33 and 35 (formerly Nos. 23 and 25) (16c.)

6538-9 † Nos. 43 and 45 (16c. & 17c.)

6540 † The Duke's Head (P.H.) (17c. with 19c. front)

KINGSTON ROAD

6541-2 † Nos. 109 and 111 (*c.* 1800)

STOKE D'ABERNON ROAD

6543 †† Patsom Cottage (16c.)

6544 † Patsom Farm Cottage (16c.)

REIGATE BOROUGH

GATTON

GATTON PARK

6545 † North Lodge (early 19c.)

6546 † Town Hall (late 18c.)

UPPER GATTON

6547 †† Crossways Farm (17c., much altered)

6548 Old Forge (16c. and later), High Road

6549 †† Old Trees (18c.), High Road

6550 † Upper Gatton Park (18c.)

MERSTHAM

GENERAL

6551 † Alderstead Farm (17c.), Alderstead Lane

6552 * Earthworks of Surrey Iron Railway

6553 Limeworks Cottage (18c.)

6554 †† Harps Oak (16c. & 17c., with modern additions), London Road North

6555-7 †† Hoaths Farm, Barn and Granary (17c.)

Borough or District Civil Parish	No.	Name or Description of Antiquity

MERSTHAM—*contd.*

GENERAL—*contd.*

6558   *Moated site of Albury Manor

6559   ¹Portions of track of The Croydon, Merstham and Godstone Iron Railway (Surrey Iron Railway), in Greystone Lime Works (1803–1805)

SCHOOL HILL

6560   ††No. 8 (The Golden Wheel Tea Rooms) (17c.)

6561   ††No. 10 (Barn Cottage) (18c.)

6562–7 ††Nos. 16 (Tudor Cottage) to 26 Parkstile Cottages (17c. & 18c.)

GATTON BOTTOM ROAD

6568   †The Rectory (18c.)

6569   ††Wellhead (17c.)

HIGH STREET

6570   ††No. 23 (Hawthornden) (early 19c.)

6571   ††No. 26 (1791)

6572–3 ††Nos. 31 and 33 (17c.)

6574   ††No. 34 (18c.)

LONDON ROAD

6575   Foxshaw (formerly Fox Inn) (17c.)

6576–7 ††The Old Saddlery and Old Tye Place (18c.)

6578   ††Weighbridge Cottage (1803–5)

QUALITY STREET

6579   ††No. 143 (Merstham Garage) (1796)

6580   ††Home Farm (late 17c., 18c. & 19c.)

6581   †Mead Cottages (16c.–18c.)

6582–3 †Old Manor (17c.) and Court Cottage (late 16c.)

6584   †Prior's Mead (formerly Parsons Mead) (17c.)

6585   ††St. Nicholas Cottage (18c., refronted)

6586   †The Old Forge (15c., restored and enlarged)

6587   †The Old School House (1816)

¹ Erected in 1951 by Surrey County Council on site adj. The Jolliffe Arms (P.H.) Brighton Road, Merstham

Borough or District Civil Parish	No.	Name or Description of Antiquity

REIGATE

GENERAL

6588 †† No. 26 (early 19c.), London Road

6589– † Nos. 6 and 10 (16c. & 17c.), Slipshoe Street
90

6591 No. 8 (16c. & 17c.), Slipshoe Street

6592 † No. 20 (The Old House) (18c.), Upper West Street

6593 †† Clayhall Farm (18c.), Clayhall Lane

6594 †† Cockshut (early 19c.), Park Lane East

6595 Flanchford Farm (formerly Flanchford Place) (16c. and later)

6596 †† Littleton Farm (18c.), Littleton Lane

6597– φ*¹Reigate Priory (13c., rebuilt 1780) and
8 ††Garden wall (18c.) P. 60

6599 † Ricebridge Farm (17c. and earlier)

6600 †† Rose Cottage, Cockshot Hill (late 18c.)

6601 Santon House (17c. and later)

6602 †† Whitehall Farm, No. 211 (Sandcross Lane) South Park (17c.)

6603 * Site of Reigate Castle

6604 † The Old Manor House (formerly Colley House Farm) (17c. and later), Clifton Lane

6605 † The Angel Inn (formerly The White Horse) (17c., restored), Woodhatch Road

BELL STREET

6606–7 †† Nos. 8 and 10 (18c. with modern shop front)

6608–9 † Nos. 15 and 15A (19c. & 20c.)

6610–1 † Nos. 16 and 18 (early 19c.)

6612–3 †† Nos. 23 and 25 (18c., with modern shop front)

6614–5 † Nos. 37 and 39 (18c., with modern shop front)

6616 † No. 38 (early 18c.)

6617 †† No. 40 (early 18c. with modern shop front)

6618–9 †† Nos. 43 and 45 (19c. & 20c.)

6620–1 †† Nos. 77 and 79 (1815)

6622 †† No. 107 (*c.* 1840)

6623 †† No. 109 (early 19c.)

6624 †† No. 111 (St. Michael's) (18c.)

¹ Main Southern Wing scheduled as an Ancient Monument, March 1951

Borough or District Civil Parish	No.	Name or Description of Antiquity

REIGATE—*contd.*

CHART LANE
6625 †† No. 1 (Delville) (1840–1850)
6626–8 †† No. 2 (Churchfelle) (*c.* 1840), ruins and stone gateway

CHURCH STREET
6629 † No. 48 (The Cottage) (early 19c.)
6630–2 †† Nos. 31, 33 and 35 (18c.)
6633 † The Barons (18c.)

REDHILL
6634–5 †† Nos. 1 and 2 (Copyhold Cottages) (17c.) Cavendish Road
6636–7 †† Nos. 82 (Claremont) and 84 (Belmont) (1830) London Road
6638 †† Chart Lodge (*c.* 1840), Nutfield Road
6639 †† The Firs (early 19c.), Brighton Road

CORMONGERS LANE
6640 †† Chilmead Farm (18c.)
6641 †† Cormongers (19c.)

LINKFIELD LANE
6642 †† No. 16 (late 17c.)
6643 † No. 36 (late 17c.)
6644–5 † Nos. 38 and 40 (late 17c.)
6646 †† No. 42 Warwick Lodge (late 18c.)

LINKFIELD STREET
6647–8 †† Nos. 73 and 73A (18c.)
6649 † Fengates House (18c.)

MILL STREET
6650 †† No. 1 (Old Garlands) (18c.)
6651–2 †† Nos. 5 and 7 (17c.)

DOVERS GREEN ROAD
6653 †† Dovers Farm (18c. and later)
6654 †† Dovers Farm Lodge (17c.)
6655 †† Ivy Cottage (18c.)
6656 † Hartswood Manor (17c. and later)
6657 †† Hartswood Manor Lodge (early 19c.)
6658 †† The Cottage (17c.)

Borough or District Civil Parish	No.	Name or Description of Antiquity

REIGATE—contd.

FLANCHFORD ROAD

6659 †† Bottle Cottage (18c. and later)
6660 † Santon Farm (formerly Gilbert's Farm) (17c. and earlier)

HIGH STREET

6661 No. 20 (17c. and later)
6662–4 Nos. 25, 27 and 29 (18c.)
6665–7 †† Nos. 28, 30 and 32 (18c.)
6668 †† No. 34 (18c.)
6669 No. 42 (17c. & 18c.)
6670–2 †† Nos. 44, †46 and ††50 (17c. & 18c.)
6673 No. 48 (17c. & 18c.)
6674 No. 51B (late 17c.)
6675 † No. 55 (The Bull's Head (P.H.)) (18c., refronted)
6676 †† No. 57 (18c., with modern shop front)
6677 † No. 65 (early 18c.)
6678 No. 67 (early 19c.)
6679 †† No. 70 (18c.)
6680–5 Nos. 72, 74, 76, 78, 80 and 82 (18c.)
6686 † No. 77 (includes Bellingham, Butchers) (18c.)
6687 *† The Old Town Hall (c. 1728)

PARK LANE

6688 †† No. 12 (Geranium Cottage) (early 19c.)
6689 † Priory Lake Cottage (18c.)

REIGATE HEATH

6690 * Group of Seven Barrows
6691 † Windmill (now a Chapel) (1765, restored 1964)

TRUMPETS HILL ROAD

6692–3 † June Farm and Cottage adjoining (17c. and later)
6694 †† Little Santon Farm (18c.)
6695 † Miller's Cottage (late 17c. and early 18c.)

Borough or District Civil Parish	No.	Name or Description of Antiquity

REIGATE—*contd.*

WEST STREET

6696 †† No. 16A (*mediaeval undercroft only)

6697–8 †† Nos. 19 and 21 (18c., refronted)

6699 ‡ No. 22 (Brown's Lodge) (*c.* 1780)

6700 †† No. 22A (St. Albans) (*c.* 1838)

6701–2 †† Nos. 27 (Blue Anchor (P.H.)) and 29 (17c.)

6703 †† No. 31 (early 19c.)

6704 †† No. 36 (Ye Olde Forge) (17c.)

6705 † No. 38 (Old West Street House) (18c.)

WRAY COMMON

6706 † The Windmill (1824)

6707 † Wray Farm (17c.)

A SHORT BIBLIOGRAPHY OF BOOKS ON SURREY

GENERAL HISTORIES

BRITANNIA. (SURREY AND SUSSEX). William Camden. 1607, translated. 1806.
THE NATURAL HISTORY AND ANTIQUITIES OF THE COUNTY OF SURREY. Richard Rawlinson.
 1719 (includes PERAMBULATION OF SURREY by John Aubrey. 1673-.)
THE HISTORY OF THE ANTIQUITIES OF THE COUNTY OF SURREY. Rev. Owen Manning and
 William Bray. 1804. 1814. 1847.
A TOPOGRAPHICAL HISTORY OF SURREY. Edward Brayley. 1841-8. 1850. revised 1878-81.
A HISTORY OF SURREY. H. E. Malden. 1900. 1920.
VICTORIA COUNTY HISTORY OF ENGLAND. SURREY. ed. H. E. Malden.
 1902-12.
THE PLACE OF SURREY IN THE HISTORY OF ENGLAND. F. J. C. Hearnshaw. 1936.

POCKET GUIDES

BLACK'S GUIDE TO SURREY. J. E. Morris. 1883. 1926.
SURREY. (Little Guide.) J. C. Cox. 1910. revised E. F. Peeler. 1952.
THE KING'S ENGLAND. SURREY. ed. Arthur Mee. 1938. (now issued as 'THE QUEEN'S ENGLAND
 SURREY').
SURREY. (Buildings of Britain), Ian Nairn and Nikolaus Pevsner. 1962.
SURREY. (Penguin Guide.) F. R. Banks. 1956.

GENERAL WORKS

FIELD PATHS AND GREEN LANES IN SURREY AND SUSSEX. Louis J. Jennings. 1877. 1907.
SURREY HIGHWAYS, BYWAYS AND WATERWAYS. C. R. B. Barrett. 1895.
OLD WEST SURREY. Gertrude Jekyll. 1904.
SURREY. Hope Moncreiff. ill. Sutton Palmer. 1906.
HIGHWAYS AND BYWAYS IN SURREY. Eric Parker. ill. Hugh Thomson. 1908. 1937.
MEMORIALS OF OLD SURREY. J. C. Cox. 1911.
A WEST SURREY SKETCH-BOOK. W. Hyde. 1913.
A PILGRIMAGE INTO SURREY. J. S. Ogilvy. 1914.
THE CHARM OF OLD SURREY. H. M. Alderman. n.d.
COMPANION INTO SURREY. L. Collison-Morley. 1938. 1949.
THE ARCHAEOLOGY OF SURREY. D. C. Whimster. 1931.
THE SURREY HILLS. W. A. Poucher. 1949.
SURREY ANTHOLOGY. Eric Parker. 1952.

TOWN AND VILLAGE HISTORIES

ALFOLD. F. W. Cobb. 1935.
BANSTEAD. Sir Henry Lambert. 2 vols. 1912.
BARNES. J. E. Anderson. 1900.
BARNES. Publications of Borough of Barnes Historical Society.
BEDDINGTON. T. Bentham. 1923.
BLETCHINGLEY. U. Lambert. 1949.
BYFLEET. Leonard R. Stephens. 1953.
CARSHALTON, HISTORY OF- G. B. Brightling. 1882.
CHARLWOOD, THE FREE MEN OF- Ruth Sewill and Elisabeth Lane. 1951.

CROYDON IN THE PAST. 1883.

DORKING AND LEATHERHEAD. J. E. Morris. 1906.

EGHAM. Frederick Turner. 2 vols. 1926.

EPSOM. Gordon Home. 1901.

EWELL AND NONSUCH. C. J. Willis. 1948.

FARNHAM, MEDIAEVAL-. Etienne Robo. 1935.

FARNHAM, BUILDINGS AND PEOPLE (enlarged from 'Farnham Inheritance'). Nigel Temple. 1963.

GODALMING AND ITS SURROUNDINGS. T. F. W. Hamilton. 1900.

GODSTONE. U. Lambert. 1929.

GUILDFORD IN OLDEN TIME. G. C. Williamson. 1904.

HASLEMERE IN HISTORY. G. R. Rolston. 1956.

KINGSTON, THE ROYAL BOROUGH OF-. Dr. W. E. St.J. Finney. 1902.

LEATHERHEAD. See Dorking.

LIMPSFIELD. See Oxted.

LINGFIELD, HISTORY OF-. Hayward and Hazell. 1933.

MALDEN, A HISTORY OF-. K. N. Ross. 1947.

MERROW, THE VILLAGE OF-. Frank Johnson. 1876.

MERSTHAM, A SHORT ACCOUNT OF THE ANTIENT PARISH OF-. R. I. Woodhouse. 1911

MERTON AND MORDEN, HISTORY OF-. Evelyn M. Jowett. 1951.

MORTLAKE. A History of the Parish. J. E. Anderson. 1886.

OXTED AND LIMPSFIELD AND NEIGHBOURHOOD. ed Lewis G. Fry. 1932.

REIGATE. Wilfrid Hooper. 1945.

RICHMOND. Kathleen Courlander. 1953.

SURBITON. R. W. C. Richardson. 1888.

SUTTON. R. P. Smith. 1960.

SUTTON AND CHEAM. C. J. Marshall. 1936.

WIMBLEDON. ILLUSTRATED DETAILS, ETC. S. C. Hall. 1872.

WOKING AND RIPLEY. Handbook. 1905.

BUILDING TYPES AND GARDENS

OLD COTTAGES AND DOMESTIC ARCHITECTURE IN SOUTH-WEST SURREY. Ralph Nevill. 1889.

OLD COTTAGES AND FARM-HOUSES IN SURREY. W. G. Davis and W. Curtis Green. 1908.

OLD SURREY WATERMILLS. J. Hillier. 1951.

SURREY GARDENS. Eric Parker. 1954.

BUILDINGS

CHERTSEY ABBEY. Lucy Wheeler. 1905.

HAM HOUSE. Mrs. C. Roundell. 1904.

NONSUCH, THE QUEST FOR-. John Dent. 1962.

(SUTTON PLACE). ANNALS OF AN OLD MANOR-HOUSE. Frederick Harrison. 1889.

WAVERLEY ABBEY. Harold Brakspear. 1905.

MISCELLANEOUS

SURREY ARCHAEOLOGICAL COLLECTIONS. Volume I. 1858 to Volume LXI. 1964. (Volumes issued yearly).

DOMESDAY BOOK. Facsimile 1861. Translation. 1862.

THE PLACE NAMES OF SURREY. (English Place-Name Society. Vol. XI.) J. E. B. Glover, A. Mawer and F. M. Stenton. 1934.

CLASSIFIED INDEX

* Indicates that a brief description is included in the Introduction.

Numbers in bold type after names are those of photographic plates.

I. PREHISTORIC SITES

(a) CAMPS.

LIST NO.	NAME	O.S. GRID REF.
5205.	Capel. *Anstiebury.*	153440.
1527.	Caterham. *War Coppice.*	329533.
127.	Chertsey. *St. Anne's Hill.*	027677.
2019.	Farnham. *Caesar's.*	835500.
4365.	Hascombe. *Hascombe Hill.*	005387.
5055.	Holmbury. *Holmbury Hill.*	104430.

LIST NO.	NAME	O.S. GRID REF.
6038.	Lingfield. *Dry Hill.*	413417.
3383.	Puttenham. *Hillbury.*	911468.
385.	Walton-on-Thames. *St. George's Hill.*	806618.
1996.	Wimbledon. *Caesar's.*	224711.

*(b) BARROWS.

LIST NO.	LOCATION	O.S. GRID REF.
3033.	Albury. Newlands Corner.	046493.
1273.	Banstead. Galley Hills. (4).	250607.
1275.	Banstead. Tumble Beacon. (once 10).	243591.
108.	Chertsey. NNW Flutters Gill Ho.	993653.
109.	Chertsey. SSW Flutters Hill.	991647.
110.	Chertsey. SE Longcross House.	983648.
13.	Chobham. Sunningdale.	953665.
76.	Chobham. 'Triple' Barrows. W. End Common. (4).	934613.
4831.	Dorking. Box Hill.	585513.
4832.	Dorking. Milton Heath.	153489.
4208.	Elstead. Triple. Crooksbury Cmn. (3).	894449.
	*Farnham. Badshot Lea Long Barrow. (Destroyed).	861480.
2023.	Farnham. Charles Hill. (5).	887449.
4315.	Frensham. E. of Great Pond. (4)	854407.
5958.	Godstone. Hillyfield. (2).	348516/8.
457.	Horsell. Woodham Lane.	027608.
6478.	Leatherhead. NE. Cherkley Court. (4).	183547.

LIST NO.	LOCATION	O.S. GRID REF.
3339.	Ockham. S. of Currie's Clump.	079588.
3382.	Puttenham. Frowsbury Mound. P. Heath.	939477.
6690.	Reigate. Reigate Heath. (7).	237505.
3476.	St. Martha's. Tyting Farm.	020487.
3492.	Seale. S. of Littleworth Clump.	9045.
3493.	Seale. Soldiers Ring.	880462.
3494.	Seale. N. of Turners Hill. Crooksbury Cmn.	891454.
3778.	Wisley. Cockcrow Hill. (2).	079592.
3779.	Wisley. W. of Cockcrow Hill.	075592.
3780.	Wisley. Foxwarren Park.	079600.
4470.	Witley. SE. of Half Moon Hill.	919402.
505.	Woking. SE. of Horsell Common. **1a.**	017598.
506.	Woking. do. **1a.**	014598.
3803.	Worplesdon. W. of Mt. Pleasant. Whitmoor Common. (2).	985534.
3804.	Worplesdon. Whitmoor Cmn. W. of A.320.	997537.
5525.	Wotton. In Deerleap Wood.	118480.

(c) OTHER EARTHWORKS.

LIST NO.	LOCATION	O.S. GRID REF.
	*Abinger. Mesolithic Pit-Dwellings.	112458.
1409.	Banstead. Banstead Heath.	230553/4.
		236555.
		237536.
5720.	Chelsham. Quernstone Wkgs. Worms Heath.	579578.
113.	Chertsey. Bee Garden nr. Childown Hall.	193581.
115.	Chertsey. Laleham Burway. (2)	048683.
		045680.
10.	Chobham. Bee Garden. Albury Bottom.	975643.
672.	Cobham. Chatley Heath. (Circular).	086587.
1581.	Coulsdon. Newe Ditch. Riddlesdown.	323606.

LIST NO.	LOCATION	O.S GRID REF.
1582.	Coulsdon. Fields. Farthing Down.	299576.
	Farnham. Mesolithic Pit-Dwellings.	851478.
2022.	Farnham. SW. of Botany Hill.	875463.
4290.	Frensham. On Golf Links. Hindhead.	862372.
5863.	Godstone. Lagham Park.	364480.
3366.	Pirbright. (Hut Circles?). Bulswater Common.	954545.
3381.	Puttenham. (Circle) near Frowsbury.	939476.
3497.	St. Martha's. (2 Circles). SSE slope of St. Martha's Hill.	028483.
1597.	Sanderstead. (Hut Circles) Croham Hurst.	337635.
6354.	Tatsfield. Cross-Valley Dyke. Cove Farm.	422539.

II. ROMAN SITES

(a) VILLAS.

LIST NO.	LOCATION	O.S. GRID REF.
6378.	Ashtead.	179602.
4026.	Chiddingfold.	979362.
3187.	Compton.	958481.

LIST NO.	LOCATION	O.S. GRID REF.
1580.	Coulsdon. (Farmstead).	288566.
2262.	Farnham. (Six Bells.) 1b.	852478.
1459.	Walton-on-the-Hill.	223556.

(b) TEMPLES.

3049.	Albury. Farley Heath.	053450.
6302.	Titsey.	421547.

III. RELIGIOUS BUILDINGS

(a) MONASTERIES. (Pre-Reformation).

LIST NO.	NAME
Austin Canons.	
1845/54.	Merton Priory.
*3471.	Newark Priory. 2a.
	Reigate Priory.
	Tandridge Priory.
Benedictines.	
*125/136.	Chertsey Abbey.
	Sandon Hospital. (Esher).

LIST NO.	NAME
Carthusians.	
	Richmond Priory.
Cistercians.	
*2193.	Waverley Abbey. 2b.
Friars.	
Dominicans.	Guildford.
Observants.	Richmond.

(b) CHURCHES & CHAPELS.

(Not in regular use for worship.)

LIST NO.	PARISH
3017.	Albury. *Cath. Apost. Church.*
3050.	Artington. *St Catherine's Chapel.*
128.	Chertsey. *St. Anne's Chapel.*
3184.	Compton. *Watts Mem. Chapel.*
274.	Egham.
737.	Esher.
1768.	Ewell.
2429.	Godalming. (*Tuesday.*)
2705.	Guildford. *St. Nicholas Ch. Loseley Chapel.*
5326.	Headley.
976.	Kingston-upon-Thames. *Lovekyn's or St. Mary Magdalen's Chantry* **3b**.
799.	Long Ditton.
4971.	Mickleham. *West Humble Chapel.*
1893.	Mitcham.
1932.	Sutton. *Lumley Chapel.*
1964.	do. *Gibson Mausoleum.*

(c) CHAPELS AND MEETING HOUSES.

(Non-Conformist).

LIST NO.	PARISH
5217.	Capel. *Friends.*
728.	Esher. *Friends*
2038.	Farnham. *Baptists.*
2559.	Godalming. *Friends.*
2867.	Guildford. *Friends.*
6061.	Lingfield. *Baptists.*
1164.	Richmond. *Bethlehem.*

IV. DOMESTIC BUILDINGS

(a) CASTLES.

LIST NO.	NAME	LIST NO.	NAME	LIST NO.	NAME
*5061.	Abinger. (Motte).	*2020.	Farnham. **3a, 12b.**	6603.	Reigate.
5002.	Betchworth.	*2027.	do.	6098.	Starborough.
5558.	Bletchingley.	5769.	Godstone. (Motte).	1460.	Walton - on - the - Hill.
4111.	Cranleigh. (Motte).	*2596.	Guildford. **4.**		(Motte).

(b) HOUSES & COTTAGES.

LIST NO.	NAME	LIST NO.	NAME	LIST NO.	NAME
103.	ABBEY BARN COTTAGE.	3460.	Apple Trees.	991.	*Ham.*
5134.	Abbotts.	6387.	Applebough.	1106.	*Petersham.*
1725.	Abell Cottages.	666.	Appleton's Cottage.	992.	Avenue Lodge Cott.
5064.	Abinger Manor.	3312.	Apps Tree Farm.	1967.	Aviary. The-
5127.	Abraham's Farm.		April Cottage.	5346.	Axes Farm. The-
646.	Acacias.	5968.	*Limpsfield.*	4271.	Aylwin's Cottage.
1041.	Ada Villa.	3538.	*Send.*		
1077.	Adam House.	3256.	Apsley Cottage.	4396.	BADGERS.
258.	Addlestone Park.	6088.	Apsley Farm.	2032.	Badshot Farm.
4325.	Admers Cottage.	6137.	Arden Green.	2034.	Badshot Lea House.
647.	Afron House.	6138.	Arden Green Cott.	5553.	Bagden Farm.
1079.	Alaric.	6139.	Arden Run Cottage.	3300.	Bailes Farm.
3022.	Albury House.	4625.	Arthurs.	5883.	Bakers Barn Farmho.
*3013.	Albury Park.	4624.	Arthurs Cottage.	5208.	Bakers Cottages.
3744.	Aldermoor Cottage.	5556.	Arthur's Seat.	3364.	Bakers Gate Farmho.
6551.	Alderstead Farm.	972.	Artington Coombe Manor House.	6472.	Ballands Hall.
3531.	Aldertons.			1778.	Ballards Garden.
5244.	Aldhurst Farm.	3070.	Artington Manor Farm.	5831.	Bank Farm Cottage.
3851.	Alfold House.			5754.	Bankside.
4209.	Alliford Cottage.	*1215.	Asgill House. **26a.**	3258.	Barcombe Farm.
2403.	Alma Cottage.	1216.	Asgill Lodge.	4078.	Barhatch Farm Ho.
4362.	Almshouse Cottages.	3673.	Ash Cottage.	2404.	Barlings Farm.
5729.	Altar Cottages.	4363.	Ashdale.		Barn. The-
1521.	Alton Lodge.	5133.	Ashcroft Farm.	1584.	*Coulsdon.*
4546.	Ambergarth.	3093.	Ashe Lodge.	6405.	*Gt. Bookham.*
4547.	Ambergarth Fm. Cott.	855.	Ashford Farm House.		Barn Cottage.
3438.	Amberley Cottage.	3309.	Ashlea.	6561.	*Merstham.*
4549.	Amberley Farm Ho.	936.	Ashleigh Cottage	4626.	*Wonersh.*
1282.	Ancaster House.	1620.	Ashley House.	5832.	Barn Gate House.
140.	Anchor House.	3089.	Ashmead.	4573.	Barnett Farm.
4395.	Aniker Cottage.	6384.	Ashtead House.	6477.	Barnett Wood Farm.
134.	Anningsley Park.	6370.	Ashtead Lodge.	5557.	Barnmoor.
5415.	Ansells Cottages.	6385.	Ashtead Pk. Fm. Ho. **21a.**	5884.	Barns Branford.
5330.	Anstiebury Farm.			6633.	Barons.
	Apple Tree Cottage.	6371.	Ashtead Park Ho.	5040.	Barracks. The-
3172.	*Compton.*	3041.	Atfield's Cottage.	6229.	Barrow Green Court.
4210.	*Elstead.*	990.	Avenue Cottage.	6232.	Barrow Green Farm.
			Avenue Lodge.	4421.	Basal Cottage.

LIST
NO.   NAME

LIST
NO.   NAME

LIST
NO.   NAME

929.	Basing House.
4153.	Basket Cottage.
6063.	Bassets Field Cotts.
3327.	Bassetts.
909.	Batchelors.
	Batchelors Farm.
6008.	*Limpsfield.*
3321.	*Ockham.*
2244.	Bath House.
	Bay Cottage.
5209.	*Capel.*
3111.	*E. Clandon.*
5014.	Bay Tree Cottage.
4100.	Baynards Park.
4232.	do.
6154.	Beacon. The-
4448.	Beagleys Cottage.
	Beam Cottage.
2271.	*Farnham.*
6276.	*Oxted.*
4397.	Bears Barn.
1012.	Beaufort House.
4052.	Beckhams.
1468.	Beddington Hall.
5717.	Beddlestead Farm.
	Bedford Farm(house).
356.	*Frimley.*
4398.	*Thursley.*
	Beech Cottage.
3181.	*Compton.*
4328.	*Hambledon.*
3621.	Beech House.
2585.	Beech Lawn.
2248.	Belfort.
375.	Belfry House.
1601.	Bellvue Cottages.
5694.	Bellwether Cottage.
6637.	Belmont.
155.	Belsize Grange.
918.	Belvedere Cottage.
761.	Belvedere House.
4126.	Belwethers.
4566.	Benacre.
667.	Benfleet Hall.
5368.	Benhams.
6280.	Bennetts.
714.	Bennett's Buildings.
5211.	Bennetts Castle.
5085.	Bennetts Grove.
5611.	Berry House.
6268.	Berry's Cottages.
5136.	Betchworth House.

2370.	Bethune House.
3689.	Beulah Cottage.
4154.	Beverley.
79.	Biddle Farm.
3690.	Bignold.
4235.	Bildens.
6163.	Billhurst Cott.
3837.	Billhurst Farmho.
1259.	Bingham House.
2422.	Binscombe.
4784.	Birch Cottage.
5390.	Birchwood Cottage.
5535.	Birketts Cottage.
5086.	Birkett's Farm.
3996.	Black Hams.
330.	Black Ho. Fm. Cotts.
5937.	Black Robins Fm. Ho.
4399.	Blackhanger Farm.
3323.	Blackmoor Heath Fm.
4155.	Blacknest Cottage.
5416.	Blanks.
4775.	Blossom Cottages.
475.	Bluegate Cottage.
458.	Bluegates.
6479.	Bockett's Farm.
3663.	Bodryn.
650.	Bog Lodge.
937.	Boldrae.
5939.	Bolthurst Fm. Ho.
5730.	Bombers Farm.
4329.	Bonners.
5211.	Bonnetts Farm.
6396.	Bookham Grove.
5316.	Bo-Peep.
3349.	Boro Hill.
4471.	Borough Fm. Cott.
4472.	Borough Farmhouse.
5455.	Boswells Farm.
6361.	Botley Hill Farm.
4071.	Botley House.
137.	Botleys.
6659.	Bottle Cottage.
4403.	Boundless Cottage.
4401.	Boundless Farmho.
1820.	Bourne Hall Stables.
2648.	Bow Cottage.
4070.	Bow Windows.
5996.	Bower. The-
5731.	Bowerland Farm.
5733.	Bowerland Park.
348.	Bowling Green Cott.
3352.	Box Cottage.

4402.	Boxalls.
911.	Boyle Farm.
459.	Boylett's.
2891.	Braboeuf Cottage.
3059.	Braboeuf Manor.
3835.	Bracken.
3647.	Bradstone Brook.
4236.	Bramblehurst.
938.	Bramham Cottage.
3925.	Bramley Lodge.
3926.	Bramley. Lo. Cott.
1709.	Bramshott House.
4834.	Branscombe.
5955.	Brasier's Cott.
74.	Brentmoor Dene.
5587.	Brewer St. Farm. **7b.**
3378.	Briar Cot.
	Briar Cottage.
3134.	*E. Clandon.*
4627.	*Wonersh.*
4785.	Brick Cottage.
5670.	Brick Kiln Cott.
3194.	Brickfield Cott.
6155.	Bricklands.
3089.	Bricklyn.
3852.	Brickyard Fm. Cott.
	Bridge Cottage(s).
4042.	*Chiddingfold.*
693.	*Cobham.*
4081.	*Cranleigh.*
4449.	*Tilford.*
3334.	Bridge End.
3335.	Bridge End. Cott.
	Bridge Farm(house).
3853.	*Alfold.*
2288.	*Farnham.*
4450.	*Tilford.*
1487.	Bridge House.
3316.	Bridgefoot Cotts.
3314.	Bridgefoot Farmho.
3427.	Bridgefoot House.
4080.	Bridgeham Farmho.
5087.	Bridgham Farm.
3959.	Brighton Cottage.
20.	Brimshot.
5249.	Bristow Cottage.
347.	Bristow Farm.
3252.	Brittain's Farmho.
5601.	Brittens Cotts.
5317.	Brittleware Farm.
4137.	Broadoak.
4285.	Broadstone Cottages.

227

229

LIST NO.	NAME
6460.	Fetcham Cottage.
727.	Few's Cottages.
5723.	Fickleshole Fm.
4169.	Field Place.
2253.	Firgrove Farm.
2255.	Firgrove House.
6639.	Firs. The-
4007.	Fisher Lane Fmho.
5353.	Fishers Farm.
5092.	Fishfold Farm.
1767.	Fitznell's Mnr. Ho.
6340.	Flagpole Cottage.
6595.	Flanchford Farm.
6287.	Flaxman Cottages.
733.	Fleetwood.
4725.	Fleur-de-Lys.
3774.	Flexford House.
3199.	Flexford Ho. Lodge.
	Flint Cottage.
1405.	*Banstead.*
4968.	*Mickleham.*
6319.	Flint House.
5850.	Flinthall Farm.
5342.	Florence Cotts.
44.	Florida House.
3227.	Flower Cottage.
3151.	Fludyers Cotts.
6074.	Ford Cottage.
6113.	Ford Estate Cotts.
3030.	Ford Farm.
4.	Ford Farm Cottage.
3360.	Fords Farm.
	Forge. The-
4195.	*Dunsfold.*
2409.	*Farnham.*
5454.	*Ockley.*
3664.	*Shere.*
3675.	*do.*
	Forge Cottage(s).
5710.	*Burstow.*
1539.	*Caterham.*
5257.	*Charlwood.*
736.	*Esher.*
2843.	*Guildford.*
5364.	*Horley.*
5983.	*Limpsfield.*
5451.	*Ockley.*
6278.	*Oxted.*
5544.	*Wotton.*
3179.	Forge House.
*273.	Fort Belvedere.
15.	Fosters Farm.

LIST NO.	NAME
4676.	Foundry Cottage.
4536.	Fowl House Fmho.
6386.	Fowler's Cottage.
11.	Fowlers Wells.
5318.	Fox Cottage.
6400.	Foxglove Cottage.
452	Foxlake Farm Ho.
6575.	Foxshaw.
6315.	Foyle Farm.
6308.	Foyle Riding.
4975.	Fredley Manor.
3700.	Freeland.
4291.	Frensham Beale Mnr.
4046.	Friargate.
6025.	Friars Cottage.
5542.	Fridays Cottages.
4581.	Friendly Cottage.
4008.	Frillinghurst Cott.
349.	Frimley Lodge.
4424.	Frith Cottage.
6050.	Frith Manor.
3844.	Frog Grove.
3845.	Frog Grove Cott.
5128.	Froggetts Farm.
5841.	Frogit Cottage.
3115.	Frogmore Cotts.
3820.	Frosbury Farmhouse.
1541.	Fryern.
5169.	Fryleigh Cotts.
6075.	Fry's Cottage.
	Fulbrook Cottage.
5258.	*Charlwood.*
4213.	*Elstead.*
3280.	Fullers Farm.
3729.	Fulvens Farm.
3867.	Furzen's Cottage.
5218.	Fylls Cottages.
3416.	GABLE COTTAGE.
6418.	Gables Cottage.
	Gables. The-
3417.	*Ripley.*
3686.	*Shere.*
4241.	Gadbridge Farm.
5172.	Gadbrook Farm.
993.	Garden Cottage.
3010.	Garden Court.
	Gardener's Cott. (The)
5071.	*Abinger.*
5168.	*Betchworth.*
3145.	*W. Clandon.*
743.	Gardener's Ho. The-

LIST NO.	NAME
729.	Garson Farm.
5801.	Garston Farm.
6162.	Garth. The-
	Gate House (The).
5190.	*Buckland.*
1022.	*Ham.*
1354.	*Richmond.*
5842.	Gatehouse Farmho.
5423.	Gaterounds Farm.
3896.	Gatestreet Farm.
3897.	Gatestreet Fm. Cott.
4552.	Gatton Cottage.
3565.	Gatwick End.
5309.	Gatwick Manor.
5570.	Gay House.
3441.	Georgian Ho. The-
6688.	Geranium Cottage.
883.	Giggs Hill Cott.
6316.	Gincocks Farm.
3294.	Glaziers.
	Glebe Cottage.
4382.	*Peper Harow.*
492.	*Pyrford.*
	Glebe House. The-
5065.	*Abinger.*
5183.	*Buckland.*
4065.	*Chiddingfold.*
5819.	*Godstone.*
4347.	*Hambledon.*
6192.	*Nutfield.*
	Glen. The-
1918.	*Mitcham.*
1119.	*Petersham.*
5896.	Glen Farm. The-
3868.	Glen Groote-fontein.
	Glenfield.
5642.	*Bletchingley.*
920.	*T. Ditton.*
4847.	Glory Farm Cott.
5259.	Glovers Wood.
1784.	Glyn House.
5067.	Goddards.
4364.	Gomers Farmho.
3530.	Goodgrove.
4505.	Goose Cottage.
	Goose Green Cotts.
3951.	*Bramley.*
700.	*Cobham.*
3953.	Goose Green Fm.
3800.	Gooserye.
1008.	Gordon House.
4170.	Gorebridge House.

231

236

237

238

242

LIST NO.	NAME	LIST NO.	NAME	LIST NO.	NAME
4673.	Woodyers.	5165.	*Betchworth.*	3276.	*W. Horsley.*
4609.	Woodyers Fmho.	5681.	*Bletchingley.*	4490.	*Witley.*
6209.	Woolborough.	5238.	*Capel.*		Yew Tree
4269.	Woolpit Farm.	5301.	*Charlwood.*		Farm(ho).
5198.	Workhouse Cotts.	4036.	*Chiddingfold.*	5866.	*Godstone.*
5528.	Wotton Hatch.	68.	*Chobham.*	5555.	*Wotton.*
5529.	Wotton House.	3112.	*E. Clandon.*	3422.	Yew Tree House.
6707.	Wray Farm.	4230.	*Elstead.*	5373.	Yew Trees.
4206.	Wrotham Hill Cotts.	1695.	*Epsom.*	5193.	Yewdells.
5378.	Wyatt's Farm.	4287.	*Ewhurst.*	4646.	Yieldhurst.
4420.	Wychmoor.	2413.	*Farnham.*	4207.	Yonder Lye.
4116.	Wykehurst Fmho.	6470.	*Fetcham.*	218.	York Corner.
4119.	Wyphurst.	2605.	*Guildford.*		York Cottage(s).
		2802.	*do.*	220.	*Chertsey.*
4270.	YARD	4719.	*Haslemere.*	5379.	*Horley.*
	FARMHOUSE.	5377.	*Horley.*	4431.	*Thursley.*
5105.	Yard Land.	6117.	*Lingfield.*		York House.
1011.	Yarrell's Cotts.	6123.	*do.*	219.	*Chertsey.*
1462.	Yeoman House.	5441.	*Newdigate.*	1750.	*Epsom.*
3110.	Yew Cottage.	6246.	*Oxted.*	5490.	Young's Farm.
	Yew Tree Cottage(s).	871.	*Th. Ditton.*		
				2249.	ZINGARI.

(c) MOATED SITES OF FORMER HOUSES.

LIST NO.	PARISH.	LIST NO.	PARISH.	LIST NO.	PARISH
5302/3.	Charlwood.	5361.	Horley. (Thunderfield Cas.).	5482.	Ockley Castle.
5745.	Crowhurst.			3543.	Send.
1607.	Cuddington.	*6486.	Leatherhead. (The Mounts).	4477.	Witley.
3213.	Effingham.			555.	Woking.
1369.	Epsom.	6558.	Merstham. (Albury Mnr.).		
2035.	Farnham.				

(d) ALMSHOUSES.

LIST NO.	PARISH	LIST NO.	PARISH	LIST NO.	PARISH
5231.	Capel.	2649.	Guildford. *Caleb Love-joy's.*	1364.	Richmond.
4837.	Dorking. *Cotmandene.*				*Bp. Duppa's*
3207.	Effingham.	4754.	Haslemere.	1313.	do. *Hickey's.*
2104.	Farnham. *Windsor.*	974.	Kingston -upon-Th. *Cleaves.*	1165.	do. *Houblon.*
2553.	Godalming. *Wyatt's.*	1852.	Merton. *Rowland Wilson.*	1365.	do. *Michel's.*
5820.	Godstone. *St. Mary's.*			1366.	do. *Queen Elizabeth's.*
*2791.	Guildford. *Abbot's. Hospital.* **16.**	1904.	Mitcham. *Tate.*		
		480.	Pyrford.	926.	Thames Ditton.

V. PUBLIC BUILDINGS

(a) TOWN & MARKET HALLS.

LIST NO.	TOWN
2310.	Farnham. *Bailiffs' Hall.*
6546.	Gatton.
2533.	Godalming. *Old Town Hall.*
*2764.	Guildford. *Guildhall.* **19.**
2760.	Guildford. *Old Corn Exchange.*
4710.	Haslemere. *Town Hall.*
4711.	do. *Town Ho.*
983.	Kingston-upon-Th. *Market Hall.*
6687.	Reigate. *Old Town Hall.*

(b) SCHOOLS & COLLEGES.

LIST NO.	NAME
3459.	Aldro School.
6468.	Badingham College.
1467.	Beddington. C. of E.
378.	Burwood Park School.
4085.	Cranleigh School.
1766.	Ewell Castle School.
1437.	Fair Dene School.
2315.	Farnham Grammar Sc. (Cott.)
2316.	Farnham Grammar Sc. (Gym.)
2350.	Farnham St. Christopher's Sc.
3642.	Gosden House School.
2866.	Guildford. Clark's College.
2807.	Guildford. K. Edward VI Grammar School.
1986.	Kings College Sc. (Jnr.).
6140.	Lingfield. Notre Dame Convent.
1269.	Richmond. Old Vicarage Sc.
3454.	Ripley Court School.
*278 (1)	Royal Holloway College. **28.**
444.	St. Maur. Convent.
2406.	Wrecclesham. C. of E.

(c) HOTELS, INNS & PUBLIC HOUSES.

LIST NO.	NAME
5051.	Abinger Hatch Hotel.
	Albion. The-
1708.	*Epsom.*
2265.	*Farnham.*
946.	Alma. The-
	Anchor. The-
6443.	*Gt. Bookham.*
3402.	*Ripley.*
2610.	Anchor & Horseshoes. The-
	Angel. The-
2738.	*Guildford.*
6605.	*Reigate.*
882.	*Th. Ditton.*
320.	Ann Boleyn Hotel. Ye-
6150.	Apsley Town Country Hot.
	Barley Mow. The-
6337.	*Tandridge.*
4447.	*Tilford.*
409.	*Walton-on-Thames.*
3260.	*W. Horsley.*
	Bear. The-
772.	*Esher.*
2701.	*Guildford.*
2408.	Bear & Ragged Staff. The-
	Bell. The-
5654.	*Bletchingley.*
4955.	*Dorking.*
811.	*E. Molesey.*
5806.	*Godstone.*
3326.	Black Swan. The-
	Blue Anchor. The-
5837.	*Godstone.*
6701.	*Reigate.*
2017.	Blue Boy. The-
3096.	Bricklayers' Arms. The-
5956.	Bull. The-
	Bull's Head. The-
2757.	*Guildford.*
6675.	*Reigate.*
3149.	*W. Clandon.*
4972.	Burford Bridge Hot.
2314.	Bush. The-
5363.	Cambridge Hotel.
2902.	Cannon Inn. The-
3405.	Cedar Hotel.
1642.	Chalk Lane Hotel.
	Coach & Horses. The-
2053.	*Farnham.*
1027.	*Kew.*

LIST NO.	NAME
	Swan. The-
252.	Chertsey.
322.	Egham.
916.	Th. Ditton.
3418.	Talbot. The-
92.	Three Mariners.
774.	Travellers' Rest. The-
156.	Vine. The-
2582.	Wagon & Horses. The-
1447.	Well House Inn. The-
	Wheatsheaf. The-
3938.	Bramley.
4862.	Dorking.

LIST NO.	NAME
2329.	Farnham.
2949.	Guildford.
5724.	White Bear. The-
5881.	White Duchess. The-
	White Hart. The-
5649.	Bletchingley.
63.	Chobham.
355.	Frimley.
5804.	Godstone.
1917.	Mitcham.
3344.	Pirbright.
4526.	Witley.
3838.	Worplesdon.
	White Horse. The-

LIST NO.	NAME
4884.	Dorking.
4373.	Hascombe.
4697.	Haslemere.
3670.	Shere.
279.	White House. The-
	White Lion. The-
713.	Cobham.
4759.	Haslemere.
1563.	Warlingham.
5779.	White Swan. The-
6459.	Windsor Castle. The-
544.	Wingfield Arms. The-
5849.	Wire Mill Hotel. The-
1634.	Woodcote Hotel. The-

(d) MILLS.

LIST NO.	PARISH	
Water-mills.		
5054.	Abinger.	Cranes Mill.
3958.	Bramley.	
446.	Byfleet.	
704.	Cobham.	
70.	Chobham.	Emmetts.
4835.	Dorking.	Castle.
4965.	do.	Milton Court
4840.	do.	Pipbrook.
3592.	Eashing.	
4223.	Elstead.	33a & b
1803.	Ewell.	Lower.
1790.	do.	Tayles.
1804.	do.	Upper.
2273.	Farnham.	Bourne.

LIST NO.	PARISH	
2276.	do.	Bourne Pla.
2274.	do.	Hatch.
2275.	do.	High.
2277.	do.	Willey.
2558.	Godalming.	Hatch.
2857.	Guildford.	Old Town Mill.
2975.	do.	Stoke.
6133.	Lingfield.	Haxted.
5006.	Milton.	Pixham.
1903.	Mitcham.	Ravensbury.
*3470.	Newark.	32b
6196.	Nutfield.	Kings.
6243.	Oxted.	
6303.	Oxted.	Coltsford.

LIST NO.	PARISH
3631.	Shalford.
3721.	Shere.
328.	Thorpe.
4604.	Wonersh.
3797.	Worplesdon.
Wind-mills.	
5578.	Bletchingley. (Site).
*5699.	Burstow. Outwood.
5229.	Capel. Shiremark.
5314.	Charlwood.
4087.	Ewhurst.
1899.	Mitcham.
6691.	Reigate. 35a
1997.	Wimbledon.

(e) BRIDGES.

LIST NO.	PARISH	
86.	Bagshot.	Brookside.
5135.	Betchworth.	
509.	Byfleet.	Goldsworth (Langman's).
510.	do.	Woodend.
1491.	Carshalton.	Butter Hill.
1500.	do.	Leoni.
1503.	do.	Ponds.
112.	Chertsey.	
133.	do.	Bourne.

LIST NO.	PARISH	
709.	Cobham.	
671.	do.	Downside.
3585.	Eashing.	5b
3586.	do.	
1769.	Ewell.	Park House.
4318.	Frensham.	Mill.
2428.	Godalming.	Boarden.
955.	Kingston-upon-Thames.	
969.	do.	Clattern. 5a
6485.	Leatherhead.	

LIST NO.	PARISH	
6307.	Oxted.	Packhorse.
4383.	Peper Harrow.	Oxenford.
4393.	do.	Somerset.
1140.	Richmond.	
3650.	Shalford.	Lemmon.
3713.	Shere.	Packhorse.
3666.	do.	Tillingbourne.
4466.	Tilford.	
4467.	do.	
3636.	Unsted.	

(f) VARIOUS BUILDINGS.

Banks.
2125. Farnham. Lloyds.
2302. do. Midland.
2136. do. Nat'l Prov'l.

Clubs.
2029. Farnham. Albion & Liberal.
2229. do. Conservative.
2790. Guildford.
1894. Mitcham. Conservative.

Factories.
1855. Merton. Liberty.
1905. Mitcham. Eagle.
1918. do. Fibre Mills.

1869. Morden. Snuff.

Hospitals.
4136. Cranleigh. Village.
1006. Ham. C. P. Cassell.
1188. Richmond. Royal.
296(1). R. Holloway Sanatorium.
2984. Stoke.

Homes.
2266. Farnham Institute.
4334. Hambledon Institute.
332. Thorpe. Spelthorne S. Mary.

Unclassified.
2943. Castle Arch Museum.

668. Chatley Semaphore Tower.
2928. Diocesan House.
2601. Guildford Wharf Crane. **36b**
Esher. Coal & Wine Tax Post. **35b**
1085. Kew Palm House. **29**
6172. Lingfield Cage. **36a**
1896. Mitcham Railway Station.
1898. Mitcham Work-house.
3183. Watts Gallery.
2904. Wycliffe Buildings.

VI. DISTRICTS & PARISHES